AF412280

PROTECTION FOR EXPORTERS

PROTECTION FOR EXPORTERS

Power and Discrimination
in Transatlantic Trade Relations,
1930–2010

Andreas Dür

CORNELL UNIVERSITY PRESS   **ITHACA AND LONDON**

First published 2010 by Cornell University Press
Printed in the United States of America

Library of Congress Cataloging-in-Publication Data
Dür, Andreas, 1976–
   Protection for exporters : power and discrimination in transatlantic trade relations, 1930–2010 / Andreas Dür.
       p. cm.
   Includes bibliographical references and index.
   ISBN 978-0-8014-4823-2 (cloth : alk. paper)
   1. United States—Foreign economic relations—Europe.   2. Europe—Foreign economic relations—United States.   3. United States—Commercial policy.
4. Europe—Commercial policy.   5. Free trade—United States.   6. Free trade—Europe.   7. Protectionism—United States.   8. Protectionism—Europe.   I. Title.
   HF1456.5.E8D87   2010
   382.0973'04—dc22   2009032773

Cornell University Press strives to use environmentally responsible suppliers and materials to the fullest extent possible in the publishing of its books. Such materials include vegetable-based, low-VOC inks and acid-free papers that are recycled, totally chlorine-free, or partly composed of nonwood fibers. For further information, visit our website at www.cornellpress.cornell.edu.

Cloth printing   10 9 8 7 6 5 4 3 2 1

To Gemma

Contents

List of Tables and Figures ix

Preface and Acknowledgments xi

List of Abbreviations xv

Introduction 1

1. Protection for Exporters 15

2. Imperial Preference and the U.S. Reaction, 1932–1947 50

3. Deadlock in Transatlantic Trade Negotiations, 1948–1957 83

4. The European Economic Community, Discrimination, and Transatlantic Trade Relations, 1958–1963 101

5. The First Enlargement of the European Community and the U.S. Reaction 131

6. The Single Market Programme and Transatlantic Trade Policies in the 1980s 159

7. Competition between the European Union and the United States for Markets, 1995–2010 185

Conclusion 211

References 223

Index 241

Tables and Figures

TABLES

1.1 Explaining excluded countries' choice of strategy   39

1.2 Summary of hypotheses   49

2.1 Imports to the United Kingdom by origin, 1927–1938   53

2.2 U.S. exporter lobbying for the RTAA   57

3.1 The removal of quantitative trade restrictions in Europe, 1953–1956   86

3.2 Transatlantic and intra-European trade, 1938–1958   87

3.3 Major U.S. trade bills, 1934–1962   90

3.4 The results of trade negotiations, 1947–1956   96

4.1 U.S. exporter lobbying for the Trade Expansion Act, 1962   111

5.1 U.S. exporter lobbying, 1969–1974   139

6.1 U.S. trade with the EC, 1980–1990   163

6.2 U.S. exporter lobbying in the 1980s   171

7.1 The EU's network of preferential trade agreements, 2009   188

7.2 U.S. exporter lobbying in the 1990s and 2000s   196

7.3 The U.S. network of preferential trade agreements, 2009   202

FIGURES

I.1 U.S. trade liberalization, 1930–2010   2

I.2 EU external trade liberalization, 1950–2000   2

1.1 A schematic representation of a two-dimensional trade-policy space   21

1.2 Bargaining over tariffs I   24

1.3 Bargaining over tariffs II   42

4.1 U.S. exports to four major European countries as a share of these countries' total imports   105

Preface and Acknowledgments

Economists have long argued that under most circumstances unilateral trade liberalization is the economically most efficient policy. Trade creates welfare gains for a country by encouraging specialization and a more efficient allocation of resources. At the same time, political economists and political scientists have persuasively demonstrated that imposing barriers to trade is a politically sensible course of action. Consumers, the prime beneficiaries of trade liberalization, fail to become politically active as a result of free-rider problems, while exporters often ignore or underestimate the potential benefits from reciprocal trade liberalization. Import-competing interests are thus expected to dominate the political arena at most times, creating a situation in which decision makers have an incentive to maintain or raise barriers to imports.

In view of this literature, an analysis of transatlantic trade relations over the last eighty years uncovers a twofold puzzle. On the one hand, liberalization has been more pervasive than most political economy accounts would lead one to expect. Since the mid-1930s, trade negotiations have led to a significant reduction of both tariff and nontariff barriers to transatlantic trade, partly causing the rapid growth of transatlantic trade flows that has taken place since World War II. On the other hand, liberalization has occurred less rapidly and less comprehensively than one would expect if policymakers were mainly concerned with economic efficiency. What is more, the process of liberalization has not been rectilinear, since in the 1950s transatlantic trade liberalization stagnated and trade barriers even slightly increased.

My decision to write this book was motivated by a series of questions that derive from this double puzzle: Why has transatlantic trade been liberalized since the 1930s? Why did the United States and European countries agree to more far-reaching liberalization at some times than at others? And why did liberalization take different forms at different times, that is, why was nondiscrimination more important from the 1930s to the 1960s than it is today? The argument presented in chapter 1, which I call the protection-for-exporters argument, provides a comprehensive response to these questions. It suggests that on many occasions import-competing interests dominate the political process. When facing a loss of market access caused by the creation of preferential trade agreements among foreign countries, however, exporters mobilize in defense of their interests, producing a shift in the balance of domestic interests. Observing this shift, governments become more eager to protect exporters' interests, often by way of a trade agreement with the member countries of the preferential agreement. The protection-for-exporters argument also allows for predictions about the form that such policies in defense of exporter interests will take and the reaction of the member countries of the preferential trade agreement to the demand for trade negotiations.

The empirical examination of this argument provides for the first comprehensive treatment of transatlantic trade relations since the 1930s. The historical narrative offers new insights into such major developments as the U.S. turn toward negotiated trade liberalization in the 1930s, the passage of the 1962 U.S. Trade Expansion Act (TEA), the move toward a single market in Europe in the 1980s, and the role of both the United States and the European Union (EU) in the new wave of regionalism. While examining the argument across six case studies, I also point out major parallels over time. It is striking to see how similar the reasons given by presidents Franklin D. Roosevelt in the 1930s and George W. Bush in the 2000s were for the need to protect the interests of U.S. exporters in the face of foreign discriminatory trade policies. This book is unique, not only in its coverage of nearly a century of trade politics, but also in its emphasis on the feedback effects between European and U.S. trade policies over this period. The prevalence of such feedback effects suggests that studies of the trade policies of one side will fall short of providing a satisfactory explanation unless they take into account the influences from the trade policies of the other side.

In developing this argument and researching its many empirical implications over a period of more than eight years, I have accumulated many debts of gratitude. The endeavor began at the European University Institute in Florence, where Daniel Verdier pushed me to be as stringent as possible in my reasoning. Many of the arguments made in this book were strengthened because of his thorough criticisms, and the book would have turned out quite differently without his influence. Colin Crouch, Walter Mattli, and Gerald Schneider made very incisive comments on the argument and the empirical evidence presented here.

Examining my argument in six in-depth case studies required extensive empirical research. I was in the fortunate position of receiving funding from the European University Institute to do research in a series of archives: the Archives Diplomatiques of the French Ministry of Foreign Affairs in Paris, the Historical Archives of the European Communities in Florence, the National Archives at College Park in Maryland, the Politisches Archiv of the German Foreign Office in Berlin, and the British Public Records Office in Kew. I would not have been able to write the empirical chapters without gaining access to these archives. The same applies to the excellent library at the University of California at Berkeley, which I took advantage of during my four-month stay at that university in fall 2002.

From 2003 to 2005, the position of research fellow at the Mannheim Center for European Social Research provided me not only with an excellent opportunity to continue with few distractions my research on the topic of this book, but also with an intellectually inspiring environment. My gratitude for giving me this opportunity goes to Beate Kohler-Koch. I would also like to express my thanks to my friends and colleagues in Mannheim, with whom I enjoyed many stimulating lunch breaks. After moving to University College Dublin in 2005, I again benefited from both an excellent environment in which to carry out my research and the support of my colleagues. On several occasions, I presented parts of this book in departmental seminars and received valuable feedback. I also discussed the theoretical argument presented here with my UCD PhD students, with whom working has always been a pleasure.

Parts of chapters 1, 2, and 4 previously appeared as journal articles. The core argument and parts of chapter 2 first appeared as "Foreign Discrimination, Protection for Exporters and U.S. Trade Liberalization," in *International Studies Quarterly* 51(2): 457–80. The European part of the argument and portions of chapter 4 were published as "Bargaining Power and Trade Liberalization: European External Trade Policies in the 1960s," in *European Journal of International Relations* 14(4): 645–69. I am grateful to audiences at conferences of the American Political Science Association, the European Consortium for Political Research, and the European Union Studies Association who gave helpful comments on drafts of these papers. Moreover, my thanks go to the referees of these publications for their helpful comments and to Blackwell and Sage for permitting me to include this material here.

Among the many people from whom I received feedback on parts of this manuscript, mostly in the form of stand-alone articles and conference contributions, I would like to single out Dirk De Bièvre, Manfred Elsig, Bart Kerremans, Stephanie Rickard, Cornelia Woll, Alasdair Young, and Hubert Zimmermann, who all gave extremely valuable feedback on several occasions. I owe particular thanks to Dirk, who not only read my first crude attempts at coming up with a theoretical argument while we were together at the European University Institute but also provided constructive comments and criticisms on an early full draft of this manuscript while sharing an office with me in Mannheim. The articles that I coauthored with him on the politics of trade further shaped my approach to this topic. I am also grateful to Leonardo Baccini with whom I coauthored a paper that contains the quantitative test of the argument presented here. The quantitative analysis forced me to further strengthen the argument. At Cornell University Press, thanks are due to Roger Haydon, who supported the project from the beginning. Two anonymous reviewers provided me with very detailed and helpful comments.

My greatest thanks go to my family. My parents supported my education for many years and provided an environment conducive to pursuing academic studies. Above all, I am indebted to my wife Gemma and son Alexander for their support during times when work conflicted with my roles as husband and father. I dedicate this book to Gemma, who has moved with me from Florence to Mannheim to Dublin and finally Salzburg. She has been at my side from the beginning to the end of my work on this book.

Abbreviations

AD	Archives Diplomatiques of the French Ministry of Foreign Affairs in Paris
HA	Historical Archives of the European Communities in Florence
NACP	National Archives at College Park in Maryland
PA	Politisches Archiv of the German Foreign Office in Berlin
PRO	British Public Records Office in Kew

PROTECTION FOR EXPORTERS

INTRODUCTION

Since the 1930s, transatlantic trade relations have undergone a significant transformation as a series of trade negotiations have dismantled trade barriers that were erected before and during the Great Depression in the early 1930s. Successive trade rounds have reduced tariffs to the point where they are of little relevance in shaping current transatlantic trade flows with respect to most products (see figures I.1 and I.2 for U.S. and European tariff levels over time). In the 1990s and 2000s, international agreements have also imposed restrictions on the use of nontariff barriers.[1] This process of transatlantic trade liberalization is arguably one of the key developments in the global political economy over the last century. As a result of this liberalization, in most developed countries trade has grown in importance relative to gross domestic product (GDP) ever since World War II. This rise in international trade flows, in turn, has been a major driving force of globalization, a process that has had far-reaching consequences for societies across the globe.

This book is about the political processes that have brought about the liberalization of transatlantic trade. Although, according to economic theory, free trade maximizes the wealth of a country (at least under most circumstances),

---

1. Alas, to the best of my knowledge, no systematic time-series data for such nontariff barriers are available. Not even Andrew Rose (2004), who lists sixty-eight measures of trade protection and liberalization, mentions time-series data on nontariff barriers. Data in Messerlin (2001, 23–23) show, however, that at least in Europe nontariff barriers are now concentrated on a few tariff lines.

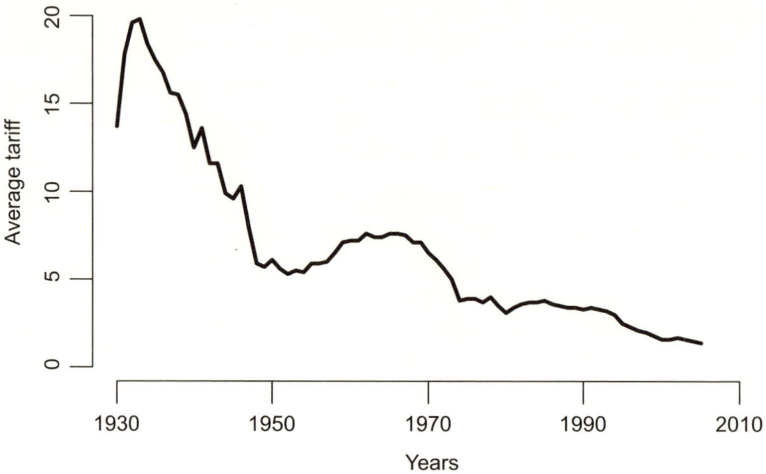

FIGURE I.1 U.S. trade liberalization, 1930–2010.

Source: U.S. International Trade Commission (2006).

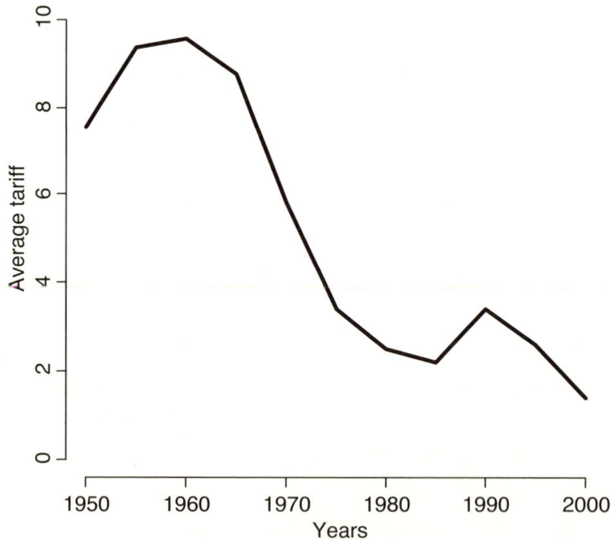

FIGURE I.2 EU external trade liberalization, 1950–2000.

Source: Calculated from data in Eurostat (various); Eurostat (2003);
Organization for Economic Cooperation and Development (various).

Note: Figures I.1 and I.2 show the U.S.'s and the EU's trade-weighted average
tariff, calculated as duties collected divided by total imports, which is the most
frequently used measure of tariff levels. For figure I.2, I used imports from
outside the EU only (but not for the period from 1950 until 1960 when duties
were still collected on intra-European trade flows), with the five-yearly data
taking into account the development in membership from EU-6 (1950–70) to
EU-9 (1975–80), EU-10 (1985), EU-12 (1990), and EU-15 (1995–2000).

the removal of policy interventions intended to limit imports is puzzling since protection seems "eminently reasonable" from a political point of view (Milner 2002, 449). The reason for this is to be found in the distributional effects of trade and the organizational advantages of the losers from increased trade flows. Lower trade barriers favor consumers and, if domestic liberalization is made dependent on foreign liberalization, exporters of goods and services; they also hurt producers and providers of goods and services that compete with imports. Collective-action problems, which arise when the benefits of an action are available to all members of a group regardless of whether they contributed to the costs of provision of the good (Olson 1965), inhibit lobbying by consumers, the main beneficiaries of trade liberalization. With protectionist forces dominating the political process, politicians have an incentive to implement policies that favor import-competing interests (Schattschneider 1935).

Scholarly understanding of protectionist policies thus is well advanced; what is less well understood is under which circumstances politicians have an incentive to liberalize trade. This book develops an explanation for trade liberalization, which I call the protection-for-exporters argument and which is based on the premise that exporters lobby more against losses than in favor of gains of foreign market access. In particular, exporters mobilize against losses inflicted on them by the discriminatory trade policies of foreign countries, such as preferential trading arrangements.[2] These arrangements, even if they do not give rise to higher external barriers, impose concentrated costs on third-country exporters in the form of trade diversion (Viner 1950; Panagariya 2000). Negatively affected exporters are likely to mobilize in defense of their interests, making it politically reasonable for the government of an excluded country to formulate trade policies aimed at the protection of exporter interests. In many cases it will seek a negotiated agreement with the member countries that lowers foreign discriminatory trade barriers. With the excluded government's desire for a negotiated agreement increased, however, it has to accept a balance of concessions in these negotiations that it would have rejected in the absence of greater exporter lobbying.

Applying the protection-for-exporters argument to six in-depth case studies, the book provides a new reading of major developments in transatlantic—understood as U.S.–European—trade relations over nearly a century. The empirical analysis extends from 1930, the high point of protectionist policies as exemplified by the passage of the Smoot-Hawley Tariff Act in the United States, until the

---

2. Throughout, I use the term "preferential trade agreement" to refer to agreements that reduce or eliminate trade barriers between two or more countries on a preferential basis, including partial and complete free trade agreements and customs unions.

early 2000s. On the U.S. side, the book discusses important developments such as the turn toward negotiated trade liberalization in the mid-1930s, the passage of the far-reaching Trade Expansion Act (1962), and the shift from a multilateral strategy to an approach that combines unilateral, bilateral, and multilateral elements, which is observable since the 1970s. On the European side, it covers developments such as the British acceptance of international trade rules in the 1940s, the European Economic Community's (EEC) first steps toward a common external trade policy in the 1960s, the international impact of the move toward a single market in the 1980s, and the EU's role in the new wave of regionalism in the 1990s and 2000s.

This book thus presents a sweeping account of U.S.-European trade liberalization. This is a particularly significant topic in that the transatlantic axis formed the center of the international trading system for much of the last century (Bergsten 1999, 25–26). The book does not provide a simple historical overview of the main developments in U.S. and European trade policies, however. Throughout the empirical chapters I test the protection-for-exporters argument against alternative hypotheses to avoid overestimating the explanatory power of my account. This process makes me concentrate on specific facets of transatlantic trade relations and give less importance to others, without neglecting any major developments altogether. The advantage of this approach is that by distinguishing the generalizable facets from the idiosyncratic ones, I highlight some persistent features in the trade relations between Europe and the United States.

Existing Approaches

The existing literature dealing with the puzzle of transatlantic trade liberalization can be divided into four broad approaches, each putting emphasis on one of four factors: societal demands, political institutions, geopolitical interests, and decision-makers' ideas and beliefs. First, some authors argue that the demands voiced by societal actors, whether this be firms, industries, or factors of production, largely determine the trade policies of a country. The preferences of economic actors are assumed to be shaped by a sector's import sensitivity or export dependence, or by the factor endowment of a country (Frieden and Rogowski 1996, 37–41). Politicians are seen either as simple intermediaries between domestic interests and policy outputs, or as having minimal impact on policies. A shift from protectionism to trade liberalization thus should take place whenever the balance of domestic interests swings in favor of the free trade forces.

Such a shift in the balance of domestic interests can come about for several reasons. For one, exogenous changes in the relative size and geographic concentration of industries may alter the political clout of different constituencies in a political system. In the United States, for example, the relocation of certain industries from the Northeast to the South during and after World War II may have resulted in changes in the constituencies represented by the Democratic and the Republican parties—increasing the importance of exporting interests for the Republicans and of import competitors for the Democrats (Hiscox 1999). By softening the stance of the Republican Party, traditionally the party of high tariffs, this shift may have allowed the United States to embrace trade liberalization in the postwar years. Alternatively, a rise in the number of firms benefiting from economies of scale may move a country's aggregate trade-policy preference toward liberaliztion (Chase 2005). These firms are internationally competitive as they can produce at low unit costs, and therefore they should have a major interest in foreign market opening. This may give them an incentive to push their government to offer reductions in domestic trade barriers in exchange for improved foreign market access.

A further prominent explanation for trade liberalization starting with societal demands emphasizes the role of multinational companies, that is, companies with production facilities in different countries (Helleiner 1977; Milner 1988). Producing in several countries may change the trade preferences of a firm by making it more vulnerable to foreign retaliation, as its production process probably depends on intrafirm trade of intermediary goods across borders. In addition, a multinational company may realize that protection benefits the domestically oriented competitors more than itself. An increase in the number of multinational companies, therefore, may shift the aggregate trade preference of a country toward freer trade. A similar outcome may result from a growth in intra-industry trade, namely the exchange across countries of like products, rather than products in which one side has a comparative advantage (Meyer 1978; Lipson 1982, 445; Verdier 1998). Since intra-industry trade does not have stark distributional effects, its increasing importance in transatlantic trade flows may have weakened the opposition to freer trade. Finally, a change in the domestic balance of interests may result if an initial step toward trade liberalization, which may come about for exogenous reasons, leads to the elimination of specific import-competing producers (Lipson 1982, 421; Bailey, Goldstein, and Weingast 1997; Hathaway 1998; Lusztig 2004). Firms that disappear as a result of market forces can no longer oppose the liberalization of trade relations, allowing free trade interests to dominate the political process.

Notwithstanding the key insights contained in the explanations that focus on societal demands, none of them provides a comprehensive explanation for the process of transatlantic trade liberalization since the mid-1930s. Some arguments' explanatory power suffers from a rather imprecise prediction of the timing of different steps of trade liberalization. Michael Hiscox's (1999) data on changes in party constituencies, for example, reveal that already in the 1920s the Republicans had a more export-oriented and less import-competing constituency than the Democrats. Nevertheless, until the late 1960s the Democrats were more supportive overall of reciprocal trade liberalization than the Republicans (Destler 2005, 31). This discrepancy limits the usefulness of changes in party constituencies as an explanatory factor for trade liberalization. The same point applies to the argument stressing economies of scale: although it is likely that the large domestic market made some U.S. sectors increasingly competitive in international markets in the late nineteenth and early twentieth centuries (Chase 2005), this gradual process can hardly explain the brisk reversal in U.S. trade policies that is evident from the short time span (four years) that divides the protectionist Smoot-Hawley Tariff Act (1930) and the far more liberal Reciprocal Trade Agreements Act (RTAA) of 1934.

The conclusion that multinational companies are more free trade oriented than other firms is not that straightforward either (Hillman and Ursprung 1993; Goodman, Spar, and Yoffie 1996). Because multinational companies can supply foreign markets by producing abroad, they may have less incentive than exporters to support trade liberalization. In fact, they may even push for the imposition of trade barriers to protect their position in foreign markets against competition from exporters. Empirical examples backing this conjecture are the U.S. chemical industry, which engaged in large foreign direct investments but remained strictly protectionist until the late 1970s, and the U.S. car producers with subsidiaries in Europe in the 1980s and 1990s, which supported barriers to imports in Europe. Finally, the argument about a rise in intra-industry trade easing protectionist pressures has not remained without challengers. Intra-industry trade, even if causing lower adjustment costs overall, may concentrate them on individual producers, creating major incentives for protectionist lobbying (Gilligan 1997b). Indeed, in 1909 60 percent of U.S. exports and 50 percent of U.S. imports were manufactured goods, suggesting that there was already considerable intra-industry trade in manufactured goods (Bordo, Eichengreen, and Irwin 1999, 13). Nevertheless, trade policies turned protectionist at that time.

Some of the explanations that start with societal demands also have difficulties in predicting the direction of the policy shift caused by changes in the economic structure. The reason is that such changes often do not only affect one of the two relevant constituencies, namely exporters and import-competing producers, but both. For example, an increase in economic interdependence makes some actors more free trade oriented, but at the same time it makes others embrace protectionism, because they face greater import competition. To improve on the societal-demands approach, therefore, a novel argument should provide a trigger that can predict the timing of changes in trade policies and a rationale for why the trigger event should change the *balance* of lobbying efforts. The aim of the protection-for-exporters argument is to achieve just this.

Second, some authors stress the role of political institutions in shaping trade policies. A change in domestic political institutions may lead to trade liberalization by introducing a bias in the system of interest-group mobilization that favors exporting interests. Following this line of reasoning, a prominent argument for U.S. trade liberalization holds that the RTAA, a trade bill by which Congress delegated authority to the president, allowing him to negotiate reciprocal trade agreements, created an incentive for exporters to mobilize (Bailey, Goldstein, and Weingast 1997; Gilligan 1997a). Reciprocal trade agreements link a reduction in domestic trade barriers to a cut in foreign trade barriers and thus concentrate the benefits of trade liberalization on exporters. The institutional change resulting from the RTAA may have "empowered" exporters (Gilligan 1997a), thus triggering the process of trade liberalization. Similarly, in the EU the delegation of trade authority to the European Commission as stipulated by the Treaty of Rome (1957) may have biased the process of interest representation. As representative of the EU in international trade negotiations, the Commission may have an incentive to seek pan-European solutions, which often may be found most easily by adopting a liberalizing stance (Woll 2008). Societal actors that support the Commission in this position—that is, the free trade forces—then have better chances of being heard than protectionist groups.

Alternatively, the institutional division between the negotiation of trade agreements, on the one hand, and the provision of protection through administrative procedures, on the other, may have enabled decision makers to engage in trade liberalization (Nelson 1989; Messerlin 2001; Chorev 2007). It may have allowed politicians to buy off import-competing interests with temporary and product-specific protection, while at the same time pushing forward with general trade liberalization. In the United States, for example, the argument has been made that in the 1970s Congress decided to facilitate access to instruments of administrative protection, such as antidumping and countervailing duties, making it easier for import-competing interests to receive protection (Chorev 2007). By doing so, they created a security valve for protectionist pressures, which enabled liberalization to continue on other fronts.

An institutional change may also increase the autonomy of decision makers from societal pressures. For the case of the United States, a substantial literature suggests that in the aftermath of the Great Depression, members of Congress decided to protect themselves from constituents' demands by delegating trade authority to the president (Bauer, Pool, and Dexter 1972; Pastor 1980; Haggard 1988; O'Halloran 1994; Destler 2005). Domestic interests may find it more difficult to influence the president, who has a far broader constituency than members of Congress. By curtailing the power of protectionist interests, the delegation thus may have paved the way for trade liberalization. Similarly, in Europe the delegation of trade-policy authority to the European Commission may have insulated policymakers from protectionist pressures (Meunier 2005, 8–9; Woolcock 2005, 247). Illustratively, Sophie Meunier (2005, 8) posits that European policymakers "chose to centralize trade policymaking in order to insulate the process from protectionist pressures and, as a result, promote trade liberalization."

The creation of an international trading regime after World War II is another institutional change—this time at the international level—that may have favored trade liberalization (Keohane 1984; Bagwell and Staiger 1999; Sherman 2002; Chorev 2007). International institutions may lower the transaction costs associated with interstate negotiations and thus facilitate the finding of efficient international agreements. An international regime may also assist in the enforcement of international agreements by providing members with information about the behavior of other members. The establishment of the General Agreement on Tariffs and Trade (GATT) in 1947 may thus have laid the foundation for the reciprocal trade liberalization that has taken place over the last several decades.

Again, as is the case with most versions of the societal-demands approach, the majority of institutionalist arguments suffer from a series of weaknesses. Hiscox (1999), for example, criticizes arguments stressing the causal role of the RTAA in propelling trade liberalization. He points out that the liberalization brought about by trade negotiations carried out under the provisions of the RTAA should have strengthened protectionist pressures, as imports started to threaten an increasing number of U.S. producers. Moreover, the studies suggesting that liberalization came about because politicians could buy off protectionist pressures mostly fail to make clear why decision makers would decide to do so in the first place. Finally, the application of the collusive delegation hypothesis to the case of the EU is put into doubt by the fact that even after delegation of trade authority to the European level, decisions concerning external trade liberalization had to be taken unanimously by the member states in the Council of Ministers (Nicolaïdis and Meunier 2002, 176). Unanimity decisions, in turn, should have empowered the forces lobbying against a change to the protectionist status quo rather than free trade interests.

The most important counterargument to the institutionalist interpretations of transatlantic trade liberalization, however, comes from their (implicit) prediction of a relatively steady reduction of tariffs after 1934, or at least after the end of World War II. Most of these interpretations point to only *one* event, an institutional change, that should have led to a reversal in trade-policy outcomes from protectionism to freer trade. From then on, in the absence of further institutional changes, the process of trade liberalization should have continued without interruption until it resulted in (almost) free trade. Yet this prediction does not withstand empirical scrutiny, as is evident from the empirical analysis in chapter 3. While a set of trade agreements led to substantial tariff reductions from the mid-1930s on, during the long decade from 1947 until 1958, the process of transatlantic trade liberalization not only stagnated but, if anything, was on the verge of reversal (Diebold 1962; Zeiler 1999). Not before the end of the Kennedy round of GATT negotiations in the mid-1960s did the tariffs of developed countries again undergo substantial reductions (see also figures I.1 and I.2 above). An explanation of this pattern of trade liberalization is likely to require several trigger events.

Third, since trade policies can have security externalities, politicians may design them with the aim of furthering the geopolitical interests of a country (Hirschman 1945; Gowa 1994; Skålnes 1998). Trade leads to a more efficient allocation of resources in an economy; to the extent that it increases trade, liberalization may thus allow a country to boost its military spending. Trade liberalization may also be aimed at strengthening a security alliance by increasing interdependence among its members, bolstering the economy of an ally by providing it with improved foreign market access or establishing a relation of dependence. Several authors stress that the hegemonic position of the United States after World War II may have made it particularly concerned with such geopolitical objectives (Nelson 1989; Eckes 1995). It may have supported the process of trade liberalization with its allies as an instrument in its conflict with the Soviet Union. This argument is in line with a version of the hegemonic stability thesis that sees the existence of a hegemon as a precondition for the liberalization of international trade (Kindleberger 1973; Krasner 1976; Gilpin 1987). Another strand of the same literature, however, argues that a hegemonic power may compel all other countries to trade freely while imposing an optimal tariff on its own imports (Conybeare 1987; Lake 1993; Pahre 1999). If so, we would expect the United States to have remained protectionist after World War II while forcing the European countries to liberalize.

Geopolitical interests clearly have had an influence on transatlantic trade relations over the last century, and especially during the cold war. Nevertheless, the explanatory power of geopolitical interests for transatlantic trade liberalization can easily be, and has often been, overestimated. What casts most doubt on the role of geopolitical interests is the stagnation of transatlantic trade liberalization in the 1940s and 1950s. All geopolitical explanations lead to the expectation that both the United States and the European countries, or at least the latter if the United States was a malevolent hegemon, should have liberalized their trade policies at a time when the potential geopolitical benefits from liberalization were strongest and U.S. hegemonic power was at its peak. As I point out in chapter 3, however, this expectation is not confirmed by the empirical evidence.

Finally, decision-makers' ideas and beliefs may influence the trade policies they pursue (Kindleberger 1975; Curzon and Curzon 1976; Goldstein 1993; Krueger 1997). Under conditions of incomplete information about cause and effect relationships, ideas can shape policy outcomes by helping decision makers determine which among several different strategies will maximize their interests. Trade liberalization, in this view, may have come about as a result of the spread of a liberal ideology among decision makers. In the United States, such a liberal ideology may have taken hold as a result of the perceived failures of the protectionist policies of the interwar years (Pastor 1983, 161; Winham 1986, 396; Goldstein 1998, 148). The possibly negative effects on economic growth of the protectionist Smoot-Hawley legislation in 1930, according to this "lesson thesis," taught legislators that they would be better off if they managed to restrain themselves from voting for trade protection. Karen Schnietz (2000), however, provides a devastating critique of the lesson thesis by pointing out that none of the members of the House of Representatives who voted for protectionism in the Smoot-Hawley tariff supported the RTAA four years later. This is a strong indication that the U.S. turn to trade liberalization in the 1930s did not come about because of a change in ideas.

In short, while the various approaches that dominate the literature on trade liberalization provide interesting insights into transatlantic trade relations in the twentieth and early twenty-first centuries, they also suffer from specific shortcomings. What is more, studies from all four approaches generally concentrate on either the United States (mainly) or the major European countries (rarely), with very few attempts at theorizing the trade policies of both sides at the same time (for exceptions, see Milner 1988; Verdier 1994; Chase 2005). This is a major shortcoming, given that developments on both sides of the Atlantic follow a similar pattern and that trade agreements between the two required concessions from both sides. My aim in this book is to provide a novel explanation of the process of transatlantic trade liberalization that, by building on the societal-demands approach, overcomes some of the shortcomings of the existing literature.

The Protection-for-Exporters Argument

I posit that the protection-for-exporters argument, developed in detail in chapter 1, achieves this objective. The basic premise of this argument, which builds on prior work on the relationship between regionalism and multilateralism (Oye

1992; Baldwin 1993, 2006; Mattli 1999), is that export interests often fail to become politically active because they are either unaware of opportunities in foreign markets or uncertain about whether their political activity will eventually be rewarded with better foreign market access. The expectation thus is for import-competing interests to dominate the political process on many occasions, a prediction that is in line with the findings of a series of empirical studies (Rodrik 1995). Going beyond this conventional finding, I hypothesize that exporters increase their political activity whenever they lobby in defense of existing market shares abroad rather than in pursuit of improved market access. In particular, exporters should mobilize whenever foreign countries threaten access to their markets by establishing a preferential trading arrangement.

In a second step of the argument, I hypothesize that the mobilization of exporters should make the governments of excluded countries engage in policies that protect exporters' interests. Excluded countries can opt for one among four distinct strategies to achieve this aim: they can threaten with retaliation, set up an alternative agreement, conclude an agreement with the member countries that liberalizes trade in a nondiscriminatory manner, or accede to the existing preferential agreement. The existing literature, while differentiating among some of these strategies, has provided few indications of why a country would opt for one or another of them. I hypothesize that the choice among these options mainly depends on the degree of vulnerability of an excluded country to changes in trade flows resulting from foreign trade policies.

The third step of the argument allows for a response to the question of why on many occasions the member countries of a regional agreement accept external trade liberalization to accommodate the demands voiced by excluded countries. I argue that the creation of a preferential trading arrangement increases the bargaining power of its member countries, enabling them to gain additional concessions in trade negotiations with excluded countries. For member-country governments, the shift in bargaining power makes it attractive to accept a trade agreement with excluded countries. On the one hand, the prospect of additional concessions makes exporters in member countries back an agreement. On the other hand, the agreement is likely to face only limited opposition from import-competing interests, since the distribution of bargaining power ensures that member countries can avoid making concessions that impose large costs on them.

Explaining Transatlantic Trade Liberalization

The empirical examination of the protection-for-exporters argument starts with the impact of the system of imperial preference, preferential trade agreements that the United Kingdom concluded with its dominions in 1932, on transatlantic trade relations (chapter 2). Several exporter lobbies sprang up in the United States during this period and pushed the administration to react to the discrimination exporters faced in foreign markets. This mobilization offers an original explanation for the passage of the RTAA that challenges a substantial existing literature. In Great Britain, the offer for trade negotiations was examined critically, with societal interests demanding that reducing imperial preference should only be accepted in exchange for substantial U.S. concessions in the form of improved market access. The historical narrative also provides a new reading for the establishment of the GATT, not as an expression of U.S. hegemony, but as an American reaction to the discrimination caused by the British system of imperial preference.

In the late 1940s and 1950s, U.S. exporters' access to the European market was relatively secure (chapter 3). As expected under these circumstances, U.S. exporters failed to become politically active. With import-competing interests dominating the domestic debate, it is no wonder that U.S. trade policies turned protectionist in that decade. Several features of the trade bills passed by Congress at that time made it impossible for the administration to offer concessions in international trade negotiations. These protectionist U.S. trade policies, while in accordance with the protection-for-exporters argument, challenge many of the explanations of trade policymaking outlined above, as they lead to the expectation of a continuation of the process of trade liberalization started by the United States in the 1930s. In Europe, in the meantime, the U.S. failure to accept reciprocal trade liberalization was one of the driving forces behind the decision to create a preferential trading zone. The weakness of exporter interests in the United States explains the administration's willingness to support this process, although its end product caused discrimination against U.S. trading interests.

The third case, dealt with in chapter 4, illustrates the major repercussions that the formation of the EEC (1958) had for transatlantic trade policies. The creation of the EEC, as a discriminatory trading arrangement, had the potential to cause substantial trade diversion. As expected, U.S. exporters mobilized in reaction to this threat to their foreign market access. The bill extending the RTAA in 1958 and the Trade Expansion Act of 1962 were both legitimized by the danger that European integration posed for U.S. exports. The U.S. administration then called for a major trade round to bring down preferential European tariffs. Initially, the member countries of the EEC showed some reluctance to accept this U.S. initiative, but they agreed to participate in the Kennedy round of trade negotiations (1964–67) once they thought they could extract substantial concessions from the United States in exchange for a lowering of their own trade barriers. In fact, the results of the Kennedy round indicate that the EEC's bargaining power had increased quite significantly as a consequence of the creation of a customs union.

In the fourth case, I suggest that neither the internationalization of production nor the breakdown of the institutional structures to protect Congress from special interest-group influence can provide a full explanation of U.S. trade politics at the beginning of the 1970s (chapter 5). Instead, I emphasize the influence of the first enlargement of the European Community (EC) in 1973 and the accompanying European preferential trade policies on U.S. trade policies.[3] I also explain why the United States reacted more assertively to discrimination than it had in previous decades, namely by passing trade legislation that included a provision that authorized the administration to use retaliation to pry open foreign markets in which U.S. exporters faced unfair barriers to trade. The U.S. strategy, however, was only partly successful, as the Europeans largely resisted unilateral concessions, again creating the need for U.S. concessions in international trade negotiations to achieve a lowering of European discriminatory trade barriers.

In chapter 6, I assess the explanatory power of the protection-for-exporters argument for the U.S. reaction to the single market programme (SMP) introduced in 1985. In doing so, it is important to take into account that beginning in the early 1980s countries from outside the transatlantic area, and in particular the emerging economies in Asia and Latin America, have had an increasing influence on U.S. and European trade policies. As a result of the growing importance of these countries for international economic relations, from the 1980s onward U.S. trade bills can no longer be seen as solely, or even mainly, a response to European trade policies. Moreover, with trade barriers already very low (and thus the possible extent of further trade diversion in the European market limited) and an altered U.S. trade position, transatlantic trade relations themselves had undergone a certain change by that decade.

Despite these far-reaching structural changes, the protection-for-exporters argument retains substantial explanatory power for developments in the 1980s. It correctly predicts the mobilization of U.S. exporters in response to the SMP. The United States used its strong position, which resulted from the large balance of trade deficit that it experienced in the mid-1980s, to prevent policies that went to the detriment of U.S. exporters. The prospect of an economic Fortress Europe, therefore, was avoided because the European side was vulnerable to aggressive

---

3. Legally, trade policy was part of the EEC until 1993 and of the European Community pillar of the European Union since then. Nevertheless, throughout I will use the name of the aggregate entity: European Economic Community (EEC) until 1967, European Community (EC) between 1967 and 1993, and European Union (EU) from 1993 onward.

U.S. trade policies. Only a few issues raised by the SMP were postponed for resolution in the Uruguay round of GATT negotiations. An analysis of the Uruguay round itself also reveals the workings of the protection-for-exporters logic: the U.S. pursuit of preferential trade policies in the early 1990s convinced European trading interests that they had to accept the conclusion of multilateral trade negotiations to forestall losses of foreign market access.

The last empirical chapter (chapter 7) asks why, after nearly a decade without delegation of trade authority to the president, the U.S. Congress finally decided to pass a trade bill that enabled the administration to engage in trade negotiations with foreign countries in 2002. The answer given is that the degree of discrimination that U.S. exporters faced in foreign markets increased over this period owing to the rapid spread of regional trade agreements among foreign countries. The chapter also explains why the U.S. administration used this new trade authority to conclude *preferential* trade agreements with a series of countries rather than privileging the multilateral approach. The EU responded with its own preferential agreements with countries such as Mexico and Chile, creating a situation in which it competes with the United States over access to emerging markets.

In short, this book presents a novel argument to explain trade-policy choices that favor export interests. Drawing on this argument, six empirical chapters provide an analysis of the process of transatlantic trade liberalization between 1930 and 2010. While the book's central aim is to provide an in-depth analysis of transatlantic trade relations, and to submit existing causal claims about these relations to a rigorous test, its argument and empirical findings potentially have implications for a range of scholarly debates. With respect to trade policy, the protection-for-exporters argument makes an addition to an emerging literature on the interdependence of trade-policy decisions. What is more, the logic presented here may also be of use in explaining the spread of international cooperation in other policy fields. It makes a strong case for policy diffusion being the result of competitive processes (for a discussion of policy diffusion, see for example Simmons and Elkins 2004). Moreover, the book contributes to the recent resurgence of interest in the study of power in international relations (Gruber 2000; Barnett and Duvall 2005). The analysis reveals that power, a factor that has been too often neglected since the institutionalist turn in political science research, plays a major role in shaping trade policies. Finally, the book has notable implications for the debate about the consequences of regionalism, as it outlines the *specific circumstances* under which preferential trade agreements set off a process of overall trade liberalization rather than mutual retaliation. In view of the recent proliferation of bilateral trade agreements across the globe, the insights reached on this question are of major relevance for policymaking.

PROTECTION FOR EXPORTERS

In this chapter, I set out an explanation for trade policy choices that favor exporting interests. My argument starts with the basic insight that under most circumstances, import competitors pushing for the protection of the domestic market dominate over exporters interested in enhanced foreign market access. In this situation, although free trade tends to be the economically most efficient policy, governments have an incentive to impose protectionist policies. I suggest that exporters increase their level of mobilization when facing losses of foreign market access, urging their governments to protect their interests. In particular, preferential trade policies among foreign countries impose costs on exporters in excluded countries. By way of trade diversion, such agreements replace imports from foreign countries with production from inside the borders of the preferential agreement. Governments thus should instigate policies aimed at the protection of exporter interests in reaction to the preferential trade policies implemented by foreign countries.

The logic underlying the protection-for-exporters argument set out here has antecedents that date back nearly a century. Already in the 1930s, S. H. Bailey (1932) stressed that under certain circumstances discrimination can have external effects by compelling excluded governments to react. He even alluded to possible differences in the reaction by the excluded country depending on the relation in which the discriminating and the aggrieved governments stand to each other. In his words, "the action of the aggrieved government will vary in degree according to the nature and motive of the discrimination, the relative position of the governments concerned, and the importance of the interests involved" (Bailey 1932, 103). Despite this early precedent, only in the last few years has more systematic attention been given to the external political—in contrast to economic—effects of trade discrimination. Among others, Kenneth A. Oye (1992) argues that since the profits reaped by the partners to a preferential agreement are at the expense of third parties, the latter have a strong incentive to enter the agreement and divert the negative externalities to other third countries. Similarly, Richard Baldwin (1993, 1997) contends that by imposing costs on outsiders, an initial step toward regional market opening can trigger further market openings. Walter Mattli (1999, 59–64) comes to a comparable conclusion but specifies that only if the economic growth of outsiders lags behind the one experienced by the members of a preferential trade agreement will they respond to regional integration. Finally, authors such as Lloyd Gruber (2000), Yoram Haftel (2004), David Lazer (1999), and Robert Pahre (2008) have further elaborated and formalized these arguments.

While these studies converge on the same basic idea that is also used in developing the following argument, the protection-for-exporters explanation goes beyond the existing literature with regard to three major questions. First, why do exporters mobilize against losses rather than in pursuit of gains? Second, what are the determinants of the excluded government's choice of strategy in response to discrimination? Third, under which conditions is an excluded government's strategy successful in protecting exporter interests? I take up these issues with the aim of developing an argument that can complement existing explanations of trade policymaking.

The resulting argument builds on two main assumptions. For one, I assume firms, governments, and individual politicians in a legislature to be instrumentally rational actors that choose the best means, given their preferences. It might be problematic to refer to firms and governments as unitary actors, but this assumption is necessary to simplify the theoretical argument. In the empirical chapters, I relax the assumption and discuss internal divisions, especially in governments. Other composite entities, such as countries as a whole, are not considered actors in my analysis. In addition, with information costly, I posit that the actors mentioned above sometimes only have incomplete information about the preferences of other actors and about economic conditions in other countries. Firms, for example, have difficulty being informed about the precise economic conditions prevailing in foreign markets. In bargaining situations, moreover, governments lack information about the exact preferences of the other side. Because of this limitation on information, on some occasions lapses from optimal choices are possible. While these assumptions clearly simplify reality (as is the purpose of assumptions), I consider them a plausible starting point for the derivation of concrete expectations that can be tested against the available evidence.

The argument as developed in this chapter also comes with certain scope conditions that are suited for the case of transatlantic trade relations. In particular, the bargaining part of the argument may have to be adapted when applied to two countries with very different capabilities, such as a large developed country and a small developing one. In this case, the simplifications made with respect to differences in bargaining skills and the (non)use of financial side payments are not necessarily appropriate (although I think that the limited fungibility of power makes sure that the argument has to be adapted only for cases involving countries with very large differences in structural power). The fact that I do not consider the revenue consequences of cutting tariffs also introduces a scope condition in time and space.

In this chapter I first discuss the political economy of trade and then set out the economic effects of preferential trade agreements for exporters in excluded countries. Next, I make clear why exporters should lobby more in defense against losses than in pursuit of gains, before showing how increased exporter lobbying should influence trade policymaking in excluded countries. In the same section, I also explain an excluded government's choice of strategy in response to discrimination. I then discuss why the member countries of a preferential trade agreement may change their trade policies in the aftermath of the creation (or deepening or enlargement) of this agreement. The chapter ends with a short discussion of the methodology used to empirically examine the protection-for-exporters argument.

The Political Economy of Trade

My explanation for trade policy starts with domestic actors that have preferences for trade policy outcomes that are in line with their material interests, an assumption supported by empirical research (Pugel and Walter 1985). International trade, while generally beneficial for a country as a whole, has distributional effects: it increases the profits and wages of some actors and decreases those of others (Alt and Gilligan 1994). Actors who gain from trade should prefer trade liberalization, while those that lose from trade should favor protectionist trade policies. Assuming that capital invested in one sector cannot easily move to another sector, the beneficiaries (and thus supporters of freer trade) should be consumers and exporters. Consumers gain from lower prices on imported goods and services resulting from lower domestic tariffs. If domestic trade barriers are linked to foreign trade barriers in a reciprocal agreement, exporters profit from better foreign market access as a result of lower trade barriers. Domestic producers of goods or providers of services that are in competition with foreign goods or services, by contrast, lose from increasing trade. They consequently should prefer the imposition or maintenance of barriers to trade.

All of these actors can opt to engage in lobbying with the objective of instigating policies that are in line with their interests. Lobbying, however, creates collective-action problems, since its benefits accrue to all members of the respective group independently of whether they contributed to the effort or not (Olson 1965; Alt and Gilligan 1994). The resulting free-rider logic makes sure that only economic interests with concentrated gains or losses can mobilize for political action. Consumers and other diffuse interests, therefore, will largely be absent from the political process. By contrast, the exclusionary mechanism favors specific industries lobbying for the maintenance of high domestic trade barriers to protect them against import competition. Exporters, who are interested in lower foreign trade barriers, may also gain concentrated benefits from lobbying (Gilligan 1997a).

Influencing Political Outcomes

If engaging in lobbying, exporters and import competitors can influence policy-making processes through a series of channels (Potters and Sloof 1996; Nownes 2001; Hall and Deardorff 2006; Dür 2008).[1] For one, they can try to affect who is in power by rallying the electorate and giving campaign contributions (Fordham and McKeown 2003). If specific societal groups manage to select decision makers who have similar preferences to their own, they can have an indirect impact on policy outcomes. By way of outside lobbying (Kollman 1998), namely mobilizing the electorate, or by way of strategic information transmission (Lohmann 1998), they may also have a bearing on the position that a politician assumes on a specific issue. Finally, through the provision of "legislative subsidies" in the form of information and other help (Hall and Deardorff 2006), lobbies may have an impact on policy outcomes by determining the intensity with which politicians pursue a specific activity.

The balance of the lobbying efforts by exporting and import-competing interests is thus likely to have a bearing on the trade policy choices of a country (Schattschneider 1935; Cassing, McKeown, and Ochs 1986; Milner 1988; Gilligan 1997a; Chase 2005). Obviously, the balance of interests in a country does not provide an exhaustive explanation for policy outcomes. Some studies draw attention to the preferences and beliefs of parties, politicians, and voters in explaining

---

1. While I formulate the argument here in terms that are peculiar to democracies, there is good reason to believe that the logic also applies to autocracies. Just as in a democracy, in an autocracy decision makers will be concerned about policies that increase opposition to the regime.

trade-policy decisions (Bauer, Pool, and Dexter 1972; Goldstein 1993; Shoch 2001). I deliberately abstract from these factors when suggesting that whenever import-competing interests dominate, a country's trade policy should give more importance to the protection of the domestic market. Whenever exporting interests dominate, the trade policy should attach more significance to the degree of foreign market openness.

This is not to say that trade policymaking processes follow a winner-take-all logic. On the contrary, I expect politicians, who care about reelection and want to maximize the distance to the next competitor, to design policies with the aim of avoiding the imposition of concentrated costs on any societal actors (see also De Bièvre and Dür 2005). Their reason for doing so is that in a situation of electoral competition they fear that discontented organized groups could induce voters to punish the incumbent politicians or parties. Policymakers thus are reluctant to reduce domestic protection to avert costs for domestic producers of import-competing goods and try to avoid foreign market closure that would hurt exporting interests. In this view, the preferences of decision makers only matter in cases in which public actors can implement policies that have no stark distributional consequences. Although clearly a simplification of the actual political process, I consider this parsimonious assumption to be plausible enough to serve as a starting point for an explanation of policy outcomes.

An alternative approach would start with the supply side, that is, the politicians who implement certain policies and then receive support from the beneficiaries (for such an approach, see for example Pahre 2008). In this view, a politician who has information about export opportunities could engage in trade negotiations, knowing that a trade agreement will benefit some domestic exporters, with the expectation of future support from these exporters. Importantly, and in stark contrast to the demand-side argument set out above, no exporter lobbying would be needed for this trade agreement to come about. The main problem with such a supply-side theory is that it is not clear why the beneficiaries of a policy should invest resources to bolster the electoral prospects of a decision maker once they have received the benefits. The approach starting from the demand side resolves this issue by assuming that societal actors and decision makers enter a deal that links groups' resources to government's pursuit of certain policies. This deal is credible because of the repeated interaction between the two sides. A group not only gains influence by making a promise of support but also by wielding the stick of punishment in case the government fails to respond to its demands.

Following the demand-side approach, a country's ideal state of trade policy is reached with relatively low domestic openness and maximum foreign openness. This ideal point can be plotted in a two-dimensional policy space, with one dimension reflecting domestic producers' exposure to foreign competition and the other dimension, domestic exporters' access to foreign markets (see figure 1.1). The home country can unilaterally determine its position along the "domestic openness" dimension; it thus is likely to choose its ideal point on that dimension. Given that exporting interests have only a secondary interest in the height of domestic barriers, this point mainly reflects the preferences of import-competing interests for protection.[2] Foreign countries determine the position of the status quo on the second dimension following the demands of their own import-competing interests for trade barriers. On this second dimension, consequently, on which home country exporters consistently prefer lower to higher values, the noncooperative status quo is likely to be far away from the home country ideal point.

If two countries want to get closer to their ideal points regarding foreign market openness, they can engage in negotiations. I assume that in this bargaining process, the use of force is not a viable option to achieve a reduction of foreign trade barriers. Other power resources—such as financial means—most often cannot be employed to gain advantages in trade negotiations either. In addition, I assume that there is no systematic variation across countries with regard to bargaining skills, attitudes to risk, or information advantages. Again, these assumptions appear to be plausible in many contexts, with the exception of negotiations between a large developed country and a small developing one, in which both financial support and differences in administrative capabilities can play a role (Drahos 2003).

In this situation, the home country has to provide concessions with regard to the dimension that it controls (domestic openness) in exchange for concessions by foreign countries on the dimension under their control (foreign openness). For an agreement that changes the status quo, the two sides have to settle on an appropriate balance of concessions. This, however, is only possible if at least one side attaches more importance to exporter interests, namely foreign market access, than to the continued protection of the domestic market. Otherwise, no set of feasible agreements exists.

Bias in Favor of Import Competitors

This condition, however, should be absent in many circumstances because, for several reasons, exporters frequently lack the necessary incentives to engage in political activity. First, potential exporters are often not aware of the opportunities

---

2. The height of the trade barriers is limited by decision-makers' concern about economic growth and import-competitors' concern about foreign direct investments increasing in the face of high trade barriers (Ellingsen and Wärneryd 1999).

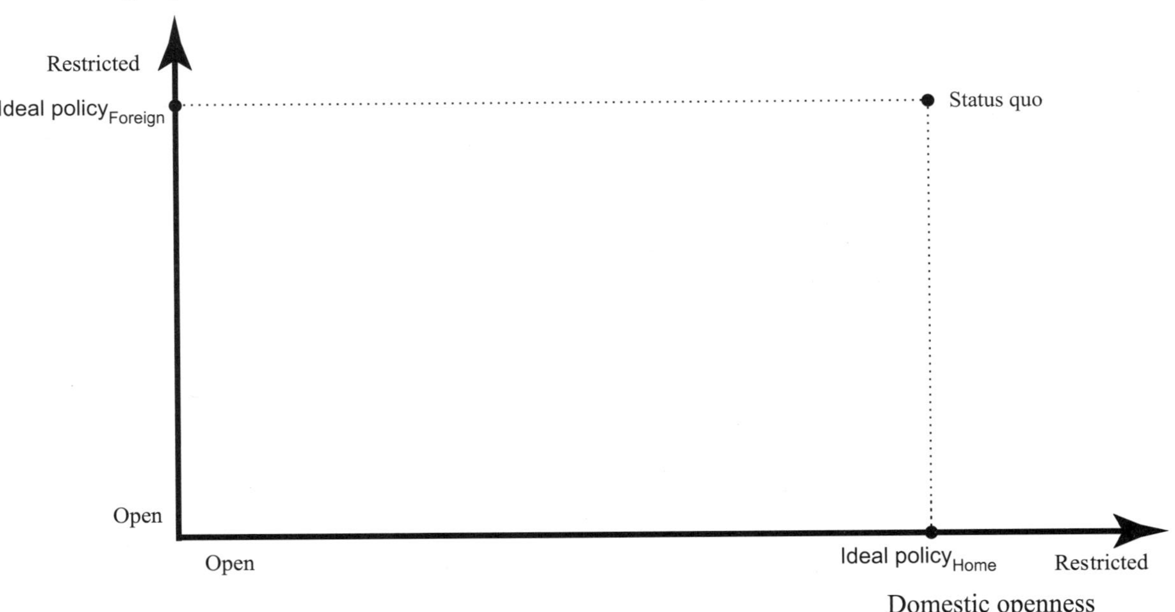

FIGURE 1.1 A schematic representation of a two-dimensional trade-policy space.

that they lose owing to high foreign trade barriers. Being fully attentive to these opportunities would require the constant scanning of foreign markets, a process that tends to be costly. A document prepared for the French government in the early 1960s presents this point quite clearly: "With regard to the perspectives for the enlargement of external markets that could result from the [Kennedy round], these often interest our industries only to a limited extent, *since they try to avoid the efforts of required exploration.*"[3] In cases in which an exploration of foreign markets is undertaken, moreover, research suggests that export opportunities are nearly always underestimated (Srinivasan and Bhagwati 2001, 14).

Second, even if exporters know of an opportunity, they cannot be certain about the benefits they would reap from lobbying, given that foreign tariffs are not under the control of the domestic government. Instead, they can only be affected by way of trade negotiations. For exporters, this is problematic, as under most circumstances they should find it difficult to judge which balance of concessions would entice a foreign government to lower its trade barriers for a specific good or service. They therefore have little idea of how probable it is that the negotiations can be successfully concluded. The need for international negotiations also introduces a considerable time lag between the moment when exporters spot an opportunity and the moment when they can possibly benefit from better foreign market access. This time lag makes prediction of the overall economic situation at the time when the agreement will have practical consequences quite demanding. Foreign governments can also enact domestic industrial policies, which may not even be in clear violation of a trade agreement but still undo its liberalizing effects.

Finally, for an exporter, it is often difficult to know whether they or rather another exporter from the same country will be able to capitalize on improved foreign market access resulting from a trade agreement. Many goods are produced and services provided by more than one domestic company, especially in large trading entities such as the United States or the EU. The problem is further compounded if a plurilateral or multilateral trade agreement gives exporters from several countries the same access to previously protected markets (Goldstein and Martin 2000, 607–8).

Exporters thus face high costs when trying to be informed about opportunities, the likelihood of and benefits from the lowering of a foreign trade barrier are uncertain, and, if there are benefits, each individual exporter does not know whether they or somebody else will reap them. For exporters, consequently, the costs of mobilization often outweigh the anticipated benefits, making them only

---

3. "Note. Préparation de la Conférence Kennedy. Opinions des producteurs français," 5 February 1964, Service de Coopération Economique, no. 930, AD (emphasis added).

rarely engage in political action to improve foreign market access. To be precise, the expectation is not for exporters to be completely absent from the political process. There will always be some that manage to overcome the obstacles just mentioned, either because they have particularly easy access to information or because they are monopolists.[4] Rather, the prediction derived from this argument is that import-competing interests should clearly dominate over exporting ones.

In two specific situations, however, exporters should increase their lobbying activity. On the one hand, I expect exporter mobilization to increase in the face of losses of foreign market access, because in this situation no exploration of opportunities is needed and the beneficiaries of political activity are clearly defined (namely the losers). On the other hand, exporters should mobilize when a foreign government approaches the home country and offers major concessions to reach a trade agreement, because in this situation the uncertainty about a foreign government's willingness to engage in trade liberalization disappears. I will take up these two arguments below.

Building on the scheme presented in figure 1.1, the consequences of exporters' weakness under many circumstances can be portrayed graphically. Figure 1.2 shows the indifference curves of two countries, which are defined by the relative importance given to import-competing and exporting interests by their governments. These curves may differ in shape across countries. A country with a major balance of trade surplus should have a curve that gives more importance to foreign market openness than a country with a balance of trade deficit. Whatever their exact shapes, however, the dominance of import-competing interests on both sides should make sure that the indifference curves of the two sides do not overlap. By extension, no negotiated agreement should be possible.[5]

So far, this discussion has followed quite closely a standard political economy approach to trade policymaking (Anderson and Baldwin 1987; Nelson 1988; Rodrik 1995). The expectation derived from such an approach is for protectionist trade policies to prevail across the globe and over time. Quite evidently, this expectation is contradicted by the empirical record, for example, the process of transatlantic trade liberalization after 1934. To resolve this discrepancy, I go beyond this standard approach by proposing that the prediction changes fundamentally whenever exporters act in defense of their existing trade shares abroad rather than in pursuit of potential gains. Above all, the creation of

---

4. As Destler and Odell (1987) show, some exporters also lobby against domestic import restrictions when they fear negative consequences of such protectionism for their exports.

5. It is important to note that the main difference between this argument and others that come to the conclusion that reciprocal trade agreements are politically efficient (see, for example, Bagwell and Staiger 2001) is that for the reasons mentioned above I expect governments to be little concerned with exporter interests in most circumstances.

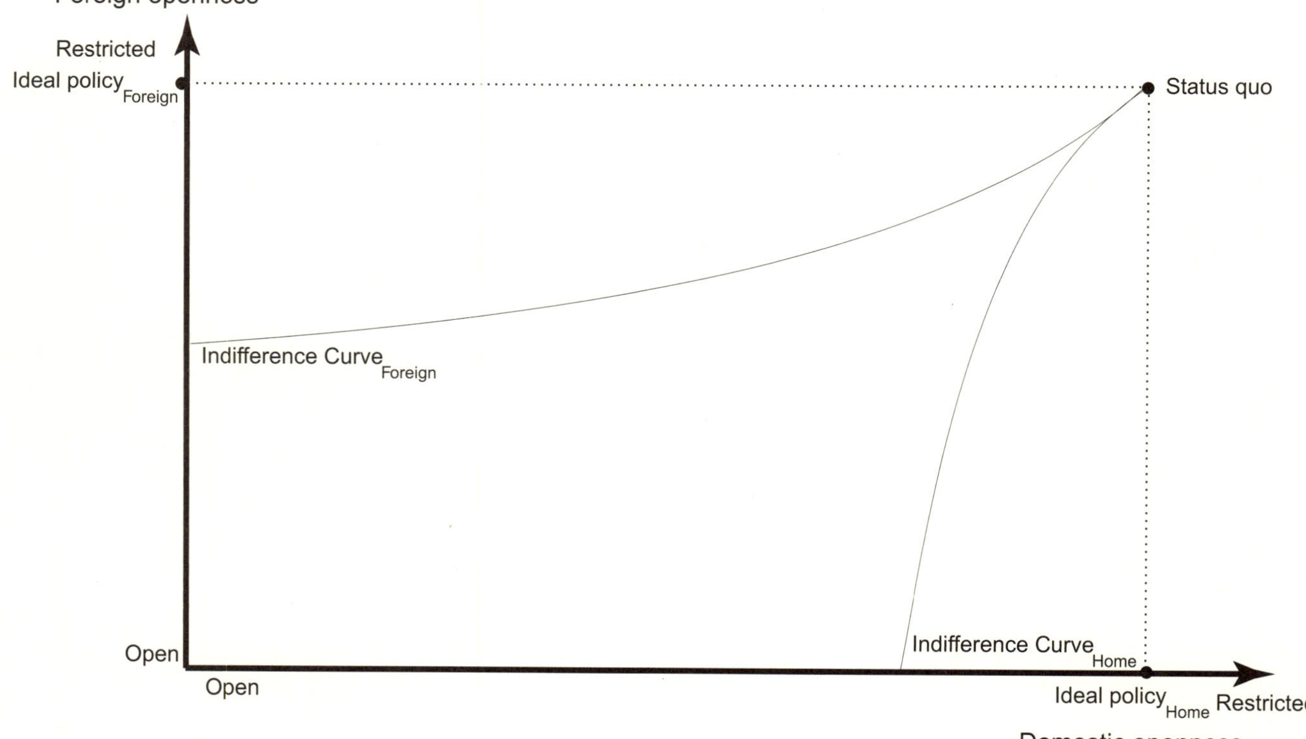

FIGURE 1.2   Bargaining over tariffs I.

Note: Indifference curve$_{home}$ and indifference curve$_{foreign}$ are the indifference curves of two governments crossing the status quo.

a discriminatory trading arrangement among foreign markets imposes costs on exporters barred from participation. Facing such costs, exporters mobilize, leading to a shift in the indifference curves of excluded countries that allows for the conclusion of liberalizing trade agreements.

Preferential Trade Policies and Costs for Excluded Countries

Economic discrimination can be described "as a situation in which deliberate government policy creates different trading and payments conditions for the residents of various foreign countries" (Hieronymi 1973, 7). Following this definition, trade discrimination comprises a broad range of policies, all of which are of concern to exporters in affected countries. As a specific type of discriminatory trade policy, preferential trade agreements remove barriers to trade between members of the agreement but keep them against excluded countries. Preferential trade policies have been widespread throughout the last centuries, although countries have tried to protect themselves against the negative consequences of such policies by including most-favored-nation (MFN) clauses in trade agreements. In Europe, MFN clauses can be found as far back as the Middle Ages (Viner 1950; Pomfret 2001). By contrast, until 1922 the United States made MFN treatment conditional on adequate foreign concessions. After World War II, all GATT contracting parties had to accept an unconditional MFN clause, according to which "any advantage, favor, privilege or immunity granted by any contracting party to any product originating in or destined for any other country shall be accorded immediately and unconditionally to the like product originating in or destined for the territories of all other contracting parties" (GATT, art. 1, par. 1).

Despite the spread of the MFN rule, significant exceptions to the unconditional MFN treatment have existed at all times. Until World War II, for example, empire preference, regional clauses, and special cases of frontier trade between countries with long common borders were acceptable exceptions. These exceptions were frequently invoked to legitimize trade discrimination, as witnessed in the spread of systems of imperial preference in the interwar years. The trading system established after World War II in the GATT also allows for various exceptions to the MFN rule (World Trade Organization 1995, 7). Among them are full free trade areas or customs unions, preferences already in existence at the time of negotiating the GATT, and preferential treatment for or among developing countries. Again, many countries have made use of these exceptions in the last fifty years. Notwithstanding the attempts to restrict their use, preferential trade policies have been a central feature of the international trading system at all times.

If under many circumstances exporters tend to be uncertain about the benefits of engaging in political action, as argued above, why do governments ever pursue preferential trade agreements? It is commonly agreed that several factors can lead a country to engage in such discriminatory trade policies (Gilpin 2001, 358–59; Pomfret 2001, 326–40). Among the ones that I consider to be the most important are protection for import competitors, competition over market access, and foreign policy aims. In some cases, preferential agreements result from an increase in trade barriers intended to protect import-competing interests, which is applied to some countries but not to others. The preferential agreements between the United Kingdom and the Commonwealth countries in the 1930s are an illustration of this mechanism. Protection for import competitors may also be upheld if preferential agreements are designed in a way that only shifts imports from one source to another (Grossman and Helpman 1995, 680). In other cases, as I elaborate on below, regional agreements are a reaction to prior preferential policies by other countries. Finally, politicians may seek preferential trade agreements in pursuit of geopolitical objectives, for example to strengthen security alliances (Skålnes 1998). Given the assumptions underlying the protection-for-exporters argument, however, this should only be possible if the agreement imposes limited costs on import-competing interests or if the agreement has some support from exporters. Such support may be forthcoming for agreements between neighboring countries, in particular, since uncertainty about opportunities in neighboring countries should be lower than about opportunities in markets that are geographically farther away.

The Static Effects

Whatever the reasons for their creation, early on it was recognized that preferential trade agreements can have a variety of economic effects (O'Brien 1976). Already in 1776, Adam Smith (1937, bk. 4: chap. 6) stressed the negative consequences of (preferential) trade treaties for merchants in the country granting preferences. Not before 1950, however, did the economic analysis of preferential trade agreements advance substantially. In that year, Jacob Viner (1950, 44) demonstrated that the direct trade effects of preferential trade agreements depend on the changes in relative prices they bring about. He showed that customs unions can both create and divert trade, depending on whether they shift the sources of supply to lower- or higher-cost sources. Trade creation shifts the supply from higher-cost domestic producers to lower-cost producers in another member country of the preferential trade agreement. Trade diversion replaces lower-cost supplies from the rest of the world with higher-cost production from within the borders of the preferential trade agreement.

For exporters in third countries, trade creation is at most of indirect relevance, as the gains from trade creation accrue to exporters in the member countries of the agreement. What is imperative in the present context, therefore, is to establish the factors that determine the extent of trade diversion. Three are of particular importance. First, the difference between the trade barriers confronting imports from within the agreement and from the rest of the world is crucial, as it determines the advantage that insiders have over outsiders. Second, the size of the agreement plays a role, with trade diversion likely increasing up to a certain size of the agreement and then reaching zero as the agreement encompasses the entire world (Krugman 1991). Finally, the degree of substitutability of a product influences the extent of trade diversion. Trade diversion will be lower, the fewer the goods produced within the preferential agreement that are perfect substitutes for imported goods. An increase in product differentiation and intra-industry trade should thus reduce the potential for trade diversion.

The gist of this discussion is that the extent of trade diversion is likely to differ from case to case. Nevertheless, there exists little doubt that in most circumstances (some) exporters in third countries will incur at least some costs from the establishment of a preferential trade agreement. Even if for a country in the aggregate these losses are small, they may be *politically* relevant as long as they are concentrated on specific economic actors.

Third-country exporters may be able to recover part of their losses by way of "secondary trade expansion" (Humphrey 1961). Such trade expansion comes about if the members of a preferential trade agreement reduce their exports outside the borders of the agreement in favor of exports to other members of the preferential trade agreement and thus open these markets for suppliers from third countries. If the creation of a preferential trade agreement allows the member countries to benefit from economies of scale and a more efficient allocation of resources, however, we may witness a net expansion of production rather than the redirection of trade away from third-country markets. Even if there is significant secondary trade expansion, for third country suppliers this should not be equal to keeping the original export market, because shifting exports to third markets can require high investments in new supply networks. Moreover, secondary trade expansion does not necessarily benefit those exporters that suffer from trade diversion.

The Dynamic Effects

In addition to these static effects, preferential trade agreements can have dynamic effects, which tend to produce ambiguous results for excluded exporters (Baldwin and Venables 1995; Panagariya 2000). For one, preferential trade agreements can cause an increase in the size of firms in member countries, helping them to achieve economies of scale and a reduction in the average cost of production (Corden 1972; Chase 2005). This can reinforce the static effects of trade creation and trade diversion. Trade diversion, for example, can allow an industry in a member country to gain economies of scale and in turn become more competitive. This may lead to a further reduction of imports from third countries. Trade diversion can also have further trade suppressing effects if the reduction in demand for imports from an excluded country leads to a loss of economies of scale and thus higher costs of production there. An increase in the importance of economies of scale in an industry, consequently, is likely to strengthen the negative effects of the creation of a preferential trade agreement for exporters in excluded countries.

Preferential trade agreements can also boost competition in an economy. In the short run, competition reduces prices, leading to an increase in consumer purchases, which may partly undo the negative effects of trade diversion. Much of the larger demand, however, may be satisfied by newly competitive domestic firms. In the long run, as has been argued by the literature summarized under the label of "endogenous growth theory" (Romer 1990), augmented competition, by spurring technological innovations, may also stimulate growth in this economy and thus foster additional demand. Again, this may alleviate the situation of exporters in third countries. The increased competitiveness of firms within the arrangement, however, may also be to the detriment of exporters in excluded countries, if it allows the former to boost their exports into third-country markets. Moreover, preferential trade agreements do not always increase competition. If a preferential trade agreement reduces the number of firms in the market by allowing for the exploitation of economies of scale, competition may actually decline. In this case, prices increase and demand weakens. The dynamic effects of preferential trade agreements thus are ambiguous, making it difficult to predict their external impact. Nevertheless, on average, it is likely that the dynamic effects add to rather than offset the negative static effects of preferential trade agreements for exporters in excluded countries.

Beyond Customs Unions

Although originally most authors dealing with the economic effects of discrimination concentrated on the case of customs unions, with a few exceptions the findings presented above can be generalized to all types of preferential trade agreements. In the case of free trade areas, rules of origin can also be a significant source of trade diversion. As the members of such an area do not agree on a common external tariff, they have to establish rules of origin to avoid trade deflection through the member country with the lowest external tariff. These rules of origin determine whether a product is considered as being produced within the free trade area or outside. If the rules stipulate very high domestic contents for tariff-free treatment, the inputs for the product have to be manufactured within the free trade area, and thus the potential for trade diversion increases.

In common markets, the harmonization of standards can create discrimination. The case of standards is noteworthy in that economic integration can have positive externalities if member countries agree on common standards that make it easier for third-country producers to export to all of the members of a preferential trade agreement under the same conditions. At the same time, a common standard can have a protective impact and thus create negative externalities if it inhibits imports from third countries. It is up to the discretion of the standard-setting body whether it establishes discriminatory standards or rather standards that give exporters from third countries the same chances of selling in this specific market. Since regulatory agencies may be captured by interest groups (Stigler 1971), at least some standards are likely to be set in a discriminatory manner.

Importantly, this discussion leads to the conclusion that it is very likely that the creation of a preferential trade agreement will hurt *some* exporters in third countries, at least in the short run, even if the overall welfare effects for an excluded country are positive (Wei and Frankel 1998). The overall size and sectoral distribution of the losses depends on the trade flows before the creation of the preferential trade agreement, the difference between the tariffs imposed on outsiders and insiders, the size of the preferential trade agreement, the commodity overlap of exports between outsiders and insiders, the degree of substitutability of goods and services, and the importance of economies of scale. The loss that an excluded exporter faces can be a loss of market share, a loss in the value of exports, or a loss in profits. By reducing the demand for imports, for example, preferential trade agreements may cut the prices of third-country exports and thus the profits accruing to exporters (Chang and Winters 2001).

Mobilizing Exporters

Exporters hurt by discriminatory trade policies abroad can react to them in three possible ways: they can try to adapt, invest inside the borders of the preferential trade agreement to avoid discrimination, or lobby their government to engage in policies that reduce the negative consequences of discrimination. Adaptation could mean exporting a slightly different product that does not face the same level of trade diversion or exporting to another market. Investing inside the borders of a preferential trade agreement to avoid trade discrimination can take the form of setting up subsidiaries, licensing foreign producers to manufacture and sell the good, and engaging in joint ventures. Finally, exporters may push their government to adopt policies that protect exporter interests.

A firm chooses among these options by comparing the utility of each alternative, which is determined by variables such as the intensity of discrimination and the size of the resulting costs it faces, the policies of foreign countries regarding direct investments, the degree of factor specificity of its investments, its access to political decision makers, and its beliefs about the strategies chosen by other actors. With this variable having a different value depending on the firm, it is likely that at any time there is variation across firms in the choice of strategies. It is even possible for individual firms to opt for more than one of the three strategies in response to discrimination. Nevertheless, it seems safe to say that for much of the twentieth century, most U.S. exporters should have chosen the third approach in response to discrimination in Europe. Up until the 1990s, there simply was no market that could have substituted for the European one, and the opportunities for foreign direct investment were circumscribed. In any case, the following argument is pertinent as long as at least some exporters opt for the lobbying strategy.

At first sight, the firms that decide on the third approach should face the problems crippling exporter lobbying that were discussed above. For two reasons, however, exporters facing losses find themselves in a situation that is substantially different from the one in which they have to decide whether to lobby for possible gains of foreign market access. On the one hand, exporters should be more easily informed about losses than about possible gains. Whereas, in the latter situation they have to scan foreign markets continuously, in the former they can rely on fire alarm–type mechanisms, making the acquisition of relevant information cheaper. On the other hand, whereas, in the proactive situation exporters are uncertain about who among them will reap the gains of better foreign market access, in the reactive situation those exporters who already supply a share of the foreign market have reason to be confident that when reestablishing the old competitive conditions they will be able to garner the benefits of maintaining their market shares. In short, exporters are easily informed about losses that result from the trade policies of foreign countries and—even more important—know who among them will benefit from lobbying that protects existing market access.

A loss of foreign market access resulting from a foreign preferential trade agreement thus increases affected exporters' expected benefits from political mobilization, making them more likely to engage in political activity.[6] This expectation is in line with existing research on the behavior of firms. As put by one author, "threat in general is a more reliable stimulus to action [for enterprises] than opportunity is likely to be" (Vernon 1966, 200). Similarly, a study of lobbying strategies comes to the conclusion that "the vast majority of corporations' political action continues to be *reactive;* companies deal with issues only *after* they become threats" (Yoffie and Bergenstein 1985, 124, emphases in original). I. M. Destler (2005, 5) also states: "It is the embattled losers in trade who go into politics," rather than "firms with expanding markets and ample profits." Finally, according to a survey, "Britain's top companies…admit they are not as good at spotting market opportunities…as they are at responding to threats" (as summarized in the *Financial Times,* 5 Jan. 1995, 14).

The reasoning so far can be stated succinctly in form of the following hypothesis:

> *Hypothesis 1: The Mobilization Hypothesis*
> Exporters increase their lobbying efforts whenever they face losses of foreign market access resulting from the formation (deepening, enlargement) of a preferential trading arrangement among foreign countries.

As discrimination differs across products, the reactions of different producers vary, as well; those exposed to the strongest discrimination should be the most eager to mobilize.

The speed with which exporters in excluded countries react to the creation of a preferential trade agreement is likely to vary from case to case. In most cases, I expect exporters to respond just after an agreement is signed or when they experience the first negative consequences. In some cases, however, mobilization may occur in parallel to the negotiation of an agreement. This is particularly likely if exporters recently mobilized in response to the conclusion of another trade agreement and learned from that experience. In the 1960s, for example, U.S. exporters reacted very early to the prospect of the United Kingdom acceding to the EEC, as they had just suffered the consequences of the creation of that trading entity. Equally, in the early 2000s, European exporters that had incurred losses from the North American Free Trade Agreement (NAFTA) mobilized to

---

6. Currency fluctuations may also produce losses of foreign market access, but their effect on mobilization levels is more ambiguous. Even if a currency appreciation makes exports more expensive, exporters may have little incentive to lobby in response, as they also gain from cheaper foreign inputs and a higher value of their assets. Exporters may also be able to hedge against the risk of currency fluctuations by investing in the spot currency market and thus do not have to rely on government intervention.

influence EU trade policy vis-à-vis Chile at the same time as the U.S. negotiated an agreement with that country.

In the absence of a new shock, the mobilization of exporters against the losses stemming from a specific preferential trade agreement should only be temporary. After a few years, exporters either should be successful in convincing their government to reach an agreement with the members of a preferential trade agreement or they should have adapted to the new situation. Again, the exact duration of exporter mobilization varies from case to case, depending on the adjustment costs exporters face and exporters' judgment about the likelihood of their demands being satisfied in the near future. Nevertheless, it seems safe to state that the observation of exporters continuing to lobby a decade after the creation of a preferential trade agreement and in the absence of a clear chance of success would be an anomaly from the perspective of the protection-for-exporters argument.

Even if import-competing lobbying in excluded countries becomes slightly more intense in parallel to—and possibly in reaction to—the mobilization of exporters, it is unlikely to increase as rapidly as exporters' lobbying in the face of losses.[7] The reason is that keeping in mind budget constraints, adding to exporters' low level of mobilization should be easier than stepping up import competitors' already high level of mobilization. Consequently, although I expect groups advocating the protection of the domestic market to prevail before the creation of a preferential trading arrangement among foreign countries, the balance of domestic interests should shift in favor of exporters once they feel the negative consequences of such an arrangement.

There are several other possibilities of theorizing a bias toward lobbying against losses. For one, it can be argued that if a government intervenes in a profitable sector, more firms will be attracted to that sector owing to the increased returns on investment, intensifying competition and causing gains to be lost again (Baldwin 1993; Baldwin and Robert-Nicoud 2007; for the underlying logic, see also Stigler 1971). Investing in lobbying thus would not pay off. Conversely, if a government invests in a declining sector, this act is unlikely to attract additional capital into that sector. Firms active in that sector, consequently, find it attractive to appeal to government for interventions that maintain current returns on investment. These different incentives facing firms in growing and in declining sectors may create a bias in favor of lobbying against losses. This reasoning, however, does not apply to sectors with (relatively) high entry barriers. In such

---

7. Import competitors in excluded countries, for example, have an incentive to increase their lobbying activity if a preferential trade agreement increases the competitiveness of exporters in the member countries.

sectors, firms do not have to fear the short-term entry of challengers, irrespective of whether the industry is declining or profitable. The reasoning is further put into doubt by empirical studies that reveal that more profitable industries do not attract more entrants than less profitable ones (Geroski 1995).

A bias in favor of lobbying against losses may also exist if fighting for gains causes less sympathy than struggling against losses. For a large firm, in particular, displaying its full weight when pushing its interests may have negative reputational consequences. A classic study of trade policy supports this argument when stating that "concern over [the companies'] public visibility and fear of being accused of throwing their weight around" inhibits lobbying (Bauer, Pool, and Dexter 1972, 259). The reasons could be "fear of public and particularly government action, fear of retaliation from business associates, [and] moral conflict over violating a fundamental concept of business ethics." A firm may therefore use its influence only on issues on which it can expect a positive reception by the public, such as defense against foreign discrimination.

Alternatively, human beings may generally underestimate potential gains. "Hysteresis in valuations," as this effect was termed by Russell Hardin (1982, 69–72), may make people overestimate the losses they suffer from a collective bad relative to the gains they can enjoy from the equivalent good. Such hysteresis is especially frequent if a good cannot easily be converted into money. Prospect theory makes a similar point when arguing that actors are loss averse: they attach more value to losses than to potential gains, and thus assume more risk whenever they perceive themselves threatened by losses (Kahneman and Tversky 1979; Fanis 2004). This makes them more likely to engage in political activity in response to losses relative to a reference point than in pursuit of gains. Also related to this is the idea that interest groups may lobby more in response to losses because their marginal utility of wealth is declining (Pahre 2008). In this conceptualization, once actors reach their "optimal" level of wealth, they reduce their lobbying effort. By contrast, if they fall below their optimal level, they increase their lobbying effort.

Finally, a government may follow a particular social welfare function that weighs losses more than gains, such as Max Corden's (1997, 74) conservative social welfare function, which reads: "Any significant absolute reductions in real income of any significant section of the community should be avoided." Knowing this government preference, firms would adapt their lobbying behavior and lobby in defense against losses rather than in pursuit of gains. All of these (and possibly other) arguments lead to a similar conclusion of exporters mobilizing more in response to losses than in pursuit of gains. While I cannot test these different explanations against each other, the uncertainty-based argument that I propose is the one that fits best with the other elements of the protection-for-exporters argument, which build on the assumptions of instrumentally rational actors and societal actors as the drivers of political processes.

Protection for Exporters

Based on the political economy model of trade policy developed above, governments should react to a mobilization of exporters with an initiative aimed at the protection of exporter interests, most likely to be achieved by way of a reduction in the discrimination stemming from the preferential trading arrangement. At the same time, to maximize the chances of reelection, decision makers should try to limit the costs imposed by such an initiative on import-competing interests. Even a mobilization of exporters, therefore, will not lead to a complete reversal of the policies pursued by a government; the continued existence of import-competing groups will influence government policies as well. In other words:

> *Hypothesis 2: The Influence Hypothesis*
> The stronger the lobbying effort of exporters, the more concerned a government should be about the protection of exporter interests, while continuing to cater to those import competitors that engage in lobbying.

Responding to Discrimination

Although it would seem easiest for a government to achieve this dual objective by subsidizing exports to an extent that allows exporters to regain the market shares lost owing to the preferential trading arrangement, this strategy is excluded by the fact that foreign countries would most likely impose countervailing duties in response. An excluded country still disposes of a series of options to provide protection to exporters: it can offer concessions, either of a preferential or a nonpreferential kind, to the member states of the preferential agreement in return for a reduction of their trade barriers; it can aim at gaining better access to the markets of third countries by establishing a rival agreement with them; and it can threaten with a closure of its own market unless the member states change their trade policies. I label these strategies "preferential access," "nondiscriminatory access," "rival agreement," and "threat."

Some examples illustrate the empirical relevance of these different options. The preferential access strategy is witnessed in the reaction by several small German states to the abolishment of tariffs within Prussia (1818). Their accession to the Prussian customs area led to a larger economic union that had a further pull effect on excluded states (Viner 1950; Pahre 2008, 309–10). The same strategy is evident in the case of the EU, to which no fewer than twenty-one countries acceded between 1973 and 2007. Similarly, the North American Free Trade Agreement was a result of the accession of Mexico to the U.S.-Canada Free Trade Agreement (Gruber 2000). The nondiscriminatory access strategy was used by the United States in the 1930s and 1940s to protect exporters' access to the United Kingdom, after the latter country had signed the discriminatory Ottawa agreements with the Commonwealth countries (1932). Likewise, in the late 1950s and early 1960s, both the United States and the United Kingdom hoped to reduce the trade diversion produced by the creation of the EEC through the MFN negotiations in the GATT-sponsored Kennedy round.

The United Kingdom put into practice the rival agreement strategy when pushing for the creation of the European Free Trade Association (EFTA), which brought together seven countries excluded from the EEC. Chile's decision to join the Mercado Común del Sur (Mercosur) as an associate member is also an example of the rival agreement strategy (Baldwin 1997, 871). In the mid-1990s, Chile suffered from exclusion from NAFTA, but could not join that agreement for lack of backing from the U.S. Congress, and thus decided to seek closer relations with Mercosur instead. Finally, in some cases excluded countries use a threat to protect their exporters. In the late 1850s, Prussia submitted a formal protest against the Austrian customs union with Modena, which contributed to its lapse in 1859. In 1904, Bulgaria and Serbia agreed to introduce free trade between the two countries and to adopt similar customs practices. When the Austro-Hungarian Empire complained that this would violate its MFN treaty with Serbia, the latter country yielded, and a simple commercial treaty replaced the free trade agreement. In 1932, lastly, the United Kingdom successfully used a threat (namely to revoke MFN treatment) to prevent the creation of a preferential trade agreement among the Benelux countries. The project consequently was realized only after World War II.

The various strategies come with advantages and disadvantages for excluded countries. Preferential concessions to the member countries that lead to an enlargement of the existing discriminatory agreement enable exporters to maintain and possibly even enhance their access to these markets. At the same time, however, accession to the preferential agreement entails costs in terms of lost protection for import-competing producers and possibly losses for exporters in third countries, if the latter move to conclude their own preferential agreements in response. Preferential concessions can also lead to the creation of a hub-and-spoke network of preferential agreements, in which excluded countries only conclude agreements with individual member countries. In this case, the costs for import-competing producers may be lower as the concessions can be tailored more precisely, but the gains for exporters also tend to be lower as such an agreement will maintain access only to one market.

Nonpreferential concessions, which can be negotiated bilaterally or multilaterally, lead to a lower level of protection for exporters in an excluded country. The concessions exchanged tend to be less far-reaching than in free trade agreements (since in the modern trading system the latter have to be compliant with GATT rules that stipulate that tariffs have to be cut to zero) and the concessions gained have to be shared with other countries. At the same time, such a nonpreferential strategy also eliminates the potential costs with respect to access to third markets inherent in the preferential strategy. A rival agreement with other countries can have a double effect: it may offer exporters alternative outlets for their products and may also push the member countries of the original preferential agreement into negotiations with the members of the new entity. Nevertheless, this strategy can backfire: if it does not encourage the countries of the original preferential agreement to seek negotiations, exporters continue to suffer from exclusion from those markets. Finally, a threat with retaliation may make the member countries change their trade policies in a favorable way, allowing an excluded country to achieve protection for exporters without having to impose any costs on import-competing interests. If the threat fails, however, an excluded country will be in an even worse situation than before, since discrimination against its exports continues while the country also has to cope with the consequences of a trade war (see also Haftel 2004, 125–26). In short, each of the various strategies has its pros and cons for excluded countries.

Choosing among Response Strategies

Several studies have already noted that excluded countries can select among these different strategies in response to foreign discrimination (Baldwin 1993; World Trade Organization 1995, 51–54; Haftel 2004, 124–25). Nevertheless, so far little theoretical work has been undertaken that aims at an explanation of why a specific country chooses one rather than another of the alternatives. Mattli (1999) is among the few to tackle this issue: according to him, countries excluded from a regional integration effort and suffering from relatively low economic growth can pursue two "integration strategies," namely entering the regional agreement or setting up a rival preferential trade agreement. In this view, excluded countries' choice between the two strategies is straightforward: they prefer accession and pursue alternative agreements because either existing members reject their accession application or they face a prohibitively high entrance price. This explanation, however, is not completely satisfactory since it simply assumes a preference for accession over the setting up of an alternative agreement.[8] Moreover, it only distinguishes two possible strategies without taking into account the other ones that excluded countries can pursue, namely threat and nondiscriminatory access.

I fill this gap with an argument that builds on an existing literature on retaliation in trade policy (Odell 1993; Bayard and Elliott 1994; Zeng 2002) and that makes explicit the *domestic* logic of the choice of response strategy. In line with the assumptions set out above, politicians' main aim is to maximize the chances of reelection. For this, the degree of discontent among organized societal actors is critical; the larger the number of such actors that are dissatisfied with policy decisions, the lower the probability of reelection. Societal actors, in turn, are discontented if policies impose large reallocation costs on them. In trade policy, politicians should thus try to minimize the reallocation costs that specific policies inflict on exporters and import competitors.

Which strategy best achieves this government objective depends on the vulnerability of a country to changes in trade flows, which in turn is a function of a series of factors.[9] Staying within the bounds of the political economy argument developed above, three are of particular importance: the bilateral balance of trade, the degree of regional concentration of exports, and the importance of the export sector for the economy.[10] First, the vulnerability of an excluded country grows as its *bilateral* trade surplus increases. The importance of this factor is best illustrated by considering the impact of a trade war on a country with a large trade surplus. Since a trade war benefits import-competing interests and hurts exporting ones, it imposes larger net costs on a country with a sizable trade surplus than on a country with a trade deficit. The government of an excluded country with a bilateral trade surplus, therefore, should be cautious about choosing a trade strategy that may lead to a trade war.[11]

Second, a country's vulnerability vis-à-vis the members of a specific preferential trade agreement increases with the share of total exports going to them.

---

8. Mattli (1999) mentions that the second integrative strategy is hardly ever successful. This might make countries prefer the first to the second strategy. The success of the many bilateral trading arrangements that have sprung up over the last years, however, seems to contradict Mattli's affirmation.

9. For the concept of vulnerability in international relations, see also Keohane and Nye (1989, 13).

10. These three factors do not directly determine the *political* vulnerability of a specific government. Rather, the impact of these factors on government's vulnerability is mediated by other variables, such as the institutional structure of a country and the regional concentration or dispersion of production. Nevertheless, they can serve as shortcuts to determine political vulnerability in the absence of a more direct measure of this variable. This is so at least for a comparison over time in the same political system (as is done in this book), where political institutions can be assumed to be constant.

11. Governments thus find themselves in the paradoxical situation of pursuing a trade surplus, as this will satisfy both import competitors and exporters, even though this weakens their position in international trade negotiations.

The more exporters are dependent on access to a certain market, the larger their reallocation costs when trying to find alternative outlets.[12] By contrast, the dispersion of exports across the globe decreases dependence on specific markets but increases dependence on generally free and nondiscriminatory world trade. Finally, the size of the export sector as a share of the economy should also affect the vulnerability of a country (Hirschman 1945; Krasner 1976, 320). The larger the export sector, the more politically important is the discontent voiced by export interests.[13] The government of a country with a large export sector, consequently, is under stronger pressure to find a compromise than that of a predominantly self-sufficient country.

In short, an excluded country that has a bilateral trade surplus with the members of the preferential trade agreements, that has its exports concentrated in the affected markets, and that has a large export sector is likely to be highly vulnerable. The government of such a country, in which exporters face high adjustment costs from the closure of the specific foreign markets, should opt for negotiations in response to foreign discrimination.[14] By contrast, a country with a bilateral trade deficit, exports that are either dispersed or concentrated outside of the preferential agreement, and a small export sector relative to its economic size is far less vulnerable to changes in trade flows caused by this specific agreement. The government of such a country is likely to choose an assertive strategy when facing foreign discrimination.[15] This discussion allows me to formulate the following hypothesis:

> *Hypothesis 3: The Choice of Strategy Hypothesis*
> The more vulnerable a country, the more likely it is to offer concessions to the member countries of a preferential agreement to maintain access for its exporters ("preferential access" and "nondiscriminatory access" strategies), and the less likely it is to threaten with retaliatory measures ("threat" strategy) or to join a rival agreement ("rival agreement" strategy).

---

12. This argument again builds on the assumption (introduced above) that exporters find it difficult to be informed about opportunities in foreign markets. Reallocation costs are thus a function of the amount of exports for which a new market has to be found and not the actual availability of alternative markets.

13. A larger export sector often goes hand in hand with more imports. My argument is not about the relative strength of exporters and import competitors, however, but about the absolute costs to decision makers of neglecting exporter interests as the size of the export sector increases.

14. Interestingly, the prediction here is for a hegemonic power, which should have a trade surplus and large exports, to be more vulnerable, and thus less likely to use a threat, than a declining hegemon. This may explain why some past hegemonic powers acted in a manner that has been described as "benevolent."

15. A large literature argues that repeated interaction between states may make them opt for cooperative strategies even if they find themselves in a momentarily powerful position (see, for example, Keohane 1984). In a political economy world, however, in which states are not unitary actors, this reasoning is not valid, as governments are expected to follow short-term (electoral) rather than long-term incentives in designing a response to foreign discrimination.

For a vulnerable excluded country, the degree of regional concentration of its exports should influence the decision as to whether the concessions exchanged with the member countries of the preferential trade agreement are of a preferential or a nonpreferential kind. The more widely dispersed the exports of a country are, the more likely it is that this country will stick to a nonpreferential access strategy, because such a country wants to make sure that when negotiating with one country, it does not lose market access in other countries. The rival agreement strategy should be particularly attractive if the excluded country's exports are concentrated in a third region. Table 1.1 summarizes this discussion and links the strategies to ideal combinations of variables. Cases with combinations of variables that are not mentioned in the table may fall into more than one category.

Overall, in this section I have explained how the mobilization of exporters should influence the trade policies pursued by excluded countries and why an excluded country may choose one rather than another strategy in response to the creation of a preferential trade agreement abroad. The next section turns to an analysis of the trade policy choices of the member countries of the arrangement and responds to the question of why they should accept the conclusion of a trade agreement with an excluded country.

Explaining the Trade Policy Choices of Member Countries

Participation in a preferential trade agreement may influence the trade policies of a member country in several contradictory ways (see Krueger 1999; Winters 1999; Panagariya 2000, 317–25; Kono 2007). For example, the costs that the liberalization of trade among members of a preferential trade agreement imposes

Table 1.1 Explaining excluded countries' choice of strategy

STRATEGY	FACTORS EXPLAINING CHOICE
Preferential access	Countries with large dependence on the markets included in the preferential trade agreement (bilateral trade surplus and regional concentration of exports)
Nondiscriminatory access	Countries with substantial exports to many markets, none of which is dominant
Rival agreement	Countries with a geographic concentration of exports outside of the preferential trade agreement and a bilateral trade surplus with the members of the preferential trade agreement
Threat	Countries with relatively low trade dependence and a bilateral trade surplus with the preferential trade agreement

on import-competing industries may make them increase their protectionist lobbying activities. Member governments then should become more willing to impose protectionist trade policies. The same effect can come about if a preferential trade agreement stimulates growth in inefficient industries (McLaren 2002). At the same time, increased competition can eliminate import-competing producers by way of "sectoral attrition" (for this term, see Hanson 1998, 61–62), making protectionist lobbying less pervasive in the long run. Such an effect is particularly probable if members' intra- and extra-agreement comparative advantages are similar (Kono 2007).

Alternatively, a preferential trade agreement may satisfy the demands of some producers for a larger market, and thus reduce free trade lobbying. Regional integration may also allow some firms to achieve economies of scale, and consequently increase their competitiveness. They then may advocate further trade liberalization (Chase 2005). Finally, if the preferential trade agreement is a customs union, protectionist groups, owing to their greater ability to overcome free-rider problems, might have an advantage over free trade forces when trying to influence the new trade policies at the regional level (Bilal 1998). The greater dispersion of protectionist industries in a regional market as compared to a national one, however, may also decrease their political clout.

With all of these effects pointing in different directions, it is no wonder that a review essay came to the conclusion that "we know little about whether, once in place, regional arrangements foster domestic support for broader, multilateral trade liberalization or whether they undermine such support" (Mansfield and Milner 1999, 604). My argument fills this gap in the literature when showing how a shift in bargaining power resulting from the creation of a preferential trade agreement can influence the trade policy choices of its member countries.

A Shift in Bargaining Power

Bargaining power is a function of a party's best alternative to negotiated agreement (BATNA) relative to the one of the other negotiating party (parties). (For the BATNA terminology, see Fisher and Ury 1981.) According to this preference-based measure of power, actors with a relatively bad BATNA have less bargaining power than those with a better BATNA. As actors' BATNA deteriorates, they start to attach a higher value to a negotiated solution, leading to a decline in their bargaining power. An improvement of the BATNA, by contrast, should make them less eager to conclude an agreement and thus should enhance their bargaining power. This reasoning is consistent with the "Nash bargaining solution" that assumes that actors split the difference between the respective BATNAs, at least as long as a set of feasible agreements exists (Morrow 1994, 114).

Returning to the political economy of trade model introduced above, the larger a country's bargaining power, the less it has to concede on the domestic-openness dimension to get closer to its ideal point on the foreign-openness dimension. The lower its bargaining power, the more costly is a favorable change of the other side's trade policies. What is critical in this context is that the creation of a preferential trade agreement influences the distribution of bargaining power between members and excluded countries. Most important, since the bargaining power of a country depends on its eagerness to achieve an agreement, it is influenced by the domestic balance of import-competing to exporting interests. The stronger the lobbying effort by export interests, the higher are the government's opportunity costs of foregoing an agreement.

For an excluded country this means that the mobilization of exporters in response to a preferential trade agreement reduces its bargaining power. It now accepts a negotiated agreement that it would have rejected in the absence of foreign discrimination given the costs that it imposes on domestic import-competing interests. In other words, discriminatory trade policies flatten an excluded country's aggregate indifference curve that links a change in foreign trade barriers to a change in domestic trade barriers by compelling it to find a solution that reduces the discrimination hurting its exporting industries.

This effect is illustrated for the case of an excluded country engaging in negotiations with a member country (figure 1.3).[16] Exporter mobilization in the excluded country leads to a shift from Indifference Curve$_{Home1}$ to Indifference Curve$_{Home2}$ (the status quo, at the same time, moves upward as discrimination limits access to the foreign market). This produces a set of feasible agreements (depicted as shaded area in the figure) which allows for a negotiated agreement that liberalizes trade between the two sides. The size of the resulting shift of bargaining power depends on the degree of discrimination a preferential trade agreement imposes on foreign countries and the third countries' vulnerability to changes in trade flows. Preferential trade agreements with very low external trade barriers or among countries with low levels of imports will not lead to a change in the indifference curves of excluded countries, whereas high trade barriers and originally large imports should cause a large shift in bargaining power. In addition, the shift will be larger if the member countries of the preferential arrangement agree on a common commercial policy, or at least coordinate their commercial policies to avoid excluded countries playing out one member state

---

16. The effect is similar when the excluded country engages in negotiations with third countries for a rival agreement, as also in this situation the country that is most negatively affected from the creation of a preferential agreement will be the one most eager to set up a rival agreement.

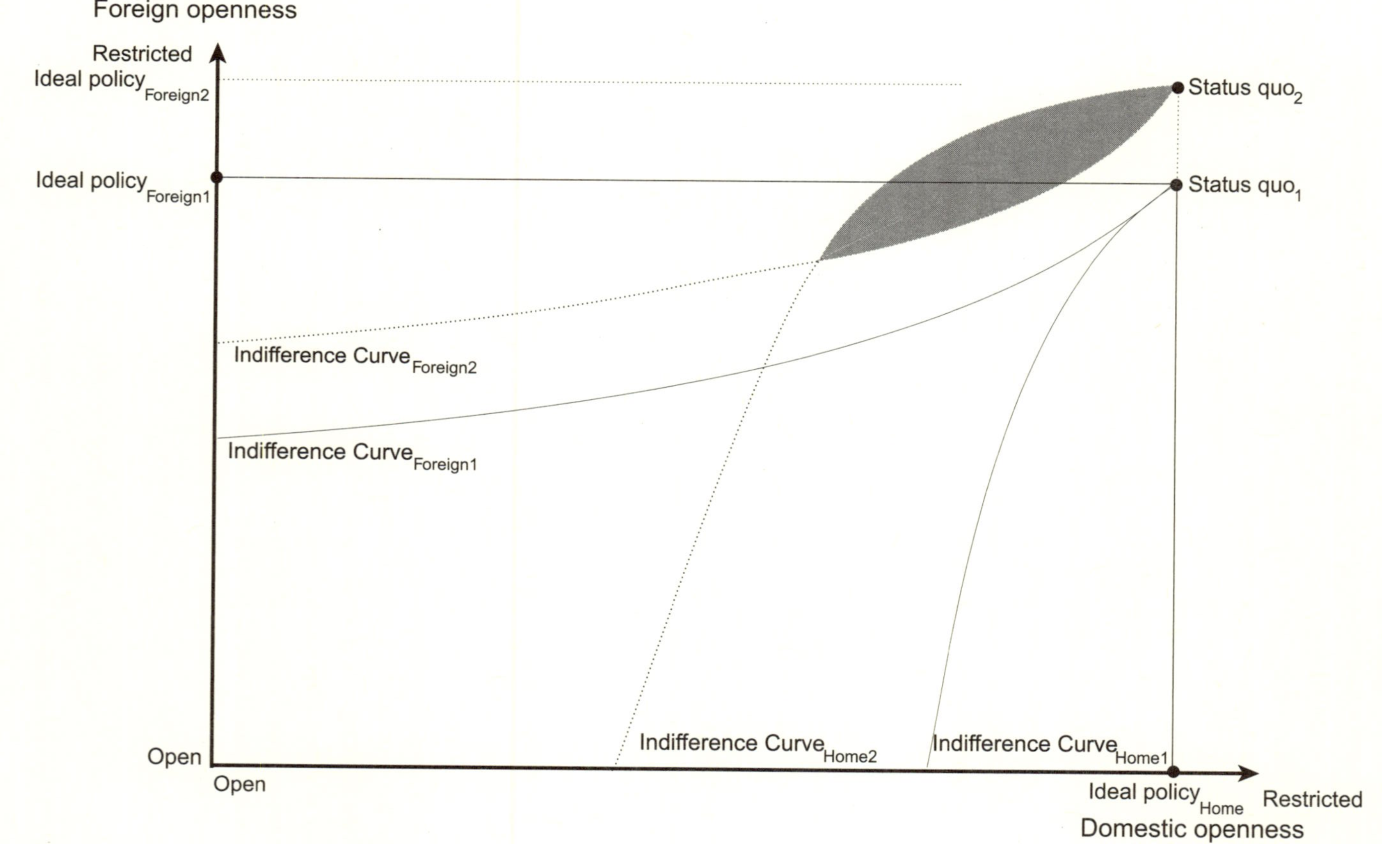

FIGURE 1.3   Bargaining over tariffs II.

Note: See the note to figure 1.2.

against the other.[17] Whatever the exact size of the shift, it goes to the detriment of the excluded country ("home" in the figure), which now accepts higher costs to reduce foreign barriers. The member countries of the preferential trade agreement ("foreign" in the figure), by contrast, can expect additional concessions.

Preferential trade agreements can also increase the leverage of members through other mechanisms. For one, the larger volume of trade represented by the members of a preferential trade agreement may enable them to get larger concessions in trade bargaining (Benoit 1961, 84; Balassa 1967b). Jacob Viner (1950, 56), for example, claimed "the larger the bargaining unit the more effective its bargaining will be." Alternatively, the creation of a customs union with a common external trade policy can increase the power of the new entity in international trade negotiations by forcing the rest of the world to propose deals that are acceptable to all members of the customs union (assuming that each has veto power over the decisions taken within the customs union). In figure 1.3 these arguments could be represented by a flattening of the indifference curve of "foreign," that is, the member countries of the preferential agreement. It is unlikely that in the absence of discrimination either of these mechanisms would bring about trade liberalization, however. Rather, the expectation is for the set of feasible agreements to remain empty.

Various historical examples illustrate the shift in bargaining power brought about by the creation of a preferential trade agreement. Concerning the Zollverein, a customs union among German states in the first half of the nineteenth century, Sidney Pollard (1974, 115) pointed out: "One of the most obvious advantages of the enlarged unit, which did not fail to impress the rest of Germany, was its power of retaliation and thus of wringing concessions from other states, to end the centuries-old political impotence of Germany." The trade relations of the German Empire with Russia in the late nineteenth century provide a further interesting example for the contention that discrimination shifts bargaining power from outside to inside countries. Because Germany had to cope with higher tariffs than France did in exporting to Russia, it first engaged in a tariff war with Russia, but finally decided to seek an agreement. In the negotiations, "Germany was *the more inclined to make terms,* because…Russia had made a commercial treaty with France (June 27, 1893) conceding most-favored-nation treatment and the reduction of some duties, which caused concern to the

---

17. Frequently, coordination is achieved by including a clause in an agreement that prohibits the signatories from reducing the margin of preference. Clauses to that effect can be found in a wide variety of contexts, such as the Ottawa agreements introducing imperial preference in the 1930s and the EEC's trade agreements with former colonies in the 1960s. In the 2000s, the EU's preferential trade agreements include a clause asking for consultations whenever a party to the agreement concludes another preferential agreement.

industrial interests in Germany" (U.S. Tariff Commission 1919, 476, emphasis added). Finally, in the 1880s, European countries tried to establish a customs union in order to increase the bargaining power of these countries vis-à-vis the United States (Viner 1950, 22–23). Individual action against the U.S. tariff was dangerous by inviting retaliation, but decision makers realized that collective action could possibly resolve this problem.

Bargaining Power and the Acceptance of Negotiated Trade Liberalization

The increase in bargaining power should make the member countries of a preferential trading arrangement expect a larger ratio of concessions gained to concessions given in negotiations with excluded countries. Gains are understood as improvements in foreign market access that favor domestic exporting interests, whereas concessions are reductions in domestic trade barriers that impose costs on import-competing interests. Obviously, most trade negotiations formally abide by the reciprocity principle. Nevertheless, formal recognition of the need for reciprocity does not exclude the workings of bargaining power. As Michael Gilligan (1997a, 7) points out, reciprocity does not guarantee a "fair" but only a "voluntary" transaction. In fact, bargaining power as used in this context defines what the parties to an agreement consider to be reciprocal concessions (Hody 1996, 146).

The expected outcome of negotiations thus moves closer to the member governments' ideal points, with the extent of the shift depending on the degree of discrimination a preferential arrangement imposes on the excluded country and that country's vulnerability to changes in trade flows. What is important about this is that with the excluded country showing a willingness to offer additional concessions to the member countries, exporters in member countries face less uncertainty about the benefits of engaging in political activity, making them willing to support an agreement under the condition that it delivers the concessions they are interested in. At the same time, the improved balance of concessions ensures that the number of import competitors lobbying against the agreement will be low. The changed balance of domestic interests makes the member governments accept negotiated trade liberalization.

As pointed out above, the excluded governments are willing to make these concessions because they find themselves in a dilemma: they know that reducing domestic protection may impose costs on import-competing producers. Yet, they cannot ignore exporters' demands for protection in the face of foreign discriminatory trade policies either. With stronger pressure from exporting interests, excluded countries are willing to make more substantial concessions to satisfy this constituency than in the absence of this pressure. Based on this discussion, I derive the final two hypotheses:

> *Hypothesis 4: The Bargaining-Power Hypothesis*
> The mobilization of exporters makes the government of a country excluded from a trade agreement accept a balance of concessions in an exchange of market access with the member countries that it would have rejected given the prior balance of domestic interests.

> *Hypothesis 5: The Member-Country Hypothesis*
> The willingness of the member countries of a preferential agreement to conclude an agreement with excluded countries increases as their ability to extract concessions increases.

Since bargaining situations are characterized by information asymmetries, however, actors engaging in negotiations do not always find an agreement, even if a set of feasible agreements exists. Occasionally, negotiations break down, as all participants have incentives to misrepresent their preferences and to exaggerate their resistance points, that is, the points at which they are willing to accept a negotiated agreement (Morrow 1992). Illustratively, when in the early 1960s the United Kingdom applied for accession to the EEC, disagreement about the appropriate entry price made the French government veto the negotiations, only for Great Britain to renew its application shortly thereafter. Equally, in the 1970s, the United States used strategies in response to the enlargement of the EC that proved ineffective. Consequently, sometimes information asymmetries limit the applicability of the bargaining part of the argument in the short run. Nevertheless, in a longer time perspective most anomalies should disappear, since countries can relaunch failed negotiations and reach an agreement in the second attempt.

Methodology

In the following chapters, I apply the protection-for-exporters argument to six cases of transatlantic trade policies from the 1930s until the early 2000s. In five cases, U.S. exporters faced losses of foreign market access, and thus should have responded with increased mobilization. The expectation for the remaining case, dealing with transatlantic trade policies in the 1950s, is that in the absence of a threat to their access to foreign markets, U.S. exporters should have failed to mobilize and no policies in protection-of-exporter interests should have been implemented. With the empirical analysis going back to the 1930s, I am able to cover the whole process of transatlantic trade liberalization from its beginning. The resulting case studies provide for novel insights into the passage of the

RTAA, the creation of the EEC, the Trade Expansion Act of 1962, the Trade Act of 1974, the external consequences of the single market programme, the recent wave of regionalism, and the Trade Act of 2002.

I heavily draw on process-related evidence to establish the internal validity of the cases studied.[18] Process-tracing "attempts to uncover what stimuli the actors attend to; the decision process that makes use of these stimuli to arrive at decisions; the actual behavior that then occurs; the effect of various institutional arrangements on attention, processing, and behavior; and the effect of other variables of interest on attention, processing, and behavior" (George and McKeown 1985, 35; see also George and Bennett 2005, 205–24). The advantage of process-tracing is that it can test several implications of an argument in a single case study. As put by Garry King, Robert Keohane and Sidney Verba (1994, 120–21), "if properly specified…our theory may have many observable implications and our data, especially if qualitative, may usually contain observations for many of these implications."

For each case, consequently, I examine the various causal links of the protection-for-exporters argument: whether exporters were confronted with losses of market access and if so which ones; the degree to which exporters became politically active; whether societal demands were reflected in trade policies; which strategies the excluded country followed in reaction to foreign discrimination; and the trade policies of the member countries of the preferential trade agreement. For each of these links, the evidence should match the expectations derived from the argument. I also test whether the historical record supports additional implications that are suggested by the protection-for-exporters argument. Obviously, such an approach requires a substantial amount of data. I thus make use of a wide variety of primary and secondary sources. Information from archives on both sides of the Atlantic and the systematic analysis of other primary sources such as newspapers and printed documents provide an excellent basis for this purpose.

Throughout the text, I also assess the explanatory power of rival explanations of specific developments. This is important to avoid overestimating the explanatory power of the protection-for-exporters argument. Since some of the potential alternative theories are underspecified in the sense of not making the causal mechanisms underlying their arguments completely clear, making them testable required some interpretation from my side. Only well-specified theories can successfully be confronted with empirical evidence. Process-tracing then can help discriminate among different theories, and may uncover anomalies that can be

---

18. See Dür (2007a) for a more detailed discussion of the tools used to establish internal validity in this book.

explained only with difficulty from the perspective of the alternative theory. The constant evaluation of predictions derived from my argument against those derived from rival theories provides for substantial rigor in the empirical analysis, and thus makes the findings plausible.

Applying the argument to the empirical cases is not always easy, as several of the variables highlighted by the protection-for-exporters argument are difficult to measure. For one, establishing the precise extent of trade diversion caused by a preferential trading arrangement is a tricky task (Frankel 1997). Since the late 1960s, relatively sophisticated econometric methods to assess the extent of trade diversion have been available. Studies using these methods, however, still tend to come to quite different conclusions. Not even the recent methodological convergence on the use of "gravity models" has changed this situation. Such models explain trade between pairs of countries based on their gross domestic products, population sizes, the distance between them, and other factors such as whether they share a common land border or whether at least one of them is an island (Frankel 1997, 40–46). The effect of a trade agreement then is assumed to be the difference between the trade flows estimated with this model and actual trade flows observed. Studies based on gravity models, however, are prone to omit important variables, have to rely on geographical distance as a proxy for economic distance, and cannot address third-country influences on trade flows in their models (Bayoumi and Eichengreen 1997, 142–43). With different authors employing diverse solutions to these problems, the models continue to produce starkly dissimilar findings. In view of this situation, I try to make my assessments plausible by relying on several studies employing alternative approaches for each of the six cases. Data on changes in trade flows complement the assessments made in econometric studies of trade diversion.

I use largely qualitative evidence to assess the extent of exporter mobilization over time. The most evident quantitative indicator, namely the number of exporter witnesses who testify before congressional committees, has to be treated with caution, as members of these committees have substantial discretion in selecting the witnesses who they want to invite. In addition, a simple counting exercise most likely does not do justice to variation in the importance of different witnesses. The chairman of the U.S. Chamber of Commerce, for example, will have greater clout than the representative of a small manufacturing company. No time-series data are available for a second possible quantitative indicator, that is, campaign spending by exporters over time. Finally, the quantitative approach taken by Gilligan (1997a), namely analyzing to what extent members of Congress representing districts with large export industries voted in favor of reciprocal trade legislation at different times, has data requirements that cannot be fulfilled in a book that encompasses seventy years. More important still, as the content of trade bills varies strongly over time, comparisons across bills have to be treated with caution. Again, the combination of a variety of indicators helps me come to a reasoned judgment on the extent of exporter mobilization.

Even more challenging than assessing the extent of exporter mobilization is to link any observable mobilization to changes in trade policy outcomes, that is, to assess the influence of domestic actors.[19] I use a combination of two research strategies to show the plausibility of the argument about lobbying influencing policy outcomes. On the one hand, in each chapter I present detailed evidence (for example, on the timing of policy changes and the rationale given by decision makers for these policy changes) that allows for an assessment of the extent to which lobbying influenced policy outcomes. On the other hand, I establish a correlation between the balance of domestic lobbying and policy outcomes across time. If domestic interests manage to exert influence, decision makers should be more concerned with policies that favor exporter interests in periods with strong exporter mobilization than in periods in which exporters are largely absent from the political process.

Finally, with respect to bargaining power, I try to assess to what degree the positions made public throughout the negotiations by the various sides are reflected in the final agreement. In the cases involving the United States and the EU, the comparison allows for a quite straightforward assessment of bargaining power, as both entities are of approximately the same size and economic weight. With structural factors controlled for, the dynamics outlined here become the most plausible explanation for any asymmetric concessions observed. In the negotiations between the United States and the United Kingdom in the 1930s and 1940s, with structural factors heavily biased in favor of the United States, even a small advantage for the United Kingdom could lead one to suspect that it disposed of additional bargaining power as a result of its preferential agreements. In all cases, I supplement this crude measure of preference attainment with judgments made by other authors.

Cautious generalizations beyond the case of transatlantic trade relations, which is the focus of this book, should also be possible. In fact, the case of the United States responding to foreign discrimination can be seen as a least likely case for the argument made here. For such a case, it is "difficult to hold that any finding confirming theory might just as well express quite different regularities" (Eckstein 1975, 118). For the last seventy years, the United States has been the economically and politically strongest power in the world. Showing that such a power switched to protect exporter interests in response to the creation of a preferential trade agreement abroad will make it plausible that many lesser powers have experienced similar influences.

---

19. Dür (2008) provides a comprehensive discussion of the difficulties of empirically measuring interest-group influence.

Table 1.2   Summary of hypotheses

Hypothesis 1	The Mobilization Hypothesis. Exporters increase their lobbying efforts whenever they face losses of foreign market access resulting from the formation (deepening, enlargement) of a preferential trading arrangement among foreign countries.
Hypothesis 2	The Influence Hypothesis. The stronger the lobbying effort of exporters, the more concerned a government should be about the protection of exporter interests, while continuing to cater to those import competitors that engage in lobbying.
Hypothesis 3	The Choice of Strategy Hypothesis. The more vulnerable a country, the more likely it is to offer concessions to the member countries of a preferential agreement to maintain access for its exporters ("preferential access" and "nondiscriminatory access" strategies), and the less likely it is to threaten with retaliatory measures ("threat" strategy) or to join a rival agreement ("rival agreement" strategy).
Hypothesis 4	The Bargaining-Power Hypothesis. The mobilization of exporters makes the government of a country excluded from a trade agreement accept a balance of concessions in an exchange of market access with the member countries that it would have rejected given the prior balance of domestic interests.
Hypothesis 5	The Member-Country Hypothesis. The willingness of the member countries of a preferential agreement to conclude an agreement with excluded countries increases as their ability to extract concessions increases.

This chapter has set out the conditions under which exporter interests should have become relevant in shaping transatlantic trade relations. The five specific hypotheses that I derive from my causal reasoning are summarized in table 1.2. They concern the mobilization of exporters in response to losses in foreign market access owing to preferential trade policies abroad; the influence that this mobilization has on the trade policies of excluded countries; the determinants of the choice of strategy by excluded countries in response to discrimination; the shift in bargaining power from excluded to member countries as a result of the creation of a preferential trade agreement; and member countries' incentives to accept a negotiated trade agreement with excluded countries. In the following chapters, I examine the explanatory power of these hypotheses for major developments in transatlantic trade relations from the 1930s until the early 2000s. Although evidently various other factors will be of relevance in explaining individual political decisions, I expect the causal mechanism outlined in this chapter to shed new light on major episodes in transatlantic trade relations throughout this period.

IMPERIAL PREFERENCE AND THE U.S. REACTION, 1932–1947

On 17 June 1930, President Herbert Hoover signed the Smoot-Hawley Tariff Act, a bill that increased U.S. trade barriers to record levels. Measured as duties collected as percentage of dutiable imports, the average tariff went up to nearly 60 percent as a result of this bill. Only four years later, Congress passed the Reciprocal Trade Agreements Act, in which it allowed the president to engage in trade negotiations with foreign countries that could lead to tariff cuts of up to 50 percent. In this arguably most significant institutional change in the history of U.S. trade policymaking, Congress delegated to the president part of the power conferred on it by the Constitution to make commercial policy. The RTAA thus indicates a shift in U.S. trade policies away from unilateral protectionism toward reciprocal agreements with the aim of opening foreign markets.

Pertinent to the importance of this institutional change, many authors have suggested explanations for why the RTAA came about and how it could be sustained. All four of the approaches presented in the introduction have been applied to this case. Several authors arguing within the societal approach base their explanations of the RTAA on the fact that the Democrats, traditionally the party of the low tariff, captured majorities in both houses of Congress in 1930 and the presidency in 1932 (Gourevitch 1986; Verdier 1994; Gilligan 1997a; Hiscox 1999; Schnietz 2000). Once in control of the decision-making institutions, they may have implemented a trade policy in accordance with their party platform.

Later, this argument goes, Congress maintained the RTAA because free trade policies led to the disappearance of some import-competing industries owing to increased competition (Bailey, Goldstein, and Weingast 1997). Authors arguing within the institutionalist approach add that the legislation persisted because it empowered exporter interests by allowing for reciprocal trade agreements (Gilligan 1997a), or because of a lock-in effect that secured its persistence even after a change in party control of Congress (Schnietz 2000). The RTAA also might have been maintained for reasons exogenous to the legislation itself. Such external influences could have been the onset of World War II and of the cold war (Verdier 1994), the rise of economies of scale (Chase 2005), or shifts in the geographical distribution of economic activities in the United States (Hiscox 1999).

Other authors explain the passage of the RTAA with the lessons that legislators learned from the Smoot-Hawley act and the following Great Depression. The logrolling that led to the protectionist Smoot-Hawley legislation, and the possibly negative effects on economic growth of this bill, according to this account, taught legislators that they would all be better off if they managed to restrain themselves from voting for trade protection. They realized that congressional tariff setting was inefficient and hence delegated trade authority to the president, who, due to his broad constituency, might give more consideration to the broader ramifications of trade policy (Pastor 1980; Baldwin 1985). In doing so, legislators may also have tried to protect Congress from the pressure of organized interests, thus increasing the autonomy of politicians to enact trade policies in accordance with their own preferences (Bauer, Pool, and Dexter 1972; O'Halloran 1994; Destler 2005).

While existing explanations of the RTAA and its maintenance capture some aspects of the puzzle, they leave several issues unresolved. The protection-for-exporters argument, by contrast, can fill existing gaps and resolve remaining ambiguities. According to this argument, the British move to establish a system of imperial preference in the Ottawa agreements in 1932 triggered the change in U.S. trade policies that is reflected in the passage of the RTAA. More specifically, I contend that U.S. exporters mobilized in response to the costs imposed on them by discrimination abroad. Their lobbying effort convinced Congress to pass legislation that allowed the administration to engage in trade negotiations with the purpose of reducing foreign discrimination. The administration, in turn, became eager to protect exporter interests by way of a trade agreement with the United Kingdom. Not before 1938, and only after arduous negotiations, however, was it able to achieve such an agreement. In fact, as predicted by the protection-for-exporter argument, the British government only accepted an agreement that was highly favorable to British economic interests. Concerns about the British system of imperial preference consequently continued until after World War II and explain both the main features of the GATT and the U.S. eagerness to engage in multilateral trade negotiations in 1947. To make this argument, I first establish the costs of foreign discrimination for U.S. exporters and then analyze

U.S. exporters' lobbying efforts. Next, I discuss how the mobilization of exporters contributed to the passage of the RTAA, before examining the interaction between British and U.S. trade policies before and after World War II.

Imperial Preference and Discrimination against U.S. Exports

U.S. exporters' foreign market access was relatively secure until the late 1920s and early 1930s, when many countries in Europe and elsewhere started to conclude preferential agreements to maintain markets for their exports in a process feeding back on itself. France, one of the first countries to move in this direction, created a free trade area with its colonies in 1928 that increased the territories' share of total French trade from 16 percent in 1928 to 27 percent in 1938 (Anderson and Norheim 1993, 94). Other countries soon followed. Initially, however, relatively few U.S. exports were affected by these moves, since the United Kingdom, the largest trading nation in the world and the largest trading partner of the United States, retained its liberal and mainly nondiscriminatory trade policy.

The situation changed when the United Kingdom started to impose tariffs on a series of non-Empire products in November 1931 (see Rowland 1987, 41–49). Four months later, the Import Duties Act imposed a general duty of 10 percent on all non-Empire imports, excluding only a few primary goods (Benham 1941, 27; Kreider 1943, 20–21). The extent of this British shift to protectionism is best illustrated by the fact that before 1931 all goods entered the United Kingdom free of duty unless they were on a (short) list of dutiable products; after March 1932, all goods were dutiable, unless they were on a duty-free list. The Imperial Economic Conference in Ottawa among the Commonwealth countries then converted these unilaterally imposed preferential trade barriers into a fully fledged system of preference in July 1932. The participants to this conference agreed on a wide-ranging system of imperial preference that was written down in twelve agreements, each valid for five years.[1] In the agreements it formed part of, the United Kingdom further increased nonpreferential tariffs on a series of products, imposed new tariffs on previously excluded imports, and submitted some imports from outside the Commonwealth to quantitative restrictions (Jones 1934, 236–37; Benham 1941, 92–94). It also pledged not to reduce its

---

1. The United Kingdom concluded seven agreements (with Australia, British India, Canada, New Zealand, Newfoundland, Southern Rhodesia, and the Union of South Africa); five more were concluded between other Commonwealth countries. Some of the British colonies and protectorates also enacted preferential tariffs. After 1937 the agreements could be terminated on six months' notice.

nonpreferential tariffs for a period of five years. In the wake of these agreements, preference for imports from Commonwealth countries increased substantially: while in 1929 only 7 percent of imports into the United Kingdom enjoyed preferential treatment, in 1937 this number stood at 60 percent (MacDougall and Hutt 1954, 237).

For many contemporary observers it was evident that the system of imperial preference would mainly work by diverting purchases away from the United States (Jones 1934, 178; *Times*, 8 June 1937, 12). Nevertheless, there was no agreement on the size of the losses that U.S. exporters would incur. At the time, losses in U.S. exports were quantified as follows: $50 million of U.S. trade with Canada (*New York Times*, 27 July 1932, 8); $65 million of manufactured exports to the Commonwealth countries (*Washington Post*, 22 August 1932, 1, 7); and as much as $200 million in total exports (*New York Times*, 28 August 1932, F9). This last figure would have meant a loss of up to 5 percent of average total annual U.S. exports in the five years preceding Ottawa. Consequently, it seems sensible to accept that U.S. exporters had good reason to be concerned about the impact of imperial preference on their access to Commonwealth markets.

In fact, post hoc analyses show that the system of imperial preference established in Ottawa had a significant influence on trade flows, causing losses for U.S. exporters and a heavy increase in the Commonwealth countries' share of total British imports. While the percentage of British imports coming from the Empire increased from 29 percent in 1930 to more than 40 percent in 1938, the percentage originating in the United States fell from around 15 percent in 1930 to around 11 percent in 1934 (see table 2.1). In absolute terms, U.S. annual exports to the United Kingdom declined from an average $734 million in the five years preceding the introduction of imperial preference to an average $421 million in the five years following this event (calculated from data in Carter et al. 2005, Ee533–50).

Table 2.1 Imports to the United Kingdom by origin, 1927–1938 (as a percentage of total imports)

YEAR	EMPIRE	NON-EMPIRE	U.S.
1927	30.1	69.9	17.3
1930	29.1	70.9	15.0
1932	35.4	64.6	12.0
1934	37.1	62.9	11.2
1937	39.4	60.6	11.1
1938	40.4	59.6	14.0

Source: Glickman (1947, 453).

An analysis of product-specific consequences buttresses the point that imperial preference hurt some U.S. exporters. At that time, the United States was a major exporter of primary products such as apples, citrus fruits, cotton, ham, lumber, pork, tobacco, and wheat to the United Kingdom (Drummond and Hillmer 1989, 10). Most of these products, with the exception of cotton, which initially remained duty free, were affected by the preferential system since they faced direct challengers from within the Commonwealth. With regard to ham, for example, the U.S. share of a decreasing amount of imports was reduced from 14 percent in 1930 to 5.3 percent in 1938 (Glickman 1947, 449–54). The reduction in wheat exports to Britain was especially grave. While in 1930 the United States provided 20.1 percent of the wheat imports of the United Kingdom, this percentage dropped to 9.4 percent in 1931 and to 4.4 percent in 1932. Over the following years, practically no U.S. exports of wheat went to the United Kingdom, and only in 1938, and already influenced by war preparations in Europe, did the U.S. share again increase to 15.3 percent. Even accepting that droughts that crippled crops in the United States in 1934 and in 1936 also played a part in this development, discrimination clearly was an important factor.

The United States also lost in various other markets due to the introduction of imperial preference. In Canada, exports of chemicals, cotton textiles, and raisins were threatened by trade diversion until the U.S. agreement with Canada in 1935 put U.S. exporters again on an equal footing with British producers (Glickman 1947, 461). Exports of timber and some other products were in danger in Australia, and exports of motor vehicles and petroleum products in New Zealand. In a mercantilist sense, the main beneficiary of these changes in trade patterns throughout the Commonwealth was Canada, since it not only supplied the formerly U.S. share of agricultural exports but also of commodities such as timber. Some Canadian domestic interests, moreover, profited from the diversion of wheat shipments from U.S. ports to Canadian ones. While before 1932 a large part of Canadian wheat was shipped through U.S. ports, after 1932 only Canadian ports could be used if the exporters wanted to avoid the payment of British import duties.

The conclusion of preferential trade agreements between the United Kingdom and countries such as Argentina, Denmark, Norway, Russia, and Sweden in 1933 further aggravated the negative economic consequences for U.S. exporters of imperial preference. These agreements led to additional restrictions to U.S. market access in Great Britain.

It was not before the late 1930s that the effects of the Ottawa agreements were diluted by British efforts to rebuild its military in the face of German aggression. A partial crop failure in Canada in these years also ameliorated the situation of U.S. wheat exporters (Kreider 1943, 30). Nevertheless, imperial preference remained threatening for U.S. exporters until the 1950s, when due to exogenous reasons the share of total British trade accounted for by the former colonies fell from 48 to 39 percent between 1948 and 1958 (Anderson and Norheim 1993, 93).

In short, the system of imperial preference imposed substantial costs on some U.S. exporters. The losses were mainly concentrated on agricultural exporters, but also some exporters of manufactured products were affected. The Ottawa agreements, however, only contributed to the trade-reducing consequences of the Great Depression and a general increase in protectionism and in the number of preferential agreements across the world. The cumulative effect of these developments on U.S. exports was substantial. All in all, between 1929 and 1932, the value of total U.S. exports fell from more than $5.2 billion to approximately $1.6 billion (see the data in Carter et al. 2005). With discrimination being a major factor contributing to this decline, if Hypothesis 1 is correct, these losses in foreign market access should have made U.S. exporters mobilize in defense of their interests.[2]

The Mobilization of U.S. Exporters after 1932

In 1929, in the hearings for the Smoot-Hawley act, import-competing firms still dominated in numbers all other kinds of witnesses. As put by the author of the landmark study of this trade legislation, "the pressures supporting the tariff [were] made overwhelming by the fact that the opposition [was] negligible" (Schattschneider 1935, 285). Yet, when foreign countries engaged in preferential trade policies at the beginning of the 1930s, as expected by the protection-for-exporters argument, U.S. exporters became active. Three factors support the hypothesis that links this mobilization to British preferential trade policies: the timing of the mobilization in the aftermath of the Ottawa agreements, the demand for reciprocal agreements rather than unilateral tariff reductions, and the complaints about foreign discrimination contained in the statements. These three factors together provide strong support for the hypothesis that discriminatory trade policies tend to give rise to the mobilization of exporters abroad.

With regard to the first aspect, the timing of the mobilization clearly backs Hypothesis 1. Interest groups started to announce their support for a reciprocal tariff policy just when the consequences of foreign discrimination were

---

2. That discrimination was important can be seen from a comparison of trade figures with other countries. The trade of other major trading countries declined as well, but no other country lost as much of its export trade as the United States, namely 69 percent. The exports of the United Kingdom, for example, decreased by 50 percent over the same period (UK data from Mitchell 1992, 562).

increasingly felt (Tasca 1938, 16–17). The export manager of the Black and Decker Manufacturing Company, for example, clearly recognized that the "export professions as a group [had] been inarticulate" before 1932 (quoted in the *New York Times*, 27 November 1932, 10). He therefore called on exporters to form a "militant group" that should ask the government for help in regaining lost foreign markets. By contrast, from 1932 onward exporters used, among other associations, the American Exporters and Importers Association, the American Manufacturers Export Association, the Foreign Commerce Club of New York, the National Automobile Chamber of Commerce, the Tariff Institute, and the World Trade League as platforms to push their demands.[3] In 1933 they hoped that the United States would be able to use the London Monetary and Economic Conference (also known as the World Economic Conference) to gain concessions to achieve a lowering of foreign preferential trade barriers (*Wall Street Journal*, 9 April 1933, N15).

By 1934 a substantial number of groups and firms supported the passage of the RTAA (see table 2.2). In the struggle over the RTAA, consequently, for "the first time in the history of legislative tariff battles" exporters mobilized in a debate over trade legislation (*New York Times*, 6 March 1934, 3). Not only the extent of the mobilization was novel but also the exporters' preferred target, namely the administration.[4] Both the secretary of commerce, Daniel C. Roper, and the secretary of state, Cordell Hull, reported substantial support for reciprocal trade liberalization.[5] In his memoirs, Hull (1948, 370) writes that, despite some opposition, "we received welcome support from many manufacturers who knew the value of exports including the automobile companies and producers of farm products." Contrary to the prediction derived from the institutionalist approach, exporters managed to mobilize even before the institutional change introduced by the RTAA.

Nearly without exception, the groups lobbied for reciprocal trade agreements rather than unilateral tariff cuts. In particular, as early as December 1931 (and one month *after* the United Kingdom imposed preferential tariffs), exporters stressed the need to use reciprocal agreements to regain foreign markets for such products as cars, cotton, tobacco, and wheat (see *New York Times*, 20 December 1931, II:19). One year later, the Foreign Commerce Club of New York maintained

---

3. See Tasca (1938, 17); Beckett (1941, 6–7); *New York Times*, 20 October 1932, 4, and 29 May 1933, 25; State Department Records, Central Files, Record Group 59, Decimal File, 1930–39, NACP.

4. This may explain why Schnietz (2000, 428; 2003, 218–19), who used archival materials of the House Committee on Ways and Means and of several legislators to study lobbying activities by trade associations, found that a substantial majority of groups took a protectionist stance.

5. Letter from the Secretary of Commerce to the Secretary of State, 7 July 1933, State Department Records, Central Files, Record Group 59, Decimal File, 1930–39, NACP.

Table 2.2 U.S. exporter lobbying for the RTAA (selection)

TYPE OF LOBBY	NAME
General business associations	Foreign Commerce Club of New York
	Foreign Trade Club of the Cincinnati Chamber of Commerce
	Foreign Trade Club of the San Francisco Chamber of Commerce
	U.S. Chamber of Commerce
Exporter lobbies	American Exporters' and Importers' Association
	American Manufacturers' Export Association
	Fair Tariff League
	Tariff Institute
	World Trade League of the U.S.
Sectoral associations	American Automobile Manufacturers Association
	National Automobile Chamber of Commerce
	Overseas Automotive Club
	Textile Export Association of the U.S.
	Western States Lumber Company
Individual companies	American Locomotive Sales Corp.
	Black and Decker
	Firestone Tire and Rubber
	General Electric
	General Motors
Agricultural interests	American Cotton Shippers' Association
	American Fruit Growers
	California Sardine Products Institute
	International Apple Association
	Pacific Vegetable Oil Company
	Southwestern Millers' League

that "the only policy which the United States can adopt to restore our foreign trade is that of mutual concessions in tariff duties accomplished through reciprocal trade agreements" (*New York Times*, 20 October 1932, 4). In 1933 a resolution published by the American Manufacturers' Export Association, which was signed by a series of large companies such as Black and Decker, General Electric, General Motors, and Standard Oil also clearly came out in favor of reciprocal trade agreements.[6] In the same year, a telegram to President Roosevelt publicized

---

6. See State Department Records, Central Files, Record Group 59, Decimal File, 1930–39, NACP. The CEO of chemical producer DuPont was the only member of the board of directors of the American Manufacturers' Export Association who opposed the resolution.

a poll of 150 manufacturers that nearly unanimously supported the negotiation of reciprocal trade agreements (Haggard 1988, 99).

Among the agricultural interests, the larger associations such as the National Farmers Union were split concerning their position on the trade-policy issue (what by itself is significant, considering the previously staunch protectionist stance of these groups). Product-specific groups like the American Cotton Shippers' Association or the International Apple Association, however, went on record in favor of reciprocal trade agreements. Quite clearly, then, the objective of this lobbying was the reduction of foreign rather than of U.S. barriers to trade (Haggard 1988, 98), with the ultimate end being the reestablishment of foreign market access. This interpretation is also supported by the fact that exporters demanded still other policies to achieve the same aim: a depreciation of the currency, the establishment of an export-import bank, the strengthening of the navy to secure trade routes, the improvement of air transport, and the diplomatic recognition of the Soviet Union.[7]

When addressing politicians, the groups explicitly complained about the negative consequences of imperial preference. In June 1933, in a telegram to President Roosevelt, the representatives of forty-one companies drew attention to the need to negotiate reciprocal agreements to avoid losses of foreign market access due to the establishment of the system of imperial preference.[8] The export manager of the Black and Decker Manufacturing Company clearly alluded to British trade restrictions as well when he argued that his company would be compelled to set up a plant in the United Kingdom, because of the restrictions hampering trade (*New York Times,* 27 November 1932, 10). Similarly, the International Apple Association, supported by the American Fruit Growers, decried the negative effects of imperial preference for their capacity to export apples to the British market.[9] Together, this evidence concerning the lobbying of U.S. exporters in the early 1930s strongly supports the hypothesis that exporters mobilized in reaction to losses of foreign market access.

Supporting the Maintenance of the RTAA

After the passage of the RTAA, U.S. exporters remained politically active and formed new pressure groups such as the National Committee for Reciprocal

---

7. In fact, Roosevelt resumed diplomatic relations with the Soviet Union to help U.S. exports in 1933 (Eckes and Zeiler 2003).

8. Telegram to President Roosevelt, 8 June 1933, State Department Records, Central Files, Record Group 59, Decimal File, 1930–39, NACP.

9. International Apple Association to Henry L. Stimson, Secretary of State, 1 September 1932, State Department Records, Central Files, Record Group 59, Decimal File, 1930–39, NACP.

Trade to push for the maintenance of this legislation (*New York Times*, 17 November 1935, F9). The Automobile Manufacturers Association explicitly supported President Roosevelt's 1936 election campaign because it hoped that Roosevelt would reduce U.S. tariffs to obtain "compensatory liberalizations from those countries which offered potential outlets" (quoted in Gardner 1964, 39). It also urged the Republican Party to change its stance on the question of reciprocal trade agreements (*New York Times*, 15 May 1936, 2). One year later, it commended the administration for "the thorough and effective work it [was] doing in consummating these reciprocal-trade agreements" (quoted in Brenner 1977, 152). Finally, in 1940, it saw the RTAA as the best instrument to end the downward trend of its exports.[10]

Other business and agricultural support for Roosevelt's trade policy was forthcoming as well. The American Manufacturers' Export Association sent letters to ten thousand exporters to ask for their backing of the new reciprocal trade policy in 1935 (*New York Times*, 17 March 1935, II:19). In 1936, as described by the *New York Times* (29 October 1936, 10; see also Ferguson 1984, 91), "at a mass meeting in the heart of the Wall Street District, about 200 business leaders, most of whom described themselves as Republicans, enthusiastically endorsed…the foreign trade policy of the Roosevelt Administration and pledged themselves to work for the President's reelection." One year later, the U.S. Chamber of Commerce supported the RTAA, arguing that the government "should have power to initiate reciprocal tariff arrangements with foreign countries where such bargaining would be clearly in our national interest."[11] Finally, around the same time the American Farm Bureau started to back the RTAA to restore export markets (*New York Times*, 12 December 1936, 11). The baseline of this lobbying, as succinctly put by a representative of the tobacco industry, was that exporters needed governmental help "to regain [their] lost trade."[12]

Exporters continued to demand a modification of the system of imperial preference in an Anglo-American trade agreement that should lead to "tariff parity" in the British market with competitors from inside the Commonwealth (Drummond and Hillmer 1989, 26). The Foreign Commerce Committee of the Chamber of Commerce was particularly active in this regard (*New York Times*, 6 October 1937, 43). When negotiations with the United Kingdom finally started, various exporter organizations, such as the International Apple Association and

---

10. U.S. Congress, January–February 1940, Hearings before the House Committee on Ways and Means, *Extension of Reciprocal Trade Agreements Act*, 1035.

11. U.S. Congress, January 1937, Hearings before the House Committee on Ways and Means, *Extending Reciprocal Foreign Trade Agreement Act*, 82.

12. U.S. Congress, January–February 1940, Hearings before the House Committee on Ways and Means, *Extension of Reciprocal Trade Agreements Act*, 2592.

lumber producers, contacted the State Department to push their demands for reductions in the British preferential system (*New York Times,* 2 August 1936, 23, and 2 January 1938, 51; Drummond and Hillmer 1989, 49). These demands for concessions in the British market were repeated in the hearings before the Committee on Reciprocity Information from March 1938 onward (*New York Times,* 20 February 1938, 41; Drummond and Hillmer 1989, 99). At that time, petitions for British concessions came, for example, from the American Institute of Meat Packers and the National Lumber Manufacturers' Association, but also from exporters of apples, milled rice, and pears. Exporters of adding machines, cars, road-building machinery, sportswear, toys, and many other manufactured goods were also hoping for reductions in British tariffs to reestablish their access to that market (*New York Times,* 2 January 1938, 51).

A historical study of the U.S.-British trade negotiations thus concluded: "There were many domestic primary producers whom the American government could placate by winning British concessions, whether on tariffs, on preferential margins, or on quantitative controls. Among the most important were the hog raisers, the citrus growers, and the producers of fresh, tinned, and dried fruit" (Drummond and Hillmer 1989, 26). A particular case was the movie industry, which opposed a British law, passed in 1936, that established quotas for movie imports into the United Kingdom, with the aim of supporting the domestic film industry (see Kottman 1968, 229–43). The American film industry, which saw a threat to its position in the British market, lobbied Washington to push for a reversal of this law in the framework of the trade talks with the United Kingdom.

Continued Lobbying by Import Competitors

Despite a significant increase in exporter lobbying in the years after the Smoot-Hawley tariff, protectionist interests in general outnumbered liberal ones (Schnietz 2003, 218–19). In addition to the American Tariff League and the Home Market Club, which were the major protectionist interest groups, such diverse groups as the American Mining Congress, the National Wool Growers, the American National Livestock Association, and the Potters' Association organized in opposition to the RTAA. During the hearings for the 1937 renewal of the RTAA, the Chemical Foundation, the National Association of Manufacturers, and some agricultural interests, especially the dairy farmers, spoke out against a renewal. The prospect of a trade agreement with the United Kingdom also stimulated protectionist lobbying (*Wall Street Journal,* 21 November 1938, 1). The cotton industry and wool producers opposed the agreement in an outright fashion. In the late 1930s, the protectionist coalition encompassed interest groups such as the National Grange (mainly representing small farmers), the United Farmers of America, the Bicycle Institute, and the Synthetic Organic Chemical Manufacturers' Association. Most opposition to trade liberalizing agreements came from the cotton-textile, fishing, glass, glove, handbag, petroleum, pottery, rubber, tanning, and watch industries.

Nevertheless, since import-competing interests were already highly mobilized before 1932 (and the level of import-competing lobbying was steady), the increase in exporter lobbying should have led to a change in the *balance* of interests. The available evidence on lobbying by the two major trade constituencies thus supports the protection-for-exporters argument. At the same time, it raises some doubts with respect to alternative explanations. The lobbying activity of import-competing interests, for example, runs counter to the argument that the RTAA could be passed and/or maintained because of a weakening of protectionist interests in the wake of the Great Depression (Ferguson 1984; Frieden 1988; Lusztig 2004). Similarly, the argument that economies of scale made some U.S. producers prefer freer trade at that time (Chase 2005) can neither account for the precise timing of the mobilization of exporters nor for the strong showing of agricultural interests. Discrimination in third markets, by contrast, provides a compelling explanation of these developments. As put by David Lake (1988, 203), "as trade shrank, the pressure for export expansion grew within the United States."

From Protectionism to Reciprocal Trade Liberalization in the 1930s

The proliferation of proposals for reciprocal trade liberalization in parallel to the mobilization of U.S. exporters suggests that the latter contributed to the changes in U.S. trade policies observable in the early 1930s (Hypothesis 2). In 1931, just when the first exporter groups started to become active, Senator Kenneth McKellar (D-TN) proposed the repeal of the Smoot-Hawley act, an immediate cut of all tariffs by 25 percent, and the offer of another cut of 25 percent for countries willing to increase their imports from the United States by an equal percentage. The link between such plans for reciprocal agreements and the trade policies of foreign countries was evident to contemporary observers. The *Wall Street Journal* (23 November 1931, 1), for example, stated: "The United States may be forced to reembark on its old policy of tariff reciprocity agreements if the present move of the British National Government leads to a permanent protective tariff policy."[13]

---

13. The "old policy of tariff reciprocity agreements," which the quotation refers to, was introduced by the Underwood Act in 1913, but discarded by Congress in 1922.

One year later, a further tariff bill discussed in Congress, known as the Collier bill, included a provision giving the president the power to negotiate reciprocal trade agreements. It is interesting to note that after the House had excluded this reciprocity provision from its version of the bill, the Senate reintroduced it with the argument that the administration would need such authority in that the United Kingdom had announced its intention to negotiate bilateral trade agreements (*New York Times*, 28 January 1932, 8). After the bill passed in Congress backed by the Democrats, however, Republican president Herbert Hoover vetoed it in May 1932, affirming that import protection was critical for the welfare of the American people (Kaplan 1996, 84).

In the same year, trade policy became a major issue in the presidential campaign between Hoover and the Democratic contender Franklin D. Roosevelt. In their speeches, Roosevelt advocated the pursuit of reciprocal trade agreements while Hoover defended the high tariff policy of his administration.[14] Against the backdrop of the Great Depression, the elections produced an overwhelming victory for Roosevelt, who followed up on his promise to change U.S. trade policy by choosing Cordell Hull (D-TN) as his secretary of state. Hull had a long record of supporting freer trade and could be expected to push this issue in his new function.

Indeed, some scholars argue that the free trade beliefs of Hull and of his collaborator Francis Sayre, who served as assistant secretary of state from 1933 until 1939, were decisive for the passage of the RTAA (Bauer, Pool, and Dexter 1964, 26n4; Gardner 1964, 25; Butler 1998). This interpretation, however, is put into doubt by the fact that others in the Roosevelt administration, such as Assistant Secretary of State Raymond Moley and George N. Peek, the president's special adviser on foreign trade, were convinced protectionists.[15] In fact, the passage of the RTAA was preceded by a struggle between these two factions within the administration (Ferguson 1984; Gourevitch 1986). The internationalist camp received support from exporting interests, while the nationalist camp was backed

---

14. In a campaign speech in September 1932, Roosevelt already set out the basic principles of the RTAA. See Medick-Krakau (1995, 76n44). Roosevelt, however, was by no means a convinced free trader. In 1932 he even stated: "I favor—and do not let the false statements of my opponents deceive you—continued protection for American agriculture as well as American industry" (quoted in Moley 1939, 51). The apparent contradiction disappears on acceptance of the view that the RTAA was not a free trade bill, but one intended to bring down *foreign* trade barriers. For Roosevelt's tariff stance during the election campaign, see Dallek (1979, 19); *New York Times*, 27 July 1932, 1.

15. For some sources concerning the economic beliefs of the Roosevelt administration see Peek and Crowther (1936); Moley (1939); Sayre (1939); Hull (1948); Allen (1953); Fusfeld (1956); Feis (1966); and Butler (1998). Peek recounts that for Hull "low tariffs [were] in the nature of a religion" (Peek and Crowther 1936, 28–29). Allen (1953) provides a far more balanced picture of Hull, stressing that the aim of protecting U.S. exports was an important stimulus in making Hull advocate the RTAA.

by import competitors. In such a setting, in which two groups with clearly defined interests oppose each other, it does not seem plausible that the beliefs of individual politicians can decisively shape policy outcomes.

For some authors, this conflict demonstrates that the Roosevelt administration initially oscillated between two different supporting coalitions (Ferguson 1984; Gourevitch 1986, 149; Lusztig 2004, 61–65). They argue that Roosevelt sought backing from the internationalists only when his initial supporting coalition among the nationalists broke down. Not all of the available evidence, however, is compatible with this account. In particular, this interpretation would lead one to expect a major shift in U.S. trade policies in the middle of the New Deal. Nevertheless, such a change did not occur. Throughout the New Deal, the trade policies enacted had features that should have appealed to both internationalists and nationalists, indicating that the administration tried to satisfy both exporting and import-competing interests at the same time. Illustratively, import-competing interests in the agricultural sector were placated both in 1933 and in 1936, and thus before and after the passage of the RTAA, when the administration backed the enactment of protectionist farm bills by Congress. Such constant concern about the demands voiced by both exporting and import-competing interests, while surprising from the perspective of alternative accounts, is completely consistent with the protection-for-exporters argument. The administration needed to design a policy that could satisfy the newly mobilized exporting interests, without imposing too high costs on import-competing interests.

Choosing a Strategy in Response to Discrimination

In the first months after taking office, Hull, who considered the Ottawa agreements to be "the greatest injury, in a commercial way, that has been inflicted on this country since I have been in public life" (quoted in Pollard 1985, 12), hoped to achieve just this objective by getting the United Kingdom to unilaterally change its preferential trade policies. This would have allowed the administration to guarantee exporters' access to foreign markets without imposing any costs on import competitors. He thus commissioned a study of the Ottawa agreements with the purpose of unearthing some arguments for a legal challenge, based on a breach of the Treaty of Commerce and Navigation concluded between the United States and Great Britain in 1815. The study, however, found that there was no basis for legal action, mainly because the MFN clause included in the British-American treaty was of a conditional nature (Rowland 1987, 180–81).

Having excluded "threat" as a possible strategy in response to British discriminatory trade policies, it became clear that the United States would have to engage in trade negotiations with the United Kingdom to achieve its aim of protecting exporter interests. The new economic adviser for international affairs Herbert Feis thus argued that the United States needed an agreement with the United Kingdom "precluding discrimination against each other's trade and making for common defense against discrimination inaugurated by third parties" (quoted in Gardner 1964, 27). From April 1933 onward Roosevelt supported this aim and pushed for trade legislation that would allow for a reciprocal trade agreement.

A major question that arose at that stage was whether or not to apply the MFN clause in a future trade agreement. Although the United States had formally adopted this principle for its trade policy in 1923, some members of the administration opposed its application. For Peek, the MFN clause even entailed "the progressive destruction of our bargaining power at a time when the conditions in international trade require that we retain the maximum freedom of action and bargaining power if our nationals are to compete on equal terms with the nationals of other countries in the markets of the world" (Peek and Crowther 1936, 32). As late as June 1934, when the U.S. administration set up a "British Empire committee" to discuss options of how to respond to the British system of preferences, several of the strategies that were taken into consideration were not consistent with an MFN approach. This particularly concerned the proposal to create a rival preferential zone excluding the United Kingdom and the Commonwealth countries (Kottman 1968, 121; Meyer 1978, 131; Rowland 1987, 186–87). The debate on the issue of the MFN clause continued until after the passage of the RTAA (Schlesinger 1959, 255–57), and only by late 1935 did it become clear that the nondiscrimination camp had won.

Compelling reasons, which are in line with the argument about choice of strategy set out in chapter 1 (Hypothesis 3), led the U.S. administration to insist on a nondiscriminatory approach. As Hull's predecessor as secretary of state Henry L. Stimson (R-NY) had already realized, a country that exports so many different products cannot "discriminate in favor of a few of its exports without producing a riot among its other exporters, and its only safety [is] in treating everybody alike."[16] Hull, moreover, stressed that the most important rationale for the MFN clause was the protection against discrimination in foreign markets that it provided (Hull 1938, 4; see also Allen 1953, 124). In essence, these remarks show an awareness of the specific vulnerability of U.S. exports at that time. This vulnerability was not least a result of the huge trade surplus that the United States had with European countries. It sold agricultural and manufactured goods to Europe and bought inputs for its industry from countries in

---

16. Memorandum on Conversation between Secretary Stimson and the Uruguay Minister, Dr. J. Varela, 15 September 1932, State Department Records, Central Files, Record Group 59, Decimal File, 1930–39, NACP.

Asia and Central America (Junker 1975, 34). Between 1930 and 1938, U.S. exports to the United Kingdom were on average three times as large as its imports from this country (calculated from data in Carter et al. 2005). Nevertheless, U.S. exports were dispersed throughout Europe, since the British market accounted for less than 20 percent of U.S. exports (calculated from data in Carter et al. 2005). In such a situation, the United States could credibly threaten neither a further closure of its own market nor a preferential agreement with other countries, although its general trade dependence was rather low (see also Oye 1992, 93–96). As expected by the protection-for-exporters argument, a highly vulnerable country with dispersed exports should pursue a nondiscriminatory strategy in response to foreign discrimination.

Toward the RTAA

In parallel to these internal discussions, the administration tried to convince the United Kingdom of the need to reduce the negative effects of discrimination. In April 1933, Roosevelt and Prime Minister Ramsay MacDonald met and published a communiqué in which they agreed to moderate existing trade restrictions.[17] The United States also stressed trade matters at the London Economic Conference that convened in June 1933, even though European countries were mainly interested in a plan for currency stabilization (Kottman 1968, 39–78; Dallek 1979, 46–57). Hull, who headed the U.S. delegation, wanted to achieve an agreement on tariff reductions, convinced that Congress would pass adequate legislation before the end of the conference (Feis 1966, 169–77). While Hull was traveling to London, however, Roosevelt decided to give priority to other legislation, such as the Agricultural Adjustment Act (1933) and the National Recovery Act (1933), which formed the core of his domestic New Deal program. Although Roosevelt's decision to postpone trade legislation created a huge obstacle for Hull's mission, the U.S. delegation still pushed the tariff issue. Only opposition from within the U.S. delegation forced Hull to discard the idea of floating a proposal for a linear cut of all tariffs by 10 percent (Feis 1966, 188–89).

After a speech by President Roosevelt in which he argued that, in the short term, the United States could not stabilize its currency, most delegations wanted to end the conference without agreement. In an attempt to avert this outcome, Hull submitted a draft resolution calling for a tariff truce for at least a year, and proposing the conclusion of bilateral treaties that should include the MFN clause and thus lead to a nondiscriminatory liberalization of trade. The conference,

---

17. The resulting declaration is reprinted in *Foreign Relations of the United States* 1933, I:492–93.

however, recessed before the plan could be discussed in detail, and did not reconvene. As the conference also failed with regard to currency matters, further competitive exchange-rate devaluations followed (Kindleberger 1973, 216–32). Although ultimately no results were forthcoming from this conference, the American attitude toward the conference illustrates an interesting fact. While before 1932 the U.S. had consistently sabotaged all conferences aimed at international trade regulation, by 1933 the United States ended up being the demander of more international cooperation on tariff matters. This supports Hypothesis 2's expectation that foreign discrimination, by changing the domestic balance of interests, can influence the trade orientation of a country.

After coming back from London, Hull continued his push for a new trade policy through the newly formed Executive Committee on Commercial Policy. Chaired by Assistant Secretary of State Sayre, but also including the protectionist Peek, this committee encouraged Roosevelt to request authority for a reciprocal trade policy. The president introduced the legislation to Congress with the following words:

> Other governments are to an ever-increasing extent winning their share of international trade by negotiated reciprocal trade agreements. If American agricultural and industrial interests are to retain their deserved place in this trade, the American Government must be in a position to bargain for that place with other governments....If [the government] is not in a position at a given moment rapidly to alter the terms on which it is willing to deal with other countries it can not adequately protect its trade against discriminations and against bargains injurious to its interests. (*Congressional Record* 1934, 3580)

Facing foreign discrimination, according to Roosevelt, the traditional policy of unilateral tariff adjustments was no longer adequate. The quotation also reveals the defensive nature of the U.S. trade strategy: Roosevelt talked about "retaining" a share of world trade as well as "protecting" American trade, rather than about *expanding* foreign market access. Similarly, Hull stated that the government needed the authority to conclude reciprocal agreements to succeed with its "policy of restoring...lost international trade."[18]

Shortly thereafter, Congress passed the RTAA with substantial majorities in both the House and the Senate. The RTAA allowed cuts (or increases) of a tariff rate up to 50 percent of the value it had in the Smoot-Hawley act in reciprocal agreements with countries that were the principal suppliers of U.S. imports for

---

18. U.S. Congress, March 1934, Hearings before the House Committee on Ways and Means, *Reciprocal Trade Agreements,* 5–6.

the good in question. Moreover, and importantly, it allowed the administration to conclude trade pacts as executive agreements that do not require congressional approval other than the authorizing legislation. Despite the quite far-reaching delegation of authority, the president remained restricted in several ways. First, he was obliged to include a most-favored-nation clause in all trade agreements. Only countries that discriminated against U.S. exports were to be barred from exporting under the lower duties agreed on in bilateral agreements with other countries.[19] Second, the delegation was for a period of three years only; after this phase, the president would have to ask Congress for a renewal.

Explaining the Passage of the RTAA

One explanation for the passage of the RTAA, known as "lesson thesis," contends that the trade contraction following the Smoot-Hawley act convinced decision makers that a change in U.S. trade policy was needed (Pastor 1980, 92; Goldstein 1993, 148; Lohmann and O'Halloran 1994). After having witnessed the negative consequences of logrolling in trade policy during the passage of the Smoot-Hawley act, they decided to delegate trade policy authority to the president in the RTAA. Yet, of the ninety-five legislators who supported Smoot-Hawley and voted on both measures, only nine changed their stance over this four-year period (Schnietz 2000, 419). If not the established politicians, was it "the new freshman Democratic class" that learned the lessons from Smoot-Hawley (Goldstein 1993, 148)? Even in this revised form, however, the lesson thesis finds it difficult to explain why legislators suddenly should have been able to implement a far-sighted solution to their collective-action problems after failing to do so for a long time.

All decisions in Congress regarding this trade legislation followed party lines, with Democrats supporting the legislation and Republicans opposing it. This cleavage reveals that the Republicans, with import-competing interests dominating their platform, would surely not have passed the RTAA. The party argument, which maintains that the RTAA came about because the Democrats, traditionally the party of the low tariff, captured majorities in both Houses of Congress in 1930 and the presidency in 1932, thus has substantial explanatory power (Gourevitch 1986; Verdier 1994; Bailey, Goldstein, and Weingast 1997; Hiscox 1999; Schnietz 2000).

---

19. For countries discriminating against U.S. exports, the Smoot-Hawley tariff levels would remain intact. Goldstein (1993, 151–52) simply discards this provision as an expression of "contradictory visions of reciprocity." Rather, I would argue that this provision was intended as a threat to achieve the reduction of foreign discrimination. This was also the interpretation given at the time. See *New York Times*, 4 April 1935, 8.

Nevertheless, two main problems limit the strength of the party explanation. On the one hand, the party account has difficulty accounting for the debate concerning the negative effects of discrimination during the passage of the RTAA. In contrast, the content of domestic deliberations strongly supports the protection-for-exporters argument. On the other hand, the party explanation is based on the assumption that Democrats wanted to achieve lower *domestic* tariffs. Reciprocity, according to this argument, was introduced to the bill mainly to make sure that lower domestic tariffs would persist even after a possible return to power of the Republicans (Schnietz 2000). Yet, if lower domestic tariffs had been the Democrats' main objective, why would they have passed the Agricultural Adjustment Act (1933), which imposed limits on agricultural imports to stabilize domestic prices, and the Buy America Act (1933), which had similar effects as higher tariffs? In addition, if Democrats' only objective was to secure the continuity of lower domestic barriers, why should they have included a provision limiting the delegation to a three-year period? Permanent delegation would have required the Republicans to gain unified control of the House, the Senate, and the presidency to repeal the RTAA. Temporary delegation, by contrast, meant that already by gaining the majority in one of the Houses, or by capturing the presidency, the Republicans had the possibility to block a renewal of the RTAA and thus further liberalization.

While problematic for existing explanations, these apparent inconsistencies are easily compatible with the protection-for-exporters argument that stresses the need to reduce *foreign* discrimination. If the aim of the RTAA was to preserve foreign market access for U.S. exporters, the imposition of trade barriers to protect import-competing interests in the United States is a complementary rather than a contradictory policy (see Hypothesis 2). The pursuit of reciprocal trade agreements, which guarded exporters' access to foreign markets, accompanied by specific provisions ensuring the continued protection of import-competing interests, was a policy that could satisfy both major trade constituencies at the same time. Protectionist policies and policies aimed at opening foreign markets, then, are two different sides of the same coin, since both are intended to protect a certain group of economic actors. Similarly, the inclusion of a time limit in the legislation makes sense in an interpretation that sees the RTAA as a response to a momentary threat to U.S. exporters' access to foreign markets, rather than a long-term strategy to keep U.S. tariffs low.

For Michael Hiscox (2002, 62), the decision to pursue reciprocal trade agreements was a compromise that reflected new disagreements in the base of the Democratic Party. The party was no longer only a party of rural voters but instead had managed to gain a new labor constituency. The compromise enabled the party to secure support from both constituencies. Nevertheless, there is little in contemporary statements that would suggest that this objective of achieving support both from rural and metropolitan districts was the main driving force in the passage of the RTAA. Instead, most decision makers referred to discrimination and foreign trade barriers as the reasons why a new trade policy was needed, and a substantial number of exporters supported this policy.

In short, whereas the protection-for-exporters argument can justify both the timing and the content of the debates surrounding the passage of this trade legislation in the United States, alternative explanations have difficulties in accounting for all of the available evidence. It thus seems plausible to argue that the RTAA was a policy intended to protect exporter interests. Francis Sayre (1940, 21), assistant secretary of state at that time, in a booklet with the telling name *The Protection of American Export Trade,* wrote: "We came to learn that a foreign commercial policy which fails to protect American export markets risks disaster for home industry and home agriculture." A contemporary article in the journal *Foreign Affairs* also stressed the defensive nature of the RTAA: "The trade agreements program is not in any sense a free trade program. It is merely an attempt…to restore…to American enterprise its natural markets abroad and at the same time reasonable protection for domestic industry" (Grady 1936, 295). More recently, the economic historian Charles Kindleberger (1973, 237) affirmed that "concern that the Ottawa Agreements might isolate the country and lose British markets to Commonwealth farmers and jobs to American firms that had established plants in Canada to come within the preference system" created support for the RTAA.

Toward a First U.S.-British Trade Agreement, 1935–1938

In line with the objective of the RTAA, the U.S. administration pursued trade agreements with a series of foreign countries in the years before World War II. Early on, in 1935, it concluded agreements with France and Canada, where U.S. exporters faced substantial discrimination (*New York Times,* 5 May 1935, F9). The focus of the U.S. administration, however, was on achieving a trade agreement with the United Kingdom that would protect the interests of U.S. exporters in this eminent market. As Jay Culbert (1987, 383) argues, the British system of preferences was seen "as costing American exporters their overseas markets and as such Imperial Preference became the object of an intense American campaign." The British government, however, reacted cautiously to the American demands for trade negotiations. Not before late 1936 did it agree to the start of negotiations, which finally led to the conclusion of trade agreements with the United

States in 1938 and 1947. While geopolitical motives are not unimportant in explaining the British acceptance of these negotiations, I argue that the recognition of increased bargaining power also played a key role. With the United States eager to achieve a lowering of discriminatory trade barriers, the United Kingdom could expect favorable terms in a trade agreement with the United States (Hypothesis 4). The expectation of disproportionate concessions, in turn, should have helped to garner support for a trade agreement with the United States in spite of the strong showing of import-competing interests in Great Britain throughout these years (Hypothesis 5).

British Trade Preferences in the 1930s

Tariff negotiations that would lead to a reciprocal lowering of tariffs were generally in the interest of British industry. Already the Import Duties Act, which established protection for British industry and agriculture, contained a section that enabled the Treasury to offer foreign countries a reduction or abolishment of duties. As Neville Chamberlain, the chancellor of the exchequer from 1931 until 1937, confirmed, this section was intended "to facilitate the lowering of tariff barriers in foreign countries by offering to reduce our own in return for an advantage of that kind" (quoted in Jones 1934, 234). In fact, the across-the-board tariff protection imposed in the early 1930s may not least have been an attempt at increasing British bargaining power to negotiate down foreign tariffs (Capie 1983, 7). Although the government continued to defend the general merits of the MFN clause, arguing that it was essential to ensure the absence of discrimination abroad, it also did not feel restrained from using preferential agreements from time to time to extract concessions from other countries.[20] Consequently, after establishing the system of imperial preference, it negotiated preferential trade agreements with, among others, Germany, Italy, and some Latin American countries.

These policies were largely in line with the demand voiced by key export interests that Britain should use its preferential trade agreements to pry open foreign markets. As early as 1932, the Federation of British Industry (FBI) passed a resolution in which it declared that Empire preference should be extended "to permit of the progressive breaking down of foreign tariff barriers by means of treaties based on mutual concessions" (*Times*, 15 January 1932, 7). Negotiations with other countries, according to the FBI, should not only be limited to tariff reductions but should also cover exchange restrictions, quotas, and the general

---

20. Walter Runciman, president of the Board of Trade in Great Britain. *Parliamentary Debates. Official Report.* House of Commons, vol. 275 (1932–33), 2019.

features of trade policy (*Times*, 7 October 1932, 7). The FBI was also convinced that the United Kingdom availed substantial bargaining power. It argued: "It should be possible to obtain from foreign countries who wish to retain their share of this market valuable concessions without any necessity for concessions on our part" (*Times*, 11 May 1933, 10). Similarly, the Association of British Chambers of Commerce adopted a resolution that argued that preferential agreements would compel outside states to join them, and thus would open up additional markets for British exports (*Manchester Guardian*, 15 November 1932, 12; *Times*, 15 November 1932, 8; Jones 1934, 241). The London Chamber of Commerce went furthest in its demands for an end to the MFN policy when asking for the establishment of barter schemes through which trade should be maintained (*Times*, 11 November 1932, 16).

Negotiating with the United States

Initially, however, the British willingness to conclude reciprocal agreements did not include an agreement with the United States. Within the British government, the Foreign Office took a more positive approach with respect to such an agreement, while the Treasury and the Board of Trade were rather opposed (Rowland 1987, 138). This split is easily explained with the different concerns of these units. The Foreign Office feared that the United States could either challenge Empire preference legally or react with retaliatory tariffs to British preferential policies (*Times*, 24 August 1932, 10). The worry was that a legal challenge by the United States could have far-reaching consequences, as it could set in motion a chain reaction in which a whole series of countries would claim compensation for damages incurred (Rowland 1987, 141). By contrast, the position of the Treasury and the Board of Trade reflected the opinion of British economic interests that were reluctant to accept a major breach in imperial preference. Such a breach seemed to be the unavoidable consequence of an agreement with the United States.

These internal conflicts came to a fore in British contacts with the U.S. administration. In February 1933, the British Embassy in Washington wrote to the Department of State that the British government "would gladly co-operate with the United States Government in pressing for a general agreement with a view to [the duties'] relaxation and their abolition as soon as possible, particularly as regards manufactures."[21] The British government thus offered to enter negotiations for an "agreement on the basis of reciprocity."[22] Nevertheless, when confronted with an American plan for the reduction of trade restrictions at nearly the same

---

21. *Foreign Relations of the United States* 1933, I:468.
22. Ibid., I:469.

time, the government argued that Britain was still in the process of setting up trade barriers and could not yet be asked to reduce them.[23] Moreover, it pointed out that trade flows with the United States were highly unequal, and that the United Kingdom could not afford to import even more from the United States than it already did. As Chancellor of the Exchequer Chamberlain affirmed in 1933, "the United Kingdom can obviously not afford to buy any larger quantity of United States goods unless the United States offer greatly increased outlets for the manufactures of this country" (quoted in Rowland 1987, 129).

Increasingly, it became clear that the acceptance of a trade agreement, but only in response to major concessions from the United States, could form the basis for a compromise between these two positions. Even in the cautious Foreign Office, the question thus arose whether "the United States [was] prepared to sacrifice some American industries in order to offer us an entrance fee in the Ottawa club" (quoted in Rowland 1987, 160). With the progress of the negotiations, the British negotiators recognized that their "position [was] even stronger than [they] previously [had] thought" (quoted in Rowland 1987, 170). It became clear that especially U.S. agricultural-export interests exercised substantial pressure on the Roosevelt administration to achieve a trade agreement. Consequently, the British ambassador in Washington, Sir Ronald Lindsay, argued that Hull would "be able to offer abundant compensation, pressed down and overflowing, for any concession he may receive" (quoted in Rowland 1987, 228). He went so far as to say that "an American hand is proffered to us, and it is full of gifts," an opinion that was shared by Chamberlain (quoted in Rowland 1987, 241).

British interest groups also alluded to the United Kingdom's strong bargaining position. In a letter published in the *Times* of London (25 June 1937, 12), Leo S. Amery from the Empire Industries Association rhetorically asked whether "the American businessmen who are at present backing up Mr. Cordell Hull's plea for a trade treaty are really more anxious to promote world trade by increasing British imports into the United States than to avoid their export markets here and in the Empire being reduced by British protection and Empire preference." He continued by arguing that Britain should use the leverage it had over the United States in an agreement with that country to achieve a better balance of trade. Other European countries, according to him, were not in such a good position, because they were bound by the MFN clause that made it impossible for them to reduce trade from the United States and at the same time increase trade with other countries. Other interests also demanded a trade agreement with benefits heavily biased in favor of British interests. The Association of British Chambers

---

23. Ibid.; Kottman 1968, 63.

of Commerce suggested that the United States should make three to four times more concessions than the United Kingdom in an agreement (*Times,* 8 December 1937, 18). Equally, the FBI made clear that it expected the United States to take a first step "to adjust the trade balance by a substantial reduction of her tariff" (*New York Times,* 10 December 1937, 2). The British textile and car industries in particular hoped to gain from concessions in the U.S. market (Drummond and Hillmer 1989, 100).

Many groups also insisted on the defense of Empire preference. The Empire Industries Association published a declaration maintaining "its emphatic objection to any action which would in any way interfere with the fuller development or even weaken the present effectiveness of our domestic and Imperial tariff system, or which would sacrifice home and Empire production for the sake of some illusory project for the revival of economic internationalism" (*Times,* 9 June 1937, 16). In May 1938, the British Empire League published a resolution asking the government not to conclude an agreement with the United States that could prove detrimental to Empire trade (*Times,* 12 May 1938, 8). Equally, the FBI sent a statement to the British prime minister arguing that there was a danger involved in granting U.S. agricultural goods improved access to the United Kingdom (*Times,* 10 December 1937, 18). This would divert trade away from the Dominions and in the end undermine the preference that British manufacturers received in Dominion markets.

As expected by the protection-for-exporters argument, the United Kingdom's position in the negotiations with the United States was one of strength. When in March 1934 British and U.S. officials met to discuss commercial policy questions, the United Kingdom straight away refused to accept the U.S. demand that Canadian grains that were transshipped through U.S. ports should benefit from imperial preference. The negotiations between the two sides continued in the following years, and from May 1935 onward the British Board of Trade put together a list of products on which the United Kingdom could make concessions. This list excluded many of the products of most interest to the United States, namely barley; canned, dried, and fresh fruits; lard; leather; lumber; rice; and tobacco, as the United Kingdom had bound preference margins on these products in the Ottawa agreements.[24] The British declared that if the United States wanted to make inroads on these products, it would have to engage in simultaneous negotiations with both the United Kingdom and Canada. This prospect was not at all welcome to the U.S. State Department, as it basically meant that the United States would have to make concessions to both countries.

---

24. For the U.S. interests, see *Foreign Relations of the United States* 1936, I:699.

Hull, in a meeting with the undersecretary of the British Treasury, even declared that "the United States had no intention of paying two for one in the matter of an Anglo-American agreement" and that "the countries which made the Ottawa Agreements must themselves be responsible for the relaxing of their provisions."[25]

In the end, however, the U.S. eagerness to achieve an agreement with the United Kingdom made it willing to compensate both Canada and the United Kingdom. What is more, the trade agreement, which the United States and the United Kingdom finally signed in November 1938, was very favorable to British domestic interests (Eckes 1999, 79).[26] It implied hardly any changes to the system of imperial preference. Despite strong pressure on the United Kingdom especially to ease restrictions on lumber and tobacco imports, the British government made only small concessions on the former and no concessions at all on the latter product. The United States, by contrast, reduced trade barriers for textiles, paper, and other manufactured goods, concessions that were of major interest for British exporters. As a result, even the FBI, which had attached strong demands to its approval of the trade agreement, welcomed it (*New York Times,* 19 November 1938, 7). By contrast, a substantial number of American economic interests expressed concerns (*New York Times,* 19 November 1938, I:6). In line with the fifth hypothesis of the protection-for-exporters argument, asymmetric concessions thus go a long way in explaining the British acceptance of this agreement.

The Role of Geopolitics

Some authors also stress the role of geopolitical interests in these events (Harrison 1984; Skålnes 1998, 595; Eckes 1999, 79). In fact, geopolitical developments, in particular the rise of the German threat in Europe, had an influence on U.S.-British trade negotiations. In the United States, Hull early on linked trade and foreign policy, since he believed that "unhampered trade dovetailed with peace; high tariffs, trade barriers, and unfair economic competition, with war" (Hull 1948, 1:81). Nevertheless, allusions to world peace were clearly less frequent than references to foreign discrimination and the economic impact of trade agreements. Moreover, to a certain extent these hints at foreign policy have to be seen in the context of relations between the president and the Congress, since trade policy is a constitutional prerogative of Congress and foreign policy, a prerogative

---

25. Ibid. 1937, II:66–68.

26. There was also a U.S.-Canada and a United Kingdom–Canada trade agreement. For the contents of the three agreements, see *Times,* 18 November 1938, 10.

of the executive. Defining a problem as belonging to the ambit of foreign policy helps the president extend his authority over it. It thus seems not very plausible to suggest that the United States made trade concessions to the United Kingdom to improve the chances of world peace.

For the United Kingdom, geopolitics played a more central role, as a trade agreement with the United States became an increasingly valuable sign of its improving relationship with that country. There also was a hope that trade concessions to the United States could favorably influence American public opinion. The British ambassador in Washington, Lindsay, stated:

> In the event of a major crisis in Europe, the factor which will most impede any measures which the American government might take in favour of Great Britain will be the Middle West, and it is just the Middle West, the centre of the agricultural community, which will be directly and favourably affected by the conclusion of a commercial treaty with the United Kingdom, improving or facilitating the export of agricultural produce from the United States to Great Britain. (quoted in Rowland 1987, 229)

In November 1937, moreover, Chamberlain stated in a letter to his sister: "The reason why I have been prepared…to go a long way to get this treaty [with the United States] is precisely because I reckoned it would help to educate American opinion to act more and more with us, and because I felt sure it would frighten the totalitarians. Coming at this moment, it looks just like an answer to the Berlin-Rome-Tokyo axis" (quoted in Kottman 1968, 205–6).

These geopolitical pressures on the United Kingdom, rather than casting doubt on the protection-for-exporters argument, make the outcome of the agreement even more astonishing. How could a country that was under strong geopolitical pressure achieve such a favorable outcome in a trade agreement? Only the different eagerness of domestic interests to reach an agreement can explain this outcome. A contemporary observer noted:

> The British undoubtedly were well aware of the possible political implications of the agreement but at the same time they were so eager to make the best possible tariff "bargain" that the political implications of the agreement were relegated to a minor position. It is clear that the British Government was certain that failure to secure an agreement would have been politically acceptable at home. (Kreider 1943, 41)

In fact, domestic interests such as the National Union of Manufacturers warned of a hurried conclusion of the negotiations with the United States for political reasons (*Times,* 6 December 1937, 19; Kottman 1968, 219).

In conclusion, two factors contributed to Britain's decision to embrace a trade agreement with the United States. On the one hand, there was the feeling that the United Kingdom could get major concessions in the trade field. With its increased bargaining strength due to imperial preference, the United Kingdom could expect substantial concessions for its industrial exports while giving minor concessions with regard to agricultural products. On the other hand, at a time when it faced disturbing developments in Europe and the Far East, the British government was also influenced by geopolitical considerations. Both factors had some bearing on British decision making, although the objective of gaining concessions seems to have been the dominant one.

Toward a Second U.S.-British Trade Agreement, 1939–1947

The persistence of the RTAA after World War II has been one of the central riddles dealt with in studies of U.S. trade policymaking. Following the protection-for-exporters argument, I suggest an explanation for this puzzle that starts from the insight that the 1938 U.S.-British agreement did not lead to a major reduction of discrimination against U.S. exporters. In the face of continued exporter lobbying against losses of foreign market access resulting from imperial preference, Congress upheld its delegation of trade authority to the president. The issue of preferential trade agreements abroad thus remained important and continued to influence U.S. trade politics into the late 1940s. As put by Susan Strange (1985, 240), "the destruction of preferential barriers against American exports was the first target of U.S. commercial policy" after World War II.

The protection-for-exporters argument thus allows for an interpretation of the establishment of the GATT that differs from well-accepted accounts that stress the importance of geopolitical interests in this decision (Gaddis 1972; Keohane 1989). Rather than being an expression of the hegemonic power of the United States at that time, the trade rules included in the GATT were defended by the United States to make sure that in the future U.S. exporters would not face discrimination as in the 1930s. The decision to multilateralize the process of tariff negotiations was also a reaction to the experience of the 1930s when two factors had blocked the trade negotiations with the United Kingdom: on the one hand, the need to provide concessions to Canada for the reduction of British preferential tariffs, and, on the other hand, the British reluctance to engage in MFN negotiations without getting concessions from all of its main trading partners at once. The multilateral approach pursued by the U.S. administration after World War II allowed it to tackle both of these problems.

From the Wartime Debates to the GATT

In the United States, the preoccupation with the system of imperial preference continued until after World War II. In the hearings on the various extensions of the RTAA during that time, exporter interests—in particular from the agricultural sector—accounted for a substantial number of witnesses. Again, they argued that their lobbying was aimed at regaining lost market shares abroad. A representative of the tobacco industry, for example, stated: "We have come before the House Committee to ask the Government to help us on the trade treaties, in order to regain our lost trade."[27] Some other agricultural associations, such as the National Farmers' Union and the American Farm Bureau Federation, came out in favor of reciprocal trade negotiations, as well (Aaronson 1996, 46). In 1945 the representative of the United States Chamber of Commerce strongly backed delegation of trade authority to the president, arguing that this was necessary to reach new agreements with the United Kingdom and Canada. He stated: "Foreign traders favor a modification of Empire preferences and Britain has indicated that she will modify Empire preferences only in return for adequate concessions."[28] Finally, the Textile Export Association stressed that U.S. textile exporters needed a change in British preferential agreements to be able to compete in Empire markets (*New York Times,* 30 December 1946, 28, and 12 January 1947, F6).

A reciprocal agreement with the United Kingdom that would reduce foreign discrimination, therefore, was needed to satisfy the interests of U.S. exporters. In line with this objective, the U.S. administration insisted on having the issue of preferences mentioned in several U.S.-British agreements during World War II. When Winston Churchill managed to include a provision in article 4 of the Atlantic Charter (14 August 1941) that asked for respect for "existing obligations," Hull (1948, 975–76) complained that it "deprived the article of virtually all significance since it meant that Britain would continue to retain her Empire preferences against which I had been fighting for eight years." In 1942 the Mutual Aid Agreement in article 7 then demanded the "elimination of all forms of discriminatory treatment in international commerce" (quoted in Evans 1971, 35). The United States and the United Kingdom also agreed that as soon as possible they would start talks about the attainment of this objective.

In autumn 1943, and then again in the summer of 1945, U.S. and British delegations met for negotiations as proposed in article 7 of the Mutual Aid Agreement to deal with the question of imperial preference (Garrett 1947, 75). In these

---

27. U.S. Congress, January–February 1940, Hearings before the House Committee on Ways and Means, *Extension of Reciprocal Trade Agreements Act,* 2592.

28. U.S. Congress, April–May 1945, Hearings before the House Committee on Ways and Means, *1945 Extension of Reciprocal Trade Agreements Act,* 2197.

negotiations, the Americans suggested that the British should abolish preferences in exchange for financial aid.[29] Despite their dependence on U.S. aid, however, the British insisted that they would only abandon preferences in a reciprocal bargain that, in the words of an official in the U.S. Embassy in London at the time of the negotiations, produced "a heavy all-round and not a 'selective' reduction of tariffs and other trade barriers" (Penrose 1953, 93). As put by the *Economist* (29 April 1944, 564), "there is no chance that the British Parliament would consent to the abolition of the system of imperial preference save possibly as part of a very large reconstruction of international trade involving concessions by other countries far larger than any that are yet in prospect." Equally, in the United States it was recognized that "the British will prove willing to abandon [imperial preference], except for token remnants—but only on the condition that America make substantial reductions in its own duties" (*Wall Street Journal*, 15 November 1943, 1).

Although at the time, given the British position as a country destroyed by war, this might have seem overly ambitious, many within the British government were convinced that the system of preferences could serve as a bargaining lever. This is evidenced by the discussions over the Overton report, published in January 1943, based on which Britain accepted negotiations on a reduction of imperial preferences, but only in exchange for a *linear* reduction of U.S. tariffs (Zeiler 1999, 29–32). James Meade, who worked for the British Board of Trade at that time, also stressed the possibility of getting concessions in exchange for a reduction of imperial preferences with the following words:

> As a practical matter, there is much to be said from the point of view of our own commercial advantages for getting now in the proposed general commercial policy convention the most we can for the virtual elimination of Preferences. We may, thereby, obtain a drastic cut not only in the American but in other high tariffs against our exports, and the removal of many quantitative restrictions against our exports.[30]

This stance was in line with interest-group demands within the United Kingdom. The Association of British Chambers of Commerce, for example, argued that only in response to "sufficient compensation" should the British government agree to abolish the system of Empire preference (*Times*, 16 November 1946, 2).

Initially, however, the United Kingdom had to bow to U.S. pressure. In December 1945, in a joint statement with the U.S. administration, the British

---

29. Top secret Cypher telegram from Washington to Cabinet Offices, 9 October 1945, BT 11/2795, PRO.

30. Note by James Meade, entitled "Imperial Preferences," 10 February 1944, PRO, T230/173. This was a position that was shared by other British officials. See Ikenberry (1992, 311–12).

government indicated that it supported the broad lines of the American text on postwar trade relations, which was published as "Proposals for the Expansion of World Trade and Employment."[31] These proposals called for the elimination of tariff preferences as the major objective of international trade cooperation. The U.S. administration then invited fifteen countries (most prominently, these were the countries that had signed the Ottawa agreements in 1932) to meet for negotiations aiming at the creation of an international trade organization. The talks of a preparatory committee started in October 1946 in London and continued in New York and Geneva until August of the next year (Wilcox 1949; Brown 1950; Kock 1969, 35–53; Gardner 1980, 361–68). Building on the "Proposals," the administration under President Harry S. Truman prepared a suggested charter for an International Trade Organization that was to form the basis for the talks (U.S. Department of State 1946). As the "Proposals" before it, the charter (art. 18, par. 1) included the objective of "elimination of tariff preferences." It stated that negotiated reductions of MFN tariffs should "operate automatically to reduce or eliminate margins of preference." In addition, it included a provision establishing a ceiling for preferences.

Although already formally committed to most of these provisions in prior agreements with the United States, the United Kingdom fought hard to avoid their inclusion in the final charter for the international trade organization. In accordance with Hypothesis 4 of the protection-for-exporters argument, this struggle proved quite successful. The provision establishing a ceiling for preferences was defeated because of opposition from the Commonwealth countries. The United Kingdom also achieved an extension of the list of preferences that could be maintained as exceptions to the MFN rule. On the issue of automaticity of preference reductions, a compromise was found according to which tariff cuts would not necessarily have to lead to a reduction of preferences. This British success in defending its preferences, while in accordance with the protection-for-exporters argument, is astonishing from the view of most alternative accounts, according to which the United Kingdom was in a weak bargaining position given its dependence on the United States in the immediate postwar years.

Even though the international trade organization envisaged by the participants in these talks never materialized, the trade rules that were agreed on have remained relevant due to their incorporation in the GATT. This discussion thus is

---

31. "Proposals for Expansion of World Trade and Employment," available at http://www.law. ku.edu/library/researchlinks/research/intltrade/GATT_WTO.shtml (accessed 15 December 2008). The agreement linked trade to a loan to the United Kingdom, lend-lease issues, and the disposal of surplus war property. For the British reaction to this compromise in 1945, see the *Economist,* 15 December 1945, 849–50, and 22 December 1945, 897–99.

of significance beyond theory testing in that it shows that the GATT, rather than being a codification of America's preferences (Goldstein 1993, 162), was strongly shaped by the United Kingdom's trade policy stance. Clearly, the United States also was highly influential. The major role given to the principle of nondiscrimination in the GATT, for example, was at least partly a result of the U.S. administration's desire to dismantle the system of imperial preference.[32] At the same time, the U.S. administration seems to have been driven by the hope of avoiding future situations in which U.S. exporters would be excluded from foreign preferential agreements as had happened in the 1930s. Ironically, however, the strong British endorsement of exceptions from the nondiscrimination principle helped six continental European countries form a customs union that would impose costs on both U.S. and British exporters only one decade later.

The 1947 Geneva Negotiations

In view of the failure to convince the United Kingdom to abolish preferences in the form of a unilateral concession, the U.S. administration called for a tariff conference in Geneva in 1947. It did so under authority granted in the 1945 trade legislation to negotiate reductions of up to 50 percent of the tariffs in effect in 1945. Already when advocating passage of that legislation, the U.S. administration had argued that it would need such authority to negotiate down imperial preferences.[33] Consequently, the Geneva trade conference was again dominated by the conflict between the United States and the United Kingdom over the Ottawa agreements (Gardner 1980, 349–61; Zeiler 1999, 89–126). According to one account, "the primary U.S. goal [in these negotiations] was to bargain away what remained of the Hawley-Smoot protective system in exchange for the elimination of British preferences and discriminations against American exports" (Eckes 1999, 78). In fact, as put in an internal document of the State Department, the United States was "far more interested in the elimination or reduction of the bound margins of preference in favor of British countries than in [the] reduction of the United Kingdom's most-favored-foreign-nation tariffs."[34]

---

32. The fact that at the same time the United States engaged in secret bilateral negotiations with Canada aiming at the formation of a free trade arrangement between the two countries (which would have run counter to the MFN principle) confirms the view that U.S. politicians did not follow economic beliefs when pushing for this rule. Beliefs may have played a more important role in the parallel negotiations in the monetary field. See Ikenberry (1992).

33. See, for example, the testimony by the assistant secretary of state for economic affairs, William Clayton, in U.S. Congress, April–May 1945, Hearings before the House Committee on Ways and Means, *1945 Extension of Reciprocal Trade Agreements Act.*

34. "The Nuclear Approach," 11 April 1945, State Department Records, Central Files, Record Group 59, Decimal File, 1945–49, NACP.

The U.S. negotiators, consequently, pushed the United Kingdom to accept a tight schedule for the abolition of tariff preferences. The British, however, rejected this demand. The problem, as put by Stafford Cripps, president of the British Board of Trade, was that even an offer of an all-round cut of U.S. tariffs by 50 percent, as permitted in the 1945 trade legislation, would not be considered sufficient compensation by the United Kingdom for a "dismantling" of Empire preference (Toye 2003, 922). Clair Wilcox, chief U.S. negotiator in Geneva, thus had to accept that London "had no intention of making concessions that involve[d] any real progress toward the elimination of preferences" (quoted in Zeiler 1999, 108). When the negotiations were close to breakdown, the Americans finally gave in. Similar to the 1938 agreement, they had to consent to an outcome that substantially reduced existing U.S. tariffs in exchange for only a breach in the system of imperial preference.

As expected by the protection-for-exporters argument, the American eagerness to reduce British preferential trade barriers enabled the British to gain valuable concessions in the U.S. market without having to provide concessions of the same magnitude. In the words of one historian, the "outcome of the negotiations represented a success for Britain, which, to a striking degree, withstood the pressure to fall in with American views on trade" (Toye 2003, 914). It is particularly interesting to note that not even the American threat to withhold economic assistance was successful in making the British give in more on trade. While some authors see the continued existence of imperial preference as a sign of a benign hegemon's acceptance of some discrimination against its exports, the historical record rather supports an explanation based on asymmetric bargaining power. The U.S. delegation pushed for strong rules limiting preferential trading arrangements but had to accept many exceptions since U.S. export interests were vulnerable to a breakdown of the negotiations.

In summary, in the 1930s, the U.S. Congress reacted to the British system of trade preferences with the passage of the RTAA. The U.S. administration used this institutional change to push for a policy in protection of exporter interests, which was to be achieved by way of a trade agreement with the United Kingdom. The latter country, however, responded cautiously to this initiative. It only accepted a trade agreement with the United States in 1938 after it had made sure that this agreement included substantial concessions for a relatively minor lowering of British preferential trade barriers. With Commonwealth preference remaining a threat to U.S. exporters, America's preoccupation with discriminatory trade policies abroad continued until after World War II, thus explaining the maintenance of the RTAA during that period. Although the trade agreements achieved in Geneva in 1947 also hardly reduced imperial preferences, in the 1950s the issue became less urgent as trade patterns started to change and Commonwealth trade lost importance relative to other trade flows.

Obviously, various causal factors were at work in producing these outcomes. Nevertheless, the narrative reveals some limitations of existing explanations of transatlantic trade policies in the 1930s and 1940s. Observing the mobilization of exporters *preceding* the passage of the RTAA, for example, it seems appropriate to state that rather than being a "magic bullet" that created support for free trade policies, the RTAA was itself made possible by a changed balance of domestic interests.[35] Neither could the political party argument provide a complete explanation of this institutional change in U.S. trade policy. Previous interpretations of U.S. negotiations with the United Kingdom, and of changes in the British trade policy stance during the 1930s, also left specific gaps. This particularly concerns the questions of why the United Kingdom accepted a trade agreement in 1938 and why it could gain asymmetric concessions in 1947.

---

35. Hiscox (1999), by referring to the RTAA as a "magic bullet," criticized the arguments that see the RTAA as the cause of an empowerment of exporters in the United States in the following decades. For these arguments see, for example, Bailey, Goldstein, and Weingast (1997) and Gilligan (1997a).

DEADLOCK IN TRANSATLANTIC TRADE NEGOTIATIONS, 1948–1957

Most existing accounts of U.S. trade policies have treated the 1950s as a period of trade liberalization. The explanations given for this supposedly liberal decade stress either the position of the United States as a hegemon in the international system or the role of geopolitical interests in determining U.S. trade policies. Some authors classify the United States during that time as a benevolent hegemonic power that supported free trade policies to achieve a variety of goals (Krasner 1976; Keohane 1989, chap. 10). Other studies have seen the objective of U.S. free trade policies as supporting U.S. allies in the conflict with the Soviet Union (Nelson 1989; Verdier 1994, 273; Eckes 1995). Some authors also have tried to provide an explanation for allegedly liberal U.S. trade policies in the 1950s based on the institutional change introduced by the RTAA. In particular, the passage of the RTAA is said to have changed the balance of domestic coalitions by empowering exporters (Bailey, Goldstein, and Weingast 1997; Gilligan 1997a; Irwin and Kroszner 1999). Because of the benefits of better foreign market access, exporter lobbying should have steadily increased over this period according to these accounts. Moreover, at a time when the United States had a huge balance of trade surplus and was technologically far superior to all other economies, free trade interests might have been dominant simply because of a lack of import competition (Hiscox 1999).

Supposedly liberal U.S. trade policies in the 1950s, then, have been taken by many authors as support for their theories. It is a particular irony, then, that the historical record contradicts the widely held view that U.S. trade policies were liberal in the 1950s. During the decade from 1947 until 1958, U.S. trade policies remained protectionist, as Congress, under pressure from domestic interest groups heavily biased in favor of import competitors, resisted delegation of trade authority to the administration. As a result, in that period, the process of transatlantic trade liberalization not only stagnated but even was on the verge of reversal (Camps 1957; Vernon 1958; Diebold 1962; Stiles 1995; Zeiler 1999). The last major tariff reductions before the Kennedy round resulted from the Geneva trade round in 1947, which—as previously discussed—was shaped by the U.S. attempt at reducing discrimination resulting from the British system of imperial preference. In the following years, although several rounds of tariff negotiations took place to allow countries to accede to the GATT, they remained largely unsuccessful in reducing the tariffs of participating countries.

In this chapter, I explain this deadlock by arguing that with Commonwealth trade losing importance for the U.S. economy, and in the absence of major discrimination in the rest of Europe, the motivation for U.S. exporters to mobilize was low in the 1950s. This is not to say that American exporters did not face any discrimination in European markets. Early on, however, U.S. exporters understood that the discrimination imposed by European governments for balance-of-payments reasons would be of a temporary nature. This proved to be true, and after 1953 most of the discriminatory trade barriers were abolished. Since U.S. exporters were not concerned about losses in foreign markets, as predicted by the protection-for-exporters argument they failed to mobilize, and consequently they were unable to influence trade policymaking in their favor. On the few occasions when politicians defended trade liberalization, therefore, they legitimized their stance by arguing that freer trade was necessary for the strengthening of the American economic and political situation, instead of maintaining that trade liberalization would help exporters secure foreign markets. The lack of policies intended to protect U.S. exporter interests in the absence of discrimination abroad provides a major confirmation of the protection-for-exporters argument.

The 1950s were also important in shaping the course of European trade policies over the next decades. In the absence of improved access to the U.S. market, the European countries developed plans for a preferential trading arrangement, which finally led to the creation of the European Economic Community in 1957. The establishment of this preferential trade zone, as shown in the next chapter, ended the deadlock in transatlantic trade liberalization by stimulating renewed exporter lobbying in the United States from 1958 onward. This chapter starts with a short examination of the extent of discrimination confronting U.S. exporters from 1948 to 1958. It continues with an analysis of lobbying patterns in the United States. The third and fourth sections discuss U.S. and European trade policies during this period.

U.S. Exporters' Foreign Market Access

While nondiscrimination was one of the central GATT tenets, discrimination did not stop after World War II (Hieronymi 1973). Three major sources of discrimination existed in Europe at that time: bilateral trade and payments agreements, the discriminatory removal of quotas, and the European Payments Union (EPU). Initially, discrimination mainly stemmed from foreign exchange–control measures, imposed by most European states for the protection of their balance of payments. Since such a system of foreign exchange–control measures was difficult to manage unilaterally, soon bilateral trade and payments agreements were concluded, in which governments agreed to grant each other export and import licenses. Imports were consequently bartered against exports. By 1947 European countries had concluded two hundred such agreements that caused a tight balancing of imports and exports with each trading partner, thus severely restricting the free flow of goods (Patterson 1966, 76). Several efforts at multilateralizing this system to provide for more flexible trade relations were crippled by a lack of dollars and the devaluation of European currencies.

At the same time, many countries also made use of quantitative restrictions to deal with balance-of-payments problems. Initially, these restrictions were used to regulate both intra- and extra-European trade. Soon, however, the newly created Organization for European Economic Cooperation (OEEC) tried to advance the objective of a reduction of quantitative restrictions on intra-European trade (Organization for European Economic Cooperation 1958; Hieronymi 1973). In November 1949, the Council of the OEEC agreed on the removal of at least 50 percent of all quantitative restrictions on private imports in each of the three sectors of food and feeding stuffs, raw materials, and manufactured goods by 15 December 1949. In January 1950, the target was raised to 60 percent by October of the same year, and by February 1951 to 75 percent of all imports with at least 60 percent in each of the three sectors. A last step in the program was taken in 1955, when the liberalization aim was raised to 90 percent of overall private imports and to at least 75 percent in each of the three categories mentioned above (Organization for European Economic Cooperation 1958, 60).[1] Initially, these steps toward liberalization were taken on a preferential basis and thus contributed to discrimination against U.S. exports (see table 3.1). However, from October 1953 forward, the OEEC also worked toward the elimination of quotas against U.S. imports.

The creation of the European Payments Union in 1950 was a final source of discrimination against U.S. exports (Patterson 1966, 75–104). The EPU was a system designed to facilitate trade between countries whose currencies were not

---

1. The base year to which the percentages refer is 1948, except for Germany for which it is 1949.

Table 3.1 The removal of quantitative trade restrictions in Europe, 1953–1956 (in percent)

	1953		1954		1956	
	INTRA-OEEC	**U.S.**	**INTRA-OEEC**	**U.S.**	**INTRA-OEEC**	**U.S.**
Belgium-Luxembourg	87	57	88	86	96	86
Netherlands	93	0	93	86	96	86
France	18	0	65	0	82	11
Germany	90	0	90	54	92	68
Italy	100	0	100	24	99	24

Note: The liberalization percentage indicates for each country the share of private imports that was free of quantitative restrictions with regard to the base year. The base year for intra-Organization for European Economic Cooperation liberalization is 1948 (except for Germany 1949). For the liberalization toward the United States, the base year is 1953. The 1956 data for Belgium-Luxembourg and the Netherlands are those of the Benelux. Percentages are calculated based on imports in 1955 (OEEC values as of 31 December, U.S. values 1953 and 1956 as of 1 January, 1954 as of 30 September).

Source: Adapted from Organization for European Economic Cooperation (1958, 180–81).

convertible and made the accelerated intra-European removal of quantitative restrictions possible. The system, however, openly discriminated against extra-European countries as it restricted the use of earnings of European currencies to purchases in Europe. Furthermore, countries that had a surplus with EPU countries had to extend credits to deficit countries. Consequently, potential surplus countries tried to redirect imports away from the United States and toward European suppliers to achieve a greater balance of their trade. Belgium, for example, in one instance had to impose new restrictions against dollar imports for the explicit purpose of reducing its surplus with other members of the European Payments Union (Patterson 1966, 93–94).

Partly due to these various sources of discrimination, the U.S. share of total OEEC imports fell from 24 percent in 1946 to 9 percent in 1953 (see table 3.2). In absolute terms, equally, OEEC imports from the United States increased from 1945 until 1947, and then fell with some ups and downs until 1953. (The decline would have been faster in the absence of U.S. foreign aid to European countries, which had to be used to buy American goods.) These numbers, however, reflected a return to the traditional trading pattern that had existed before World War II, rather than a loss of established market shares. After 1953, moreover, because of the relaxation of most discriminatory arrangements, the share rose until it reached 14 percent in 1957, a value substantially higher than in prewar years. The share fell in 1958, owing to a devaluation of the French franc and to a slowdown of the American economy, only to pick up again in the next years, until the consequences of the creation of the EEC were being felt.

Other data also suggest that European policies did not have a detrimental impact on U.S. exports in the 1950s. In particular, at that time, European countries

Table 3.2 Transatlantic and intra-European trade, 1938–1958 (in million dollars and percent)

		SOURCE OF OEEC IMPORTS		
YEAR	TOTAL	OEEC	U.S.	U.S. SHARE OF TOTAL
1938	12,519	4,934	1,378	11
1946	13,648	4,188	3,323	24
1947	21,482	6,417	5,072	23
1948	24,735	7,942	4,405	18
1949	24,843	8,787	4,296	17
1950	24,233	9,797	3,135	14
1951	33,690	13,028	4,422	13
1952	32,298	13,220	3,972	12
1953	31,460	13,594	2,971	9
1954	33,810	15,005	3,300	10
1955	38,735	17,197	4,513	12
1956	42,727	19,203	5,329	12
1957	46,417	20,710	6,454	14
1958	43,331	20,206	4,807	11

Source: Hieronymi (1973, 131).

still traded less with each other than their geographical proximity would lead one to expect (Aitken 1973, 885). In addition, the growth of trade among the future EEC members between 1953–55 and 1956–58 was not higher than the growth of trade among other countries over this period (Bayoumi and Eichengreen 1997, 149). Overall, therefore, especially from 1953 onward, European trade policies allowed U.S. exporters better access to European markets, rather than imposing losses on them.

The Lack of Exporter Mobilization in the United States

If Hypothesis 1 is correct, this discussion of U.S. exporters' access to foreign markets leads to the expectation of a lack of exporter mobilization at that time. In fact, U.S. exporters remained largely aloof from trade-policy debates in the 1950s. Detroit and New York, with their strong export orientation and supposedly the geographical hubs for the supporters of a liberal trade policy, were barely active in lobbying for foreign market access (Bauer, Pool, and Dexter 1972, 251–64, and 277–87). Accordingly, the number of exporters testifying in the hearings of the Committee on Ways and Means was very low in the late 1940s and early 1950s (fewer than five), and only slightly increased in 1953 and 1955 (to about ten) when some exporter groups—mobilized by the Venezuelan Chamber of Commerce (Bauer, Pool, and Dexter 1972, 375–76)—opposed the imposition of oil import quotas. It is no wonder then that some officials within the U.S. administration stressed the need to give a voice to exporter interests by supporting the establishment of an exporter organization, thus balancing the lobbying effort from import competitors.[2] Indeed, shortly thereafter the Dwight D. Eisenhower administration encouraged the creation of the Committee for a National Trade Policy, which became important in later trade-policy debates. In the 1950s, however, according to all accounts, this organization remained largely ineffective, with one book even classifying it as "a relatively diffuse, educational, statement-releasing operation" (Bauer, Pool, and Dexter 1972, 380).

The weak lobbying effort by exporters is further demonstrated by the fact that before the trade negotiations of 1950 in Torquay, UK, the Committee for Reciprocity Information received testimony from import-competing interests, now filling thirty-three boxes at the National Archives, while the few exporter statements could be packed into only three.[3] The few politically active free trade interests, moreover, legitimated their lobbying effort, not with respect to gaining or maintaining foreign market access, but rather by emphasizing the general welfare effects of freer trade policies (Bauer, Pool, and Dexter 1972, 143–52). Only very selectively, in response to specific discriminatory measures abroad, did some exporters mobilize. For example, there was some concern in the U.S. steel industry about the consequences of the creation of the European Coal and Steel Community (Romero 1996, 106). In addition, the U.S. oil industry complained about restrictions on its business activities within the sterling area, which included the United Kingdom and a group of Commonwealth countries that pegged their currencies to the British pound (Hieronymi 1973, 168). This was far from amounting to a major mobilization of exporters, however.

Why were U.S. exporters so passive in the 1950s after they had vigorously pushed for trade negotiations in the two preceding decades? One possibility is that they simply did not see an advantage in getting better access to European markets crippled by wartime destruction and a lack of dollars. In fact, however, by 1948 practically all countries in Europe other than Germany had reestablished or even exceeded the 1938 levels of national income and productivity, and their economies were growing rapidly (Postan 1967, 12–13). Consequently, Europe remained the principal market for U.S. exporters even in the postwar

---

2. Memo, 23 July 1952, State Department Records, Central Files, Record Group 59, Decimal File, 1950–54, NACP.

3. Records of the Committee for Reciprocity Information, Record Group 364.2, NACP.

years.[4] The reasoning is also unconvincing because in the 1930s, when most European countries were suffering from the consequences of the Great Depression, U.S. exporters were eager to conclude trade agreements. U.S. exporters may also have failed to mobilize because they realized that the European current account would further suffer from reciprocal trade liberalization, making such liberalization unsustainable. A trade agreement, however, could have stimulated European exports to the United States by as much as U.S. exports to Europe.[5]

Import-Competitors' Continued Lobbying Effort

Particularly notable from the perspective of the protection-for-exporters argument is that the low level of exporter mobilization did not reflect a general decline in interest-group activity after World War II. On the contrary, protectionist lobbying remained strong (Vernon 1958, 6). A wide variety of import-competing industries, some of them represented by the America's Wage Earners' Protective Conference; American Tariff League; National Labor-Management Council of Foreign Trade Policy; and Nation-wide Committee of Industry, Agriculture, and Labor on Import-Export Policy, were adamant in defending the maintenance of trade barriers. The American Tariff League, for example, asked for an indefinite postponement of any international trade conference (*New York Times,* 11 September 1950, 46). O. R. Strackbein, who first represented America's Wage Earners' Protective Conference and later the National Labor-Management Council of Foreign Trade Policy, was the protectionist leader who received most public attention. Instead of declining, protectionist lobbying even increased during the 1950s. In the mid-1950s, bicycle makers, the chemical industry, coal producers, cotton manufacturers, dairy farmers, potters, watchmakers, woolgrowers, and many more united in opposition to the extension of the RTAA.[6] The *Washington Post* (5 January 1958, L10) thus could write: "Protectionist sentiment appears to have gained steadily in the last few years."

This stark contrast between minimal exporter and omnipresent import-competing lobbying in the 1950s casts substantial doubt on the institutionalist argument that the RTAA empowered U.S. exporters (Gilligan 1997a; see also

---

4. Between 1948 and 1958, the share of total U.S. exports going to France and Germany was constantly between 7.3 and 11.5 percent. Calculated from data in Carter et al. (2005, table 5–537).

5. In 1952 as many as 570 U.S. tariffs on manufactured goods exceeded the average of the four largest West European countries (Asbeek Brusse 1997, 136). Reducing these tariffs should have substantially increased European exports to the United States.

6. See, for example, *New York Times,* 24 May 1953, E7; *Washington Post,* 14 September 1954, 15; U.S. Congress, January–February 1955, Hearings before the House Committee on Ways and Means, *Trade Agreements Extension;* Watson 1956, 691.

Bailey, Goldstein, and Weingast 1997). The observations also contradict the prediction that past trade liberalization should increase future free trade lobbying (Hathaway 1998). Rather than increased free trade and reduced protectionist lobbying, what can be observed in the early 1950s is just the opposite. The strength of import-competing interests, moreover, is difficult to reconcile with Michael Hiscox's (1999, 685) point that a "drastic, temporary reduction in import-competition for U.S. manufacturers" after World War II should have reduced the pressure for protectionism. With regard to domestic interests, therefore, the years after World War II remain a puzzle for existing theories of trade policymaking. By contrast, the argument that exporters lack the incentives to become politically active in the absence of threats to their foreign market access can well account for the observation of little exporter mobilization at that time.

Protectionist U.S. Trade Policies

In the 1950s, reflecting the bias in favor of import-competing interests within the United States, Congress passed several fairly protectionist trade bills that severely limited the president's discretion to engage in international trade negotiations (see table 3.3). Four elements of the trade bills passed between 1948 and 1958 made sure that the administration could not give meaningful concessions in trade negotiations. First, in 1948 Congress introduced a peril-point provision, which

Table 3.3 Major U.S. trade bills, 1934–1962

YEAR	TIME LIMIT (IN YEARS)	TARIFF CUTS ALLOWED (WITH BASE YEARS FOR CUTS IN PARENTHESES)	OTHER KEY FEATURES OF THE BILLS
1945	3	50% (1945)	
1948	1	50% (1945)	Peril-point provision included
1949	3 (retroactive from 1948)	50% (1945)	Removal of the peril-point provision
1951	2	50% (1945)	Escape clause and peril-point provision included
1953	1	50% (1945)	
1954	1	50% (1945)	National-security clause
1955	3	5% annually (1955)	Strengthened national-security clause
1958	4	20% (1958)	
1962	5	50% (1962)	Peril-point provision eliminated, linear tariff reductions allowed

restricted the president's discretion to reduce tariffs below levels that the Tariff Commission deemed necessary to protect U.S. producers from injury. Although Congress removed this provision only one year after it was imposed, the following trade bills reintroduced it, and not before 1962 did Congress permanently repeal it. The peril-point provision led to a situation in which an exchange of concessions based on the comparative advantage of countries was made impossible.

Second, Congress obliged the president to include an escape clause in all trade agreements that authorized the withdrawal of concessions in case imports damaged American producers. Between 1948 and 1962, the president used this clause to increase duties on fifteen products, among them bicycles, carpets, glass, and watches (Diebold 1962, 360). Third, a national security clause, first introduced in 1954, enabled the imposition of quotas on imports that allegedly threatened to impair national security. Finally, five of the six trade bills passed in that decade required renewal after one or two years, a period too short to allow for major trade negotiations. Together, these four elements made sure that the administration would not be in a position to offer concessions to foreign trading partners that would be valuable enough to them to engage in reciprocal trade liberalization.

While these features of the trade bills satisfied import-competing interests, little in them—beyond the fact that the principle of the RTAA was maintained—could appeal to exporter interests. The lack of concern for exporter interests is also reflected in the debates in the President's Commission on Foreign Economic Policy (also known as the Randall Commission after Clarence Randall, who was chosen to head the commission), which was established in 1953 to prepare a new trade bill (Bauer, Pool, and Dexter 1972, 40–49; Kaufman 1982, 18–26; Medick-Krakau 1995, 204–13). In these debates, there was literally no allusion to the idea that trade liberalization could help exporters secure foreign markets, an argument that was important in the 1930s as well as in the 1960s. On the contrary, the liberal side defended freer trade only with the arguments that it would lead to a more efficient use of resources and that consumers should not be taxed for the benefit of a few producers.

Moreover, the liberals claimed that continuing the reciprocal trade agreements program would help stabilize the European economies, an important task in the cold war. Providing foreign countries improved access to the U.S. market would also help close the dollar gap that was seen as a major problem for European economic development. Since the liberal side was unable to point out how reciprocal trade liberalization would favor specific organized interests, it was weak and not very influential. As a result, the final suggestions were modest: extending the RTAA by three years and authorizing the president to cut tariffs by 5 percent a year. The peril-point and escape-clause provisions should be retained. A minority report, supported by the Republican chairman of the House

Committee on Ways and Means, Daniel Reed, even questioned the desirability of a further extension of the RTAA (Barrie 1987, 140n24).

The only exception to this general principle of little concern for exporter interests are some specific policies intended to avoid costs to U.S. exporters as a result of discriminatory trade policies abroad. Within the GATT, for example, the United States contested the decision of the sterling area to cut dollar imports by 25 percent. The U.S. administration also supported American oil companies in their efforts aimed at the abolition of discriminatory regulation of their business activities in the British market. The negotiations led to several agreements with major U.S. oil companies ending discrimination in return for some concessions by those companies. In addition, although the United States had supported the creation of the European Payments Union, it complained about discriminatory measures taken under its umbrella. When, in 1951, Belgium introduced new discriminatory restrictions against dollar imports, for example, the U.S. government protested, and argued that Belgium should have used other measures to avoid the threat of inflation caused by surpluses within the payments system. Shortly thereafter, Belgium decided gradually to relax the relevant restrictions. The U.S. administration also protested plans for preferential tariff cuts among European countries that started to surge in the early 1950s (Lynch 1997, 132–33). Consequently, when in the 1954 GATT review session Belgium proposed an amendment to the GATT to allow for regional discrimination, the U.S. administration strongly objected to this proposal, and Belgium had to withdraw it (Patterson 1966, 105–10).

The Failure of Alternative Theories

In short, in the 1950s U.S. trade policies had little regard for the interests of exporters, a finding that is in line with Hypothesis 2 of the protection-for-exporters argument in a case in which exporters were not mobilized. By contrast, the developments are difficult to explain from the perspective of alternative theories. Several authors emphasize the role of geopolitics in U.S. trade politics after World War II (Nelson 1989; Eckes 1995). Indeed, the various administrations constantly stressed the geopolitical aspects of the trade negotiations program. In 1947 President Truman in his address to Congress requesting trade legislation had stated that new presidential trade authority was necessary to organize the world for peace.[7] The task was not only to avoid Communist takeovers in Europe but also to prevent the fallback of Europe into the habit of nationalistic policies.

---

7. U.S. Congress, March 1947, Hearings before the House Committee on Ways and Means, *Reciprocal Trade Agreements Program*, II:301.

In later debates about U.S. trade policies, similar arguments were put forward. The Eisenhower administration, for example, announced its program to be "trade, not aid," meaning the substitution of aid payments with improved access for European products to the U.S. market (Eckes 1995, 164; Medick-Krakau 1995, 192; Zeiler 1999, 192). The proposal was a response to fears that the Europeans would look to the Soviet Union for help if they were barred from selling in the U.S. market (*Wall Street Journal,* 23 May 1952, 1). Evidently, however, this talk did not make U.S. trade policies more liberal (Medick-Krakau 1995, 269). On the contrary, Congress insisted on restricting the president's autonomy to engage in trade negotiations. Geopolitical arguments were even used to legitimate barriers to imports: the 1950 Defense Production Act, for example, imposed restrictions on the import of fats and oil, including in dairy products.

These and other observations also cast doubt on some variants of the hegemonic stability theory (Kindleberger 1973; Krasner 1976; for the doubts, see also Stiles 1995). In particular, Congress twice rejected plans for an international trade organization, although a benevolent hegemon supposedly should have shouldered the costs of international cooperation.[8] Congress neither ratified the "Havana Charter" that foresaw the creation of an International Trade Organization(Kock 1969, 59–60; Gardner 1980, 371–78; Medick-Krakau 1995, 105–10), nor the Organization for Trade Cooperation, which was to be the result of the 1955 meeting of GATT contracting parties (Medick-Krakau 1995, chap. 8). The latter episode is particularly telling: in the negotiations, the U.S. administration vigorously pushed for an organization that would be acceptable to Congress. Illustratively, it fought for an escape clause at the level of the GATT and the limitation of the scope of the new organization to a very narrow definition of commercial policy. Despite foreign countries' acceptance of these demands, in the end there was little support for the Organization for Trade Cooperation in Congress. This was not because Congress preferred the existing trade regime organized around the GATT: on the contrary, between 1951 and 1958 all U.S. trade agreement bills included a GATT disclaimer, which stated that passage of the bill did not imply Congressional "approval or disapproval" of the GATT. As a result of this particular situation, the GATT had to draw on the Interim Commission of the International Trade Organization for secretarial support, a situation that did not change until the creation of the World Trade Organization (WTO) in 1995.

---

8. Some advocates of hegemonic stability theory argue that a hegemon should engage in "monopolistic predation," that is, compel other states to engage in free trade while itself imposing an optimal tariff (Conybeare 1984; see also Pahre 1999). This could explain the U.S. reluctance to accept more imports; however, it cannot explain why the United States was not more insistent on prying open European markets to the advantage of U.S. exporters.

U.S. trade policy, therefore, was not driven by a desire to strengthen U.S. allies in the cold war, nor was it aimed at providing the public good of international openness and economic stability. Rather, it seems to have been intended to satisfy the preferences of (import-competing) domestic actors. To achieve this aim, Congress constantly closely monitored the negotiators from the State Department, going as far as asking the executive to submit biographies of the negotiators who would represent the United States in international trade talks (Hudec 1971, 1319n44). This evidence contradicts Stephen D. Krasner's (1979, 494) claim that in the postwar years "the United States used its power most forcefully to promote general political goals rather than specific economic interests."[9]

One explanation for the more protectionist stance of Congress in that decade stresses party politics, especially the fact that for the first time since 1932 the Republicans gained control of Congress from 1947 to 1949 and from 1953 to 1955 (and in the latter period they also controlled the presidency). The Republicans traditionally had defended a more protectionist stance than the Democrats, as the former represented import-competing producers of machinery in the north and the latter consumers of machinery and exporters of commodities in the south. It may not come as a surprise, then, that in 1948 a Republican-dominated Congress passed an RTAA bill that made further trade negotiations virtually impossible. Only at the last moment did the Senate exclude a provision from the bill that would have allowed Congress to veto all trade agreements concluded by the administration.

While powerful, the party account fails to provide a complete picture of the developments. In fact, what happened in the 1950s was a convergence of party positions (Watson 1956; Bauer, Pool, and Dexter 1972; Hiscox 1999). This convergence mainly occurred because some Democrats abandoned their previous support for reciprocal trade liberalization. A first indication of this is that it was a Democratic majority that failed to approve the Havana Charter, discussed above, in 1949 and 1950 (Gardner 1980, 371–78; Medick-Krakau 1995, 105–10). Moreover, of six rather protectionist trade bills adopted in this decade (1948, 1949, 1951, 1953, 1954, and 1955) half were passed while the Democrats controlled Congress (1949, 1951, and 1955). In 1951, for example, a Democratic majority passed a protectionist amendment to the Trade Agreements Extension Act that determined that any past or future trade agreement would be subordinated to

---

9. U.S. support for Japan's accession to the GATT might provide more support for a hegemonic reading of U.S. trade policies (Eckes 1995, 169–76). Nevertheless, with Japan only supplying a relatively small share of U.S. imports at that time (2.7 percent of total U.S. imports in 1954, as calculated from data in Carter et al. 2005, table 5–543), Japanese membership in the GATT was unlikely to stimulate major fears among import-competing interests in the United States, thus allowing decision makers to implement policies in accordance with other interests.

the provisions of the Agricultural Adjustment Act (1938), thus inhibiting the administration from negotiating on the quotas restricting trade in agricultural goods. The trade bill also included other protectionist features, such as a peril-point provision and an escape clause, which allowed import-competing industries to petition for protection in case of injury from imports. The voting records show that a substantial number of the Democrats voted in favor of these protectionist provisions.

The interpretation given here also contrasts with Michael Hiscox's (1999; see also Irwin and Kroszner 1999) emphasis on the conversion of the Republican Party in the postwar years. This conversion, according to Hiscox, was a result of changes in the constituencies represented by the Republican Party, which were increasingly export oriented. It is undeniable that the Republicans did give up their outright rejection of the RTAA program in favor of a limited approval of the principle of presidential authority over tariff setting. Yet the conversion in the Republican position was largely limited to accepting the idea that Congress should not engage in unilateral tariff setting, which could lead to (across the board) increases in U.S. tariffs. Republican support for the 1948 trade bill, for example, is not very remarkable when considering the starkly protectionist features of this bill. The Democratic and Republican positions thus converged in a rather protectionist stance at a time when the United States was the economically most powerful country in the world, an observation that remains puzzling from the point of view of Hiscox's account. Moreover, why would both parties have supported the passage of the much more liberal RTAA of 1958 and the Trade Expansion Act of 1962 only a few years later? While challenging Hiscox's interpretation, these observations are completely consistent with the protection-for-exporters argument. In the 1950s, in the absence of exporter lobbying, the Democrats had little reason to continue pushing for policies in protection of exporter interests. In the 1960s exporters mobilized, providing an incentive for both parties to support liberal trade policies.[10]

In short, the observations confirm a largely "isolationist" reading in which the United States neither showed a particular interest in opening European markets nor was willing to open the U.S. market for imports. This policy mix is difficult to explain using the available alternative theories: if geopolitics had been important, one would expect a greater willingness to accept foreign competition in the U.S. market. This is especially so since the competitive advantage of the U.S.

---

10. The protectionist stance of some Southern Democrats in the 1950s partly reflected demands made by the textile and oil industries in such states as Oklahoma, South Carolina, and Texas (Watson 1956, 698). But why would these demands determine trade policies in the early 1950s but not in 1958 and in 1962?

economy at that time was such that even a complete and unilateral opening of the market would not have created much damage to U.S. industries. According to one report, paying the salaries of all employees possibly negatively affected by U.S. unilateral free trade would have been less costly than the payments made to European countries through the Marshall Plan (*New York Times*, 20 July 1952, E7). Institutionalist arguments also fall short of providing a convincing explanation of these trade policies, as they predict more concern for exporter interests in the aftermath of the passage of the RTAA than can be observed. Given the failure of these alternative theories, the balance of domestic interests in the United States seems to be the most plausible explanation for the specific features of U.S. trade policy in the 1950s.

Stagnation in Transatlantic Trade Talks and Economic Integration in Europe

As a result of this U.S. protectionist stance, and despite several rounds of tariff negotiations that took place in the 1950s to allow new countries to accede to the GATT, GATT contracting parties hardly reduced their tariffs at that time (see table 3.4). As the data convincingly show, after the 1947 negotiations the average duty reductions in these negotiations were minimal and limited to a few product categories. The reductions in average U.S. tariffs were in line with these data for all participating countries: 2 percent in 1949, 3 percent in 1950–51, and 3 percent in 1956 (U.S. Tariff Commission 1969, 238). What is more, the United States made concessions mainly for products for which no increase in imports could be expected, because it had a clear competitive advantage (Krause 1959, 549). It is no wonder, then, that these tariff reductions did not have a discernable impact on U.S. imports (Krause 1962).

A possible rival explanation for this stagnation asserts that European countries were not interested in reciprocal tariff reductions since they needed breathing space to recover their economies after World War II. In fact, as can be expected

Table 3.4   The results of trade negotiations, 1947–1956 (in percent)

NEGOTIATIONS	YEARS	DUTIABLE IMPORTS SUBJECT TO REDUCTIONS	AVERAGE TARIFF CUTS OF PARTICIPATING COUNTRIES
Geneva I	1947	54	21
Annecy	1949	6	2
Torquay	1950–51	12	3
Geneva II	1956	16	2

Source: Adapted from Lavergne (1983, 32–33).

based on the protection-for-exporters argument, the degree of exporter mobilization in Europe was limited at that time. Nevertheless, throughout the 1950s most of the governments of the larger European countries anticipated gains from a reduction in the still very high U.S. trade barriers. Illustratively, in September 1951 the French minister of foreign trade, Pierre Pflimlin, proposed a quite ambitious plan for tariff reductions (Curzon 1965, 89; Asbeek Brusse 1997, 125). As adopted by the GATT contracting parties in 1953, this plan would have led to a linear reduction of tariffs of about one third. The hope for a lowering of U.S. duties, however, was disappointed first by the modest recommendations included in the report of the Randall Commission (Bauer, Pool, and Dexter 1972, 49) and then by the very moderate delegation of negotiating authority to the U.S. president in 1955, which did not allow for an implementation of the plan. The U.S. negotiators consequently objected to a mentioning of linear cuts in the GATT (Medick-Krakau 1995, 305). Instead of reducing trade barriers, the United States even used the 1955 meeting of GATT contracting parties to push through a waiver for its protectionist measures in the agricultural sector (Warley 1976, 346–48), and Congress never approved the Organization for Trade Cooperation that was supposed to be the foremost result of that meeting.[11]

It was thus mainly American unwillingness to move ahead with liberalization that impeded more significant advances in international trade negotiations in the 1950s. In support of this argument, Sidney Dell maintained that U.S. inability "to participate in the programme [of multilateral trade liberalization] blocked it for the other countries as well—unless the latter were prepared to reduce their tariffs against the United States unilaterally, which hardly seemed reasonable" (Dell 1963, 111). European countries had to accept that rather than "trade, not aid," what they could expect was "aid, not trade" (*New York Times*, 1 May 1953, 1). With the domestic costs of increased imports concentrated on a few industries, and those of foreign aid payments thinly dispersed across many tax payers, this outcome is in line with the political economy model set out in chapter 1.

At the same time as transatlantic trade negotiations were deadlocked, European countries considered preferential trade agreements among themselves. Already in the late 1940s, France and Italy put forward a plan for the creation of a Franco-Italian customs union, which however failed due to lack of support among French industrial sectors (Lynch 1997, 106). Shortly thereafter, the French

---

11. Tellingly, in the same meeting the U.S. admnistration also called for a prohibition of quantitative barriers to imports, which restricted U.S. exports to European countries. When other countries pointed out that its request for a protectionist waiver was inconsistent with this demand for foreign liberalization, the United States decided to push for the waiver (satisfying import-competing interests) and settle for an unambitious clause calling for "consultations" on quantitative barriers (of little use to exporting interests).

minister of finance, Maurice Petsche, launched a new plan, called Finebel (and initially Fritalux), that foresaw the removal of quantitative controls on the cross-border flows of capital, goods, and labor in traditional sectors of the economy. The agreement was to encompass France, Italy, and the Benelux countries. Given some opposition, especially from the Dutch government, which demanded the creation of a full customs union and the inclusion of West Germany in the plan, however, the Finebel negotiations suffered the same fate as the earlier proposal (Milward 1984, 235–43; Asbeek Brusse 1997, 60–63).

In 1950 Dirk Stikker, the Dutch minister of foreign affairs, proposed the "Stikker Plan of Action" that was supposed to lead to the gradual removal of tariffs and other barriers to trade within Europe (Milward 1984, 344–50; Asbeek Brusse 1997, 100–104). The idea was that all barriers to trade, whether tariffs or quantitative ones, should be eliminated through a sector-by-sector approach. The sectors to be liberalized should be chosen by a three-quarters majority in the Council of the OEEC. The plan engendered two immediate counterproposals. Italy's more conservative proposal was that multilateral negotiations should lead to preferential tariff reductions in the OEEC. The outcome of these negotiations should be subjected to two automatic tariff cuts of 15 percent that should be three years apart. France suggested reducing intra-European tariffs by a fixed percentage.

In view of these different proposals, the July 1950 meeting of the Council of the OEEC decided to establish a special working party to continue the debate. The discussions on the Stikker plan started with studies of the textile and paper and pulp sectors, but it was soon realized that this approach would be extremely difficult to carry through; no major results were forthcoming from the other two plans either (Milward 1984, 448–51). In December of the same year, consequently, the French secretary of state for finance Robert Buron tried to break the stalemate by suggesting the creation of a "high political authority" with the power to reduce tariffs within the OEEC by 10 percent each year over a period of five years. Again, however, no agreement could be found on the basis of this plan.

Although initially unsuccessful, the discussions accompanying these and other projects in the end led to the signature by six countries of the Treaty of Paris, which created the European Coal and Steel Community (ECSC), in April 1951. The treaty stipulated the abolition of all barriers to trade in the coal and steel sectors and the harmonization of external tariffs for these products. With this project being successful, some European countries started to ask for more comprehensive and longer-term preferential policies. France, for example, openly stated that European countries should deepen preferential trade ties, even if this would lead to discrimination against U.S. exports (Patterson 1966, 96). More comprehensively, the Ohlin plan, which in February 1952 was supported by the

Council of Europe, proposed—among other measures—that the European contracting parties of the GATT should eliminate the barriers to trade among themselves (Asbeek Brusse 1997, 128–30).

The pressure for preferential trade policies intensified when an increasing number of European trading interests became convinced that, at least in the short term, a multilateral trade agreement would not be forthcoming. In particular, the small European countries and export-dependent Germany needed an instrument to increase intra-European trade in the absence of progress in the GATT tariff rounds (Milward 1992). The June 1955 meeting in Messina of the member governments of the European Coal and Steel Community brought agreement on the general aim of a step-by-step creation of a customs union and on sectoral integration in transport, conventional energy, and atomic power. The governments also decided to set up a committee under the chairmanship of the Belgian foreign minister, Paul-Henry Spaak, to discuss various unresolved issues. In April 1956, this committee produced a text that already resembled the future Treaty of Rome.

The last hopes for a lowering of U.S. duties, which survived until the mid-1950s (*Wall Street Journal*, 2 February 1955, 1), were disappointed by the 1955 U.S. trade legislation. The governments of the European countries still attended the GATT tariff conference called by the United States in 1956, but they received the American delegation with harsh criticism (Gantzer 1956). As was predictable given the lack of adequate negotiating authority on behalf of the U.S. negotiators, the conference only led to minor tariff cuts, and most participants regarded it as a failure. One observer remarked that since "the U.S. [remained] a prisoner of its domestic legislation and the U.K. true to the belief that Commonwealth trade was more important than trade with the continent of Europe, the delegates from continental countries went home with a feeling of frustration" (Curzon 1965, 95; see also Kock 1969, 85–86). This lack of progress in multilateral trade liberalization convinced continental European export interests that the multilateral path of tariff reductions had ended and that alternatives were needed. Only one week after the 1956 Geneva tariff conference, six European countries met in Venice, where they approved the plan presented by the Spaak Committee for the establishment of a common market. Since European countries could not bring down highly protective U.S. tariffs, they decided to undertake a regional project that would provide benefits to their exporters while excluding the United States.[12]

---

12. Implicitly, this is also the position taken by the European Commission (Commission of the European Communities 1973), when stating that "the fact that [in the 1950s] a great many small and medium sized partners were confronted by a much stronger one" contributed to the creation of free trade areas and customs unions.

The existing literature on these developments emphasizes the assistance provided by successive U.S. administrations for regional integration in Europe (Romero 1996; Lundestad 2003). Indeed, the available evidence clearly shows that such support was forthcoming. This observation does not contradict the protection-for-exporters argument, however. On the contrary, as long as American exporters did not face losses, they failed to mobilize, providing the U.S. administration with some flexibility and the ability to pursue certain foreign policy objectives by encouraging European integration. At the same time, whenever U.S. exporters faced losses, for example when Belgium pushed for preferential trade among the OEEC countries, the United States was quite vigorous in defending exporters' interests. In short, the combination of strong import-competing and weak exporting interests in the United States in the 1950s contributed to the European choice for a preferential trading agreement (Dell 1963, 112).

In this chapter I have summarized the most important developments in transatlantic trade policies from 1947 to 1958. Since the discrimination emanating from the system of imperial preference had declined, and the European countries had not yet established a preferential trading zone, U.S. exporters lacked an incentive to mobilize. Protectionist interests, by contrast, were very vocal. This balance of interests had two major consequences for U.S. trade policies. On the one hand, the U.S. administration lacked support to push for further tariff reductions in the GATT. On the other hand, it had some leeway to support European initiatives for regional integration. The combination of these policies created a situation that was very propitious for the establishment of a preferential trade agreement, explaining in part the six European countries' decision to found the EEC. The case, therefore, provides support for the protection-for-exporters argument. In contrast, possible alternative theories of trade policymaking face substantial problems in explaining this case. They consistently lead to the expectation that the United States should have continued its pursuit of trade liberalization started in the mid-1930s, while actually protectionism was dominant.

THE EUROPEAN ECONOMIC COMMUNITY, DISCRIMINATION, AND TRANSATLANTIC TRADE RELATIONS, 1958–1963

Ending a period in which it had pursued largely protectionist trade policies, the United States undertook two major initiatives to obtain lower foreign trade barriers in the late 1950s and early 1960s. First, in 1958 Congress passed the Reciprocal Trade Agreements Act of 1958 that provided the president with increased powers to engage in trade negotiations. The administration used this authority to engage in the Dillon round (1960–62) of GATT negotiations that led to some reciprocal tariff reductions on industrial goods. Second, and even more important, in 1962 Congress passed a major trade bill called the Trade Expansion Act (TEA), which allowed the president to cut U.S. tariffs *linearly*—rather than following the item-by-item procedure required before—by as much as 50 percent in a reciprocal agreement. Moreover, it enabled the president to negotiate the reduction to zero of tariffs on a large range of products in case of the United Kingdom's accession to the newly created EEC (1957). Using this authority, the United States engaged in the Kennedy round (1964–67), which resulted in the most far-reaching tariff reductions up to that time.

Compared to the tightly circumscribed trade bills of the early 1950s, the RTAA of 1958 and the TEA of 1962 signify a major change in U.S. trade orientation. As pointed out by Raymond A. Bauer, Ithiel de Sola Pool, and Lewis A. Dexter (1972, 77) in a classic book about U.S. trade policy, the TEA represented "the most significant turn in American trade policy in thirty years." Nevertheless, U.S. trade liberalization in the 1960s has so far attracted little research by political scientists. Most studies of U.S. trade policies overlook this renewed shift toward liberalization that took place in the late 1950s. In fact, many existing theories of U.S. trade liberalization find it difficult to account for the TEA, as they put a lot of emphasis on the institutional changes introduced by the RTAA of 1934. By contrast, the protection-for-exporters argument, as I show in this chapter, can offer a plausible explanation of the developments in the late 1950s and early 1960s. The mobilization of exporters in response to the discrimination caused by the creation of the EEC, in this view, goes a far way in explaining the increase in tariff-cutting authority contained in the two bills.

In making this argument, I take issue with a series of potential rival explanations. From an institutionalist perspective, Susanne Lohmann and Sharyn O'Halloran (1994) suggest that unified government allowed for the far-reaching delegation of trade authority to the U.S. president contained in the TEA. As I show in this chapter, however, the TEA was only a continuation of a process started in the RTAA of 1958 that was passed by a Democratic Congress for a Republican president. Equally, an explanation based on geopolitical considerations (Verdier 1994; Eckes 1995) has difficulties in accounting both for the timing of the U.S. shift in trade orientation and the form that this shift took. Since the cold war was at its peak in the 1950s, if security considerations are important in shaping trade policy, the U.S. should have given most trade concessions to its European allies in that decade. In the 1960s, by contrast, the easing of tensions with the Soviet Union and the rising economic power of the EEC and Japan (Keohane 1984, 197–200) should have made the United States more cautious with regard to trade liberalization.

The main explanation for the European acceptance of trade liberalization in the 1960s has been that the delegation of trade-policy authority to a supranational entity, namely the European Commission, increased decision makers' autonomy from protectionist pressures (Meunier 2005, 8–9; Woolcock 2005, 247). Following this "collusive delegation argument," decision makers used an institutional change to overcome opposition from domestic interests to trade liberalization. The empirical evidence, however, reveals that the trade policies implemented by the EEC were tightly in line with the demands voiced by societal actors. The protection-for-exporters argument provides an alternative interpretation that calls attention to the boost in bargaining power that the member governments of the EEC experienced after the creation of this trading arrangement. The discrimination generated by the EEC made foreign countries eager to safeguard their exporters' access to European markets. The EEC, consequently, could gain disproportionate concessions from excluded countries in exchange for a smaller reduction of extra-EU trade barriers in trade negotiations. In this situation, agreeing to trade liberalization became attractive for European countries.

The EEC and Discrimination against U.S. Exports

For the last four decades scholars have debated the exact consequences of the creation of the EEC for trade flows. The general thrust of this literature is that the creation of the EEC had the potential to hurt some exporters in both excluded countries in Europe and the United States, although no agreement exists on the precise extent of trade diversion (Bayoumi and Eichengreen 1997). One problem for econometric analyses is that the multilateral trade liberalization that took place in the 1960s counteracted trade diversion, making it difficult to know what would have happened in the absence of these negotiations. Nevertheless, what is important here is that in the late 1950s and early 1960s nearly all observers predicted that the preferential lowering of tariffs and the increase of some tariffs in the process of establishing the common external tariff of the EEC would have a negative impact on the export chances of producers excluded from the EEC. Even the United Kingdom, which at that time still had notable trade links with the Commonwealth countries, was expected to suffer from trade diversion (Economist Intelligence Unit 1957, 14).

With about one-third of total U.S. exports going to the EEC countries in 1958, the prospect of export losses was a serious matter also for American exporters (Krause 1968). In absolute terms, in that year the United States exported to the EEC products valuing nearly $2.5 billion, a number that went up to nearly $3.5 billion in 1960. Two features of the Treaty of Rome particularly threatened to curtail these exports: the introduction of a common external tariff combined with the preferential abolition of internal barriers and the common policies in the agricultural sector.

Concerning tariffs, although the EEC simply averaged the tariff levels existing in the six member countries, the discrimination inherent in the establishment of a customs union threatened to exclude U.S. exporters from their most important markets. The averaging meant that tariffs were raised in the countries that previously had had relatively low trade barriers and thus had imported most from the United States. In fact, econometric studies undertaken after the creation of the EEC show that export losses were particularly significant in trade with Germany and Belgium, countries that had to increase their trade barriers when moving toward a common external tariff (Truman 1969; European Free Trade Association 1972, 54; Verdoorn and Schwartz 1972, 332–33). For some products, moreover, tariffs were not averaged, but higher tariff levels were agreed on. For exporters in third countries, consequently, not only the traditional effects as predicted by customs union theory were worrying, but also the trade effects engendered by changing external tariffs.

The expectation was that, in particular, exports of electrical and industrial machinery, machine tools, certain chemicals, and cars would likely suffer from trade diversion (Piquet 1958, 133; Kreinin 1959, 618; Benoit 1961, 172). A study by the Committee for a National Trade Policy, beyond mentioning the above products, also showed concern about potential losses regarding petroleum products (especially if the United Kingdom entered the Common Market); drugs and plastic materials (especially in the Benelux countries); paper and paperboard; textile yarn; iron and steel products; technical and musical instruments; and aircraft.[1] For these products, U.S. exporters both held significant market shares in the EEC and faced competition from common market producers. Other products were affected more by the upward adjustment of tariff levels in the low-tariff countries to the common external tariff than by the preferential reduction of internal tariffs.

U.S. exporters of agricultural products had even more cause for concern. The EEC's Common Agricultural Policy (CAP) introduced target prices for a series of agricultural products. These target prices were maintained in the market through two different mechanisms. On the one hand, government agencies could buy or sell products on which the domestic market price had fallen below or risen above a specified intervention price. The purchased products were either stored or exported at world market prices. On the other hand, variable levies, which were adjusted upward or downward depending on price movements in the domestic market, made sure that imports could not undermine this system (Piquet 1958; Patterson 1966, 198–217). By January 1962, the CAP was applied to a series of agricultural products such as cereals, eggs, fruits, pork, poultry, and vegetables (Curtis and Vastine 1971, 21). At the end of 1964, the EEC also implemented common provisions for beef, veal, rice, and milk products. The target prices, however, on which the protective effect of the policy depended, were not agreed on before 1967 and 1968.

The CAP was expected to lead to an increase in agricultural production, which not only would displace imports but eventually would even make the EEC an exporter of agricultural goods and thus increase competition in world markets (*Wall Street Journal*, 24 January 1962, 1). Initially, however, the consequences varied across products. The situation turned out to be most difficult for exporters of poultry, who had to experience a rapid reduction of exports after the EEC imposed a variable levy on this product in early 1962 (Preeg 1970, 74–77). In addition, exporters of pork and beef suffered substantially, while exporters of grains actually benefited from the larger demand for feed grains in Europe that resulted from an increased production of meat. The detrimental effects of the CAP were thus felt by grain exporters only from the late 1960s onward.

---

1. U.S. Congress, July 1962, Hearings before the Senate Committee on Finance, *Trade Expansion Act of 1962*, 334–44.

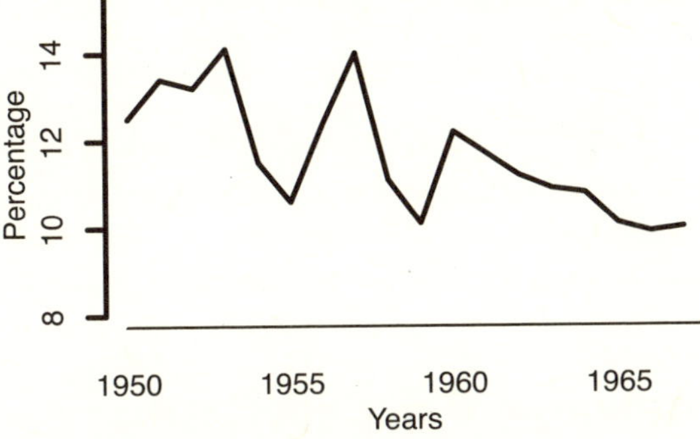

FIGURE 4.1   U.S. exports to four major European countries as a share of these countries' total imports.

Source: Author's calculations on data for U.S. exports from Carter el al. (2005). Data for total European imports and Italian imports from the U.S. are from Mitchell (1998), with national trade data converted into dollars using exchange rate data from http://www. measuringworth.org/exchangeglobal/ (accessed 1 April 2009).

Note: The graph reports American exporters' access to four major European markets, calculated as the sum of U.S. exports to France, Italy, the United Kingdom, and West Germany divided by the sum of these countries' total imports.

Nevertheless, witnessing the negative consequences of the CAP for exporters of other products, they had good reason to be concerned about the EEC as well.

Overall, trade diversion may have amounted to $650 million of U.S. exports to the EEC already in the first few years (Truman 1969). Trade diversion further increased in the following years as the gradual elimination of trade barriers among the EEC members augmented the preference differential (Aitken 1973), particularly for food, chemicals, and other manufactured goods (Balassa 1967a). Between 1958 and 1970, trade diversion may have reduced U.S. exports by as much as $2.2 billion (Krause 1968, 222). While the common market's higher growth rates may have compensated some U.S. exporters for their losses, at least a few sectors of the U.S. economy probably could not recuperate their losses. Among them were exporters of agricultural goods, automobiles, chemicals, and some types of machinery. The parallel creation of the European Free Trade Association (1960) among seven European countries, including the United Kingdom, should also have hurt U.S. exporters.

It is not astonishing, then, that trade data shows that beginning in the late 1950s U.S. exporters suffered significant losses of market access in Europe that continued into the mid-1960s (see figure 4.1). This contrasts with the long decade following World War II, when they had been able to increase their share of the European markets—with the exception of 1955 when France moved to stabilize its currency by limiting dollar imports. A British accession to the EEC and the creation of a European-wide free trade zone bringing together the EEC and the EFTA member countries was expected to impose even further trade diversionary costs on U.S. exporters (Kreinin 1959, 623–24). The expectation then is for U.S. exporters to have mobilized, pushing politicians to engage in policies aimed at the protection of exporter interests.

The Mobilization of U.S. Exporters

Already in 1957, an article in the *Wall Street Journal* (30 July 1957, 1) suggested a connection between fears about the creation of the common market and increasing support for a more liberal trade policy: "Groups backing more liberal trade see some favorable omens on their side. They believe the European Common Market and other developments have made businessmen feel the need of a liberal foreign trade policy." In fact, a substantial increase in the number of exporter witnesses in the hearings for the RTAA of 1958 and the TEA to thirty-three and thirty witnesses, respectively, illustrates the mobilization of U.S. exporters in response to the threat created by the EEC.[2] This number was substantially larger than in 1953 and 1955.

Besides farmers, exporters of airplanes, cars, electrical machinery, electronic goods, machine tools, and paper were especially politically active (Barrie 1987, 200–213). Large groups such as the Committee for a National Trade Policy (CNTP), including about two thousand members, and the U.S. Chamber of Commerce lobbied Congress and the administration in favor of a trade policy that would take into account exporter interests (*New York Times*, 3 May 1962, 1; 4 May 1962, 32; *Wall Street Journal*, 27 February 1962, 9). Illustratively, the CNTP organized a conference on trade policy with President John F. Kennedy as the main speaker and set up a Coordinating Council of Organizations on International Trade Policy with the former secretaries of state, Christian A. Herter and Dean Acheson, as honorary members. Even the banking sector increased its mobilization in favor of a new approach to trade policymaking.[3]

---

2. U.S. Congress, February–March 1958, Hearings before the House Committee on Ways and Means, *Renewal of Trade Agreements Act;* U.S. Congress, March–April 1962, Hearings before the House Committee on Ways and Means, *Trade Expansion Act of 1962.*

3. Bauer, Pool, and Dexter (1972, 283) write with regard to the banking community: "In 1962, it must be conceded, [financial firms] were somewhat more active.... They shared the general alarm over exclusion from the Common Market."

Lobbying against Losses of Foreign Market Access

Not only the timing of the exporter mobilization but also the content of statements shows that the lobbying effort was a response to losses of foreign market access, this time caused by the creation of the EEC. As early as 1957, the U.S. Council of the International Chamber of Commerce predicted discrimination resulting from the establishment of the EEC. It stressed that the "importance of the nations forming the Common Market for American exports" made it essential that the U.S. administration "be armed with ample negotiating authority for dealing with the situation as it develops."[4] In the hearings for the 1958 renewal of the RTAA, moreover, the representative of the U.S. Chamber of Commerce exhibited great apprehension when he declared: "The threat of being shut out of traditional European markets by high tariffs is of acute concern to United States businessmen. [The establishment of a customs union] will place American exporters to the area at an increasing disadvantage vis-à-vis their competitors within these countries."[5] The representative of the Caterpillar Tractor Company added that the administration had the task "to preserve for American industry a worthwhile place in the great new integrated market which will arise in Europe."[6] Agricultural interests were even more anxious about the consequences of the common market for their business interests. Accordingly, the American Cotton Shippers Association insisted that American cotton exporters could "be seriously hurt in cotton's most important and most promising export market" because of the EEC's agricultural policies.[7]

An analysis of lobbying for the Trade Expansion Act in 1962 reveals a similar picture. In December 1961, in the hearings of a subcommittee of the House of Representatives, "Europe was a principal topic of interest;…U.S. objectives were often defined in terms of assisting [organizations testifying in hearings] to gain better access to the Common Market" (Pastor 1980, 111; see also Evans 1971, 150). The U.S. Council of the International Chamber of Commerce, which counted the Ford Motor Company, Pepsi-Cola, several banks, tobacco companies, the Motion Picture Association of America, Standard Oil, and Gillette among its members, summarized the situation as follows:

> We are confronted today with the swift fusion of other countries into major trading blocs. The six-country European Economic Community

---

4. Letter by the U.S. Council of the International Chamber of Commerce to Secretary of State John Foster Dulles, 8 July 1957, State Department Records, Central Files, Record Group 59, Decimal File, 1956–57, NACP.

5. U.S. Congress, February–March 1958, Hearings before the House Committee on Ways and Means, *Renewal of Trade Agreements Act*, 639.

6. Ibid., 255.

7. Ibid., 434.

> and the seven-nation European Free Trade Area are already in existence. The Sino-Soviet trading bloc is an accomplished reality. A customs union of four Central American countries is launched, and a Latin American Free Trade Association is beyond the talking stage. Similar projects are under consideration in southern Asia, North Africa, West Africa, and the Middle East. All of these arrangements have some bearing on our commercial policy. (U.S. Council of the International Chamber of Commerce 1961, 2)

The NFTC concluded that facing such challenges, the U.S. president would need new authority to engage in trade negotiations with the aim of reducing the discrimination stemming from these preferential trading arrangements, and in particular from the EEC.[8] Only with a lower external tariff could U.S. exporters maintain their market share in the EEC. Henry Ford, the chairman of the Ford Motor Company, also argued that the existence of the EEC made it necessary for the president to have greater powers to bargain effectively and hence minimize Europe's external trade barriers (*New York Times,* 18 January 1962, 12). Finally, the American Paper and Pulp Association complained about the prospect of an eventually enlarged EEC including its foremost competitors from Scandinavia.[9]

These statements are only a small sample of a large number that all came to the same conclusion: U.S. trade policies had to change in response to the creation of the EEC. In fact, in 1962 as many as eighteen of the thirty exporter witnesses in the Committee on Ways and Means explicitly mentioned the threat of exclusion from the Common Market as the main reason for their lobbying effort. A survey carried out for *Business Week* (9 December 1961, 25–26), moreover, found "considerable business support for free trade with Europe and a widespread recognition that [the U.S. needs] some kind of change in tariff policy if only to maintain [its] bargaining position." From the 150 executives interviewed, 25 percent strongly favored freer trade with Europe, and an equal percentage opposed it. The support came from car manufacturers, business-machine makers, machinery and appliance manufacturers, electronics firms, and international oil companies. The chemical, copper and brass, rubber, glass, cement, watch, and pottery industries voiced opposition. Finally, a poll of executives conducted by

---

8. "Final Declaration of the Forty-Eighth National Foreign Trade Convention (New York), October 30–November 1, 1961," State Department Records, Central Files, Record Group 59, Decimal File, 1960–63, NACP.

9. U.S. Congress, March–April 1962, Hearings before the House Committee on Ways and Means, *Trade Expansion Act of 1962,* 1614.

the Research Institute of America and published in June 1962 found that 57 percent of the respondents were in favor of far-reaching trade legislation, and only 25.7 percent were opposed to it (*New York Times,* 27 June 1962, 11).

Not all companies concerned about the discrimination stemming from the EEC, however, also contributed to the lobbying effort. Some engaged in foreign investments instead, leading to a substantial increase in U.S. foreign direct investment (FDI) in Europe in the wake of the creation of the EEC (Krause 1968, 121). The share of U.S. FDI going to Europe that was invested outside of the United Kingdom increased rapidly from 43 percent in 1960 (nearly the same number as in 1950) to 64 percent in 1970 (Wilkins 1996, 357). Some anecdotal evidence suggests the importance of discrimination in this process. The CEO of the well-known food processing company H. J. Heinz, for example, maintained: "I believe strongly that it was necessary for us to go into the Common Market before there was an equality of tariffs between the countries and equalization of all kinds of other matters which are the objectives of having the 'club,' and in fact, which is not obviously an easy thing for a manufacturer to face."[10]

The agricultural sector, with the exceptions of the cattle and dairy sectors, which feared competition from Canadian farmers, was a further strong advocate of a reciprocal trade agreement with the EEC. Already in 1960, the U.S. Feed Grains Council expressed great urgency for action to maintain market access in Europe.[11] Equally, the American Farm Bureau Federation, the National Farmers' Union, the U.S. National Fruit Export Council, and the Florida Citrus Commission complained about the trade diversionary consequences of the CAP. They endorsed increased delegation of trade authority to the president because they hoped that trade negotiations would help them maintain their access to the EEC market. Citrus interests were particularly worried about the prospect that various Mediterranean countries could be associated with the EEC. Even the traditionally rather protectionist National Grange supported a change in U.S. trade legislation because of concerns about the EEC's agricultural policies. In the hearings on the TEA, the Grange's representative affirmed that the organization's members were "gravely concerned over the proposals of the European Common Market countries to increase their import control measures against U.S. agricultural commodities."[12] While some agricultural associations

---

10. Ibid., 2805.

11. Letter to Christian Herter SoS, U.S. Feed Grains Council, 15 November 1960, State Department Records, Central Files, Record Group 59, Decimal File, 1960–63, NACP.

12. U.S. Congress, March–April 1962, Hearings before the House Committee on Ways and Means, *Trade Expansion Act of 1962,* 2656.

thus demanded trade negotiations with the EEC, others called on the president to threaten retaliation if the EEC did not take into account American interests. Along the latter lines, the U.S. National Fruit Export Council proposed that the United States should make "equivalent withdrawals" if the EEC took "action to nullify or impair concessions granted" to the United States.[13]

From January 1962 onward, the so-called Chicken War (1962–63) contributed to the burgeoning of concerns in the American agricultural sector (Talbot 1978; Zeiler 1992, 135–39). This "trade war" erupted because a variable levy on poultry imports, which in July 1962 came into effect as part of the EEC's agricultural policy, led to a decline in U.S. poultry exports, especially to the German market. As the EEC was not willing to compensate the United States for this decline, the conflict escalated and could only be resolved after the ruling of a GATT panel. In this context, the Institute of American Poultry Industries was very active in making U.S. politicians aware of what they perceived to be a serious problem. The president of the National Farmers' Union even directly contacted President Kennedy expressing his concern about the consequences of the EEC's farm policies (Talbot 1978, 53). Many in the agricultural industry shared this concern; however, not all of them were as radical as the manager of the export division of a food producer who characterized the EEC as an "uncommon common market" and a "Frankenstein monster."[14]

Continued Lobbying by Import Competitors

This evidence provides strong backing for Hypothesis 1 by showing that European discriminatory trade policies led to a mobilization of American exporters in the late 1950s and early 1960s. (See table 4.1 for an overview of some of the major actors in the exporter camp.) Import-competing industries, represented by groups such as the Trade Relations Council and the Nation-Wide Committee on Import-Export Policy, also engaged in substantial lobbying activity (*New York Times*, 18 January 1962, 1). The wool, bicycle, and glassware producers, along with some agricultural groups, spearheaded the protectionist lobbying campaign. The strong showing by import competitors in these debates refutes a standard explanation for congressional delegation of trade authority to the president, namely that Congress tries to protect itself from the lobbying of special interests (Destler 2005). If delegation was intended to achieve insulation, the continued strength of protectionist interests in the hearings in 1958 and 1962 suggests that Congress was utterly unsuccessful in reaching its objective.

---

13. Ibid., 3160.

14. U.S. Congress, 5 February 1963, Hearings before the Senate Committee on Finance, *Statements on Impact of Common Market Regulations*, 14.

Table 4.1 U.S. exporter lobbying for the Trade Expansion Act, 1962 (selection)

TYPE OF LOBBY	NAME
General business associations	Chicago Association of Commerce and Industry
	Commerce and Industry Association of New York
	Greater Detroit Board of Commerce
	U.S. Chamber of Commerce
	U.S. Council of the International Chamber of Commerce
Exporter lobbies	Committee for a National Trade Policy
	National Foreign Trade Council
Sectoral associations	American Book Publishers Council
	American Paper and Pulp Association
	Fountain Pen and Mechanical Pencil Manufacturers Association
	Tobacco Institute
Individual companies	Caterpillar Tractor
	Ford Motor
	Gillette
	Hewlett-Packard
	International Telephone and Telegraph (IT&T)
Agricultural interests	American Farm Bureau Federation
	Florida Citrus Commission
	National Farmers Union
	National Grange
	Poultry industry
	U.S. Feed Grains Council
	U.S. National Fruit Export Council

Despite large exports to the EEC, and despite the danger that trade diversion could hurt chemical exports, the U.S. chemical industry was also largely opposed to the TEA (*New York Times,* 26 February 1962, 38; Preeg 1970, 52). A series of large companies, among them Dow Chemical, DuPont, and Monsanto, came out in opposition to the bill, and continued their protectionist lobbying effort throughout the Kennedy round. American Cyanamid, Baird Chemical, Cabot Corporation, and Pfizer International were among the few producers of chemicals that supported the TEA (Zeiler 1992, 149). This generally protectionist stance of the chemical industry is troubling both for the protection-for-exporters argument and for Helen Milner's (1988) argument that multinational companies should support liberal trade policies. Interestingly enough, the internationalization of this industry may provide the best explanation for the chemical industry's opposition to the aims of the legislation. From 1958 to October 1959, thirty U.S.

chemical companies set up new plants in Europe (Economic Research Department 1959). By producing inside the EEC, these companies may have become less interested in negotiating lower trade barriers. As a result, those parts of these large companies that depended on import protection could determine the firms' trade preferences in the absence of counterpressures.

With this notable exception, the evidence largely confirms the expectations derived from the protection-for-exporters argument. Alternative explanations, by contrast, find it difficult to account for several aspects of the lobbying effort by both exporters and import competitors. A rapid increase in exporter lobbying took place at the end of the 1950s, completely independent of an institutional change, which runs counter to the expectations originating from institutionalist approaches. Moreover, the mobilization of exporters came at a time when American competitiveness vis-à-vis European and Japanese competitors was diminishing. This observation casts doubt on a possible explanation of the increase in exporter lobbying based on the favorable trading position of the United States.

The U.S. Reaction to the Creation of the EEC, 1958–1963

In the first half of the 1950s, as discussed in the previous chapter, Congress failed to pass trade legislation that would have allowed the administration to negotiate far-reaching trade agreements. In the late 1950s and early 1960s, by contrast, Congress passed substantial trade bills. I suggest that this shift in U.S. trade policies was at least partly a reaction to the mobilization of exporters that took place in the wake of the creation of the EEC (Hypothesis 2). The repeated statements by decision makers that U.S. trade policies had to change to protect the interests of exporters, the strong similarity between interest-group demands and policies enacted, the presence of several provisions in the TEA that were explicitly aimed at the EEC, and the U.S. concentration in trade negotiations on maintaining access to the EEC all support this contention.

In the immediate aftermath of the creation of the EEC, the U.S. administration stressed the geopolitical importance of this step toward regional integration in Europe, and maintained that some commercial discrimination should be accepted as a price for achieving the objective of European unity. As the then U.S. president Dwight D. Eisenhower (1965, 125) remarked in his memoirs: "Though some provisions of the Rome treaty might serve to restrain trade between Europe and the outside world, the possible building of a powerful United States of Europe was a dream, that some day, I hoped to see realized." Soon, however, exporters started to leave their imprint on U.S. policies. Already in 1958, when the administration requested from Congress the authority to cut tariffs by 20 percent in reciprocal trade agreements, it legitimated this request with the need to alleviate the consequences for American exporters from European integration. The U.S. undersecretary of state C. Douglas Dillon, for example, maintained:

> Whatever the level of the Common Market tariff is to be, its general nature will be settled within the next 4 to 5 years. Any reductions which the United States and other countries may seek, even on a reciprocal basis, will be much harder to obtain if the Common Market area has already become accustomed to the operation of a higher tariff. The best chance we will have to achieve the reductions that are important to our export trade will be to negotiate them before the new tariff has become solidly established.[15]

The trade bill passed in 1958 enabled the administration to engage in negotiations with the EEC in the Dillon round. In this round, the United States tried to secure unilateral concessions on industrial tariffs and reciprocal reductions of trade barriers in the agricultural sector from the EEC (Curzon and Curzon 1976, 168–75; Eckes 1995, 180–83). The EEC, by contrast, suggested a 20 percent reciprocal and linear cut in industrial tariffs, but no change in agricultural protection. With the U.S. negotiators inhibited by a lack of appropriate negotiating authority, and the EEC negotiators arguing that as long as they had not agreed on a common agricultural policy internally they could not negotiate on it externally, neither side was able or willing to give in. The Dillon round, consequently, while producing some trade liberalization, did not satisfy U.S. exporters who were eager to safeguard their access to EEC markets.

Toward the Trade Expansion Act

In view of this failure to reduce the discrimination stemming from the EEC's external trade barriers, the U.S. administration soon contemplated the start of a new, more far-reaching round (Pastor 1980; Winand 1993, 173–90; Diebold 1999). It seriously considered two proposals for trade legislation that would allow the United States to engage in such a round. On the one hand, the special assistant to the president for trade policy, Howard Petersen, suggested that the president should receive authority to cut tariffs by 50 percent. He stressed the

---

15. U.S. Congress, February–March 1958, Hearings before the House Committee on Ways and Means, *Renewal of Trade Agreements Act,* 2647.

importance of the EEC for U.S. trade policy, as "goods from outside the Community will face a growing measure of discrimination."[16] Petersen hinted at the possibility that the president would need even more authority to reduce discrimination, but deemed a more sweeping request politically unfeasible. On the other hand, a report written under the guidance of the undersecretary of state for economic affairs, George Ball, recommended replacing the existing RTAA legislation with a radically new trade bill that would allow for across-the-board tariff cuts.[17] According to this proposal, the president was to allow for sufficient preparation by asking Congress for the bill only in 1963. Ball considered such a new approach vital because the creation of the EEC would "unlock new political pressures from various directions—from U.S. exporters, from Latin American countries, from the British Commonwealth, and from the European Economic Community itself."[18] He continued: "If the differential between external and internal tariffs [of the EEC] is to be substantially lowered (and we must reduce this differential if we are to avoid having our exports placed at a major disadvantage) the common external tariff of the EEC must also be reduced on an across-the-board basis."[19] The two proposals clearly illustrate the role of discrimination against exporters in stimulating a shift in the trade policies of the United States.

On 1 November 1961, George Ball, in a speech before the NFTC, emphasized the need for new trade legislation and outlined his proposal. As the reaction to this test was largely positive, Kennedy began to support the Ball approach (Taber 1969, 64–65). From this date onward, President Kennedy clearly stated his demand for a substantial delegation of trade authority: "I think that, quite obviously, we have to realize how important the Common Market is going to be to the economy of the United States. [If] the United States should be denied that market we will either find a flight of capital from this country to construct factories within that wall, or we will find ourselves in serious economic trouble"

---

16. Letter by Howard C. Petersen to George W. Ball, 4 October 1961, enclosed: "Proposals for 1962 United States Foreign Trade and Tariff Legislation," State Department Records, Central Files, Record Group 59, Decimal File, 1960–63, NACP. There was some confusion in previous studies about the contents of Petersen's proposal, given that the relevant archival source was classified and only released for consultation on demand.

17. On Ball's role in the passage of the legislation, see Ball (1982) and W. Michael Blumenthal's oral history, printed in Eckes (2000). Blumenthal, who was deputy assistant secretary of state for economic affairs at that time, calls Ball "a Europeanist first and foremost" (55). Winand (1993) stresses the importance of the Europeanists around Ball in determining the U.S. administration's course vis-à-vis the EEC.

18. Memorandum for the President by Dean Rusk, 24 October 1961, attached are two memoranda prepared by Ball, State Department Records, Central Files, Record Group 59, Decimal File, 1960–63, NACP. The quote is from the first memorandum.

19. Ibid. The quote is from the second memorandum.

(quoted in the *New York Times,* 9 November 1961, 14). Because of the urgency of the matter, Kennedy decided to ask Congress to pass the new trade legislation in 1962 rather than in 1963 as originally suggested by Ball. The final request thus combined the more ambitious elements of the two proposals set out before. Speeches that he made before the Committee for a National Trade Policy (20 November), the National Association of Manufacturers (6 December), and the federation of labor unions (7 December) gave Kennedy strong impressions of support for the new trade legislation (Preeg 1970, 46).[20]

Throughout the following months, officials directly alluded to the concept of trade diversion in their statements—as did exporters as outlined above. In this line, Secretary of State Dean Rusk, in a speech to the Chamber of Commerce in February 1962, asserted: "A manufacturer in Detroit selling to a customer in Hamburg will, of course, be under some disadvantage as against a manufacturer in Rome; he will have to sell his goods over a common external tariff while the manufacturer in Rome will not" (*Department of State Bulletin,* 12 March 1962, 403–9). Similarly, when Kennedy gave an overview of his trade program in an address to Congress on 11 January 1962, he characterized the development of the EEC as "the greatest challenge of all" (*Department of State Bulletin,* 29 January 1962, 159–63). Two weeks later, he sent the draft legislation to Congress. In the message introducing the trade bill to Congress, the president again alluded to the EEC and to trade diversion:

> But as the new external tariff surrounding the Common Market replaces the internal tariff structure, a German producer—who once competed in the markets of France on the same terms with our own producers—will achieve free access to French markets while our own producers face a tariff. In short, in the absence of authority to bargain down that external tariff, as the economy of the Common Market expands, our exports will not expand with it. They may even decline. (reprinted in Preeg 1970, 287)

The discrimination stemming from the creation of the EEC thus was a recurrent factor in the reasons given for the need for more far-reaching trade legislation. This mirrors the demands voiced by private interests.

Both the House and the Senate passed the TEA with clear majorities (298:125 and 78:8 respectively).[21] The resulting bill delegated to the president authority to

---

20. The speeches to the National Association of Manufacturers and the American Federation of Labor and Congress of Industrial Organizations are reprinted in *Department of State Bulletin,* 25 December 1961, 1039–52.

21. For the debate in Congress, see Barrie (1987, 237–62).

make 50 percent cuts of tariffs in reciprocal trade agreements. *Linear* tariff cuts became possible since the bill changed the peril-point provision by making peril points only suggestions to the president outlining the potential consequences of the reduction of a specific tariff, rather than restrictions on the president's authority. A special rule permitted the complete abolition of duties for industrial goods for which the United States and the EEC together accounted for at least 80 percent of world exports, excluding intra-EEC trade, in a reciprocal agreement with the EEC. If the United Kingdom had joined the EEC in the early 1960s, as seemed probable at that time, this provision would have covered 50 percent of U.S.-EEC trade (Curzon and Curzon 1976, 179).[22] It would have removed tariffs on the industrial products for which observers expected trade diversion to be most significant, including agricultural machinery, aircrafts, photographic supplies, railway vehicles, and motor vehicles.[23] The provision with its focus on the EEC provides strong support for the protection-for-exporters argument. To tackle the challenge of the EEC, Congress thus decided to increase the discretion granted to the president in trade negotiations.

Why Nondiscrimination?

The United States chose to use MFN negotiations to minimize the discrimination caused by the creation of the EEC. What explains this choice of strategy? In the United States, the question of how to respond to European integration was intensively discussed, with some advocating such diverse options as threatening retaliation, creating an alternative preferential agreement, and joining the EEC. The advocates of retaliation won out in the poultry sector, only to see the United States confronted with counterretaliation by the EEC in what has come to be known as the Chicken War. Others suggested the creation of a rival transatlantic free trade area that would have included the EFTA countries, Canada, and the United States (*Washington Post*, 8 November 1965, C8). Finally, the former

---

22. The Senate, with the probability of British entry markedly lower when the bill was discussed in that chamber, actually passed an amendment that was to give the president authority to use the 80 percent provision even if the United Kingdom did not enter the EEC (Douglas 1966, 132). It is remarkable that this amendment passed despite opposition from the administration, which feared that it could be seen as influencing negotiations in Europe between the EEC and the United Kingdom. Only in the conference between the House and the Senate was the amendment finally dropped. The incident contradicts explanations of U.S. trade policies that see the administration pushing a reluctant Congress toward the president's objective of trade liberalization with foreign countries. Quite to the contrary, in response to such a significant external challenge as posed by the EEC, the Senate was just as (if not more) eager to achieve far-reaching trade liberalization as the administration.

23. Several non–high technology products were also included, such as coal, confectionery, furs, glass, leather, paint, rubber goods, and tobacco.

secretary of state, Christian A. Herter, and the former undersecretary of state, William L Clayton, went so far as to advocate U.S. membership in the EEC in a report to Congress (Ilgen 1976, 175–76). Similar demands were also voiced by some economic interests, with the president of the Motion Picture Association of America maintaining: "If we fail to join, the Common Market will become an economic threat; our jobs, our wages, our security, our future are at stake" (Johnston 1962, 153).

Yet, resistance to these plans soon crystallized. As a result, President Kennedy, in an address to the National Association of Manufacturers in December 1961, felt compelled to take an explicit stance in opposition to these options:

> I am *not* proposing—nor is it either necessary or desirable—that we join the Common Market, alter our concepts of political sovereignty, establish a "rich-man's" trading community, abandon our traditional most-favored-nation policy, create an Atlantic free-trade area, or impair in any way our close economic ties with Canada, Japan, and the rest of the world. (*Department of State Bulletin,* 25 December 1961, 1046, emphasis in original)

Whereas Kennedy stressed the dangers of these strategies for American trade relations with third countries, the State Department was concerned that concluding a deal without the EEC would not bring the United States any closer to the objective of lower EEC barriers to trade (*New York Times,* 12 October 1965, 67 and 79). Ball, finally, excluded threat as a possible strategy, fearing that retaliation "could very well set off a chain reaction that would bring about the closing of markets against our exports all over the world" (*Wall Street Journal,* 17 August 1962, 10).

In fact, trade data for the early 1960s shows that the United States still had a significant surplus in its total trade and in particular in its trade with Western Europe, making it vulnerable to a deterioration of international trading relations. On average, the U.S. trade surplus with the EEC accounted for nearly 4 percent of total U.S. trade in the years from 1958 to 1962 (calculated from data in *Survey of Current Business,* October 1972). In addition, while the regional concentration of U.S. exports in the EEC was relatively high, with about 17 percent of total U.S. exports going to the six member countries in 1960 (and another 11 percent to the EFTA countries) (U.S. Tariff Commission 1969), the United States still had major export interests outside the EEC. This situation made a preferential agreement excluding the EEC equally unattractive as joining the EEC. In the former case, it would have meant no progress in protecting exporters' access to their most important market. In the latter case, exporters' access to third markets could have been hurt. With neither preferential trade policies nor the threat of retaliation being a feasible strategy, engaging in multilateral negotiations was the politically most efficient policy that the U.S. government could pursue.[24] The choice of the nondiscriminatory access strategy is in line with the expectation summarized in Hypothesis 3.

Alternative Explanations

Some authors, in line with the institutionalist approach, base their explanations of the passage of the TEA mainly on the administration's skilful handling of different constituencies (Bauer, Pool, and Dexter 1972, 78; Pastor 1980, 117). They point out that several economic sectors were opposed to an opening of the U.S. economy to international competition. First among them was the textile industry that had strong support from Southern Democrats in Congress (Zeiler 1992, 79–88). By negotiating an international agreement with the countries exporting textiles to the United States to restrict textile imports, the Kennedy administration bought off this major opponent to trade liberalization. Further sectors that requested protection were the carpet, glass, lumber, and oil industries. All of these sectors received some concessions to reduce their opposition to the trade program. In March 1962, for example, Kennedy decided to raise tariffs on carpets and glass to appease those industries, even though he expected the EEC to retaliate (Alkema 1999, 222–26). The president also chose to include an adjustment assistance provision in the TEA that granted assistance to workers in industries hurt by a rise in imports, a provision aimed at securing the support of the labor unions for the passage of the bill.

While evidently the administration's specific policies contributed to the large majorities in favor of the bill in Congress, an account that solely emphasizes this factor falls short of providing a satisfactory explanation of events. First, it fails to explain why the administration attached so much importance to this bill that it felt compelled to invest substantial time and energy in securing its passage. That is, an administration's effort to secure the passage of trade legislation should be endogenous rather than exogenous to an explanation. Second, in some instances the strategy of buying off opponents was also used in the 1950s, but the trade bills were nevertheless less ambitious than the TEA. Finally, the buying-off explanation ignores the link between the TEA and the trade legislation passed in

---

24. Other countries chose different options. An article in the *New York Times* (4 November 1962, 24) points out that excluded countries reacted in six different ways to the creation of the EEC: membership application (the United Kingdom), application for associate membership (Greece), trade negotiations on a limited list of items (Israel), larger tariff-cutting bargaining (U.S.), condemnation (Communist countries), and occasional protest (Latin America).

1958, when the administration was not particularly active in pushing for the passage of the trade bill but was still able to receive more far-reaching negotiating authority than on previous occasions. From the point of view of the protection-for-exporters argument, the policies in favor of import-competing interests are not particularly astonishing. In fact, the expectation set out in Hypothesis 2 is for politicians to satisfy as far as possible the demands of all concentrated interests. The mobilization of exporters simply made the maintenance of foreign market access in some sectors more important, without eliminating consideration of other interests.

The president's allusion to the geopolitical interests of the United States in some of his speeches was also taken as an indication of the importance of geopolitics in the passage of the TEA. In particular, Kennedy mentioned the necessity to counter a Soviet trade offensive that promised economic assistance to less-developed countries and the importance of preserving support from the European allies in the cold war. Moreover, the legislation was presented as part of Kennedy's Grand Design for a new Atlantic partnership of equal partners (Zeiler 1992, 154). Again, several observations cast doubt on the alternative interpretation emphasizing geopolitics. For one, while geopolitical rhetoric always accompanies the passage of trade legislation in the United States, in many cases the aim of such rhetoric is to garner additional support for a bill that actually closely follows the demands voiced by organized domestic actors. In this specific case, officials in the State Department even explicitly recognized that the TEA had to be "sold in foreign policy terms" to achieve maximum support.[25]

What is more, in the case of the TEA, exporters explicitly opposed a use of the bill to pursue geopolitical interests that would run counter to their interests. As stated in the *Wall Street Journal* (27 September 1962, 12), the possibility that the TEA may be used as "an instrument of international politics…is most troubling to export-minded industrialists who look to future U.S.-Common Market negotiations as a means of opening the burgeoning consumer market of Western Europe to American products and thus stimulating growth here." Finally, Congress's insistence on the creation of the Office of the Special Trade Representative, which took over the responsibility for carrying through the negotiations from the State Department, casts doubts on a geopolitical explanation. The main reason for this institutional change was Congress's desire to make sure that the negotiations would be carried out in the interest of U.S. exporters rather than following the geopolitical concerns of the State Department. The existence of

---

25. W. Michael Blumenthal to Mr. Schaetzel, 14 November 1961, State Department Records, Central Files, Record Group 59, Decimal File, 1960–63, NACP.

this office made sure that "after 1962 U.S. commercial objectives were likely to dominate daily decisions to a greater extent on average" (Odell and Eichengreen 1998, 201).

A final possible explanation for the passage of the TEA maintains that the Democratic majority delegated more authority to the executive because the president also came from the Democratic Party (Lohmann and O'Halloran 1994, 615). This argument, however, cannot explain the contents of this bill, which was clearly directed at the EEC. Moreover, it fails to account for the fact that the TEA cannot be analyzed independently of the RTAA of 1958. In this earlier legislation, facing the challenge of the EEC, a Democratic majority delegated increased authority to a Republican president. Finally, if partisan politics had been that important, why would support for the bill have been largely bipartisan in both houses of Congress (although a slight majority of Republicans in the House opposed the bill)?

In short, it seems plausible that the mobilization of exporters in response to the creation of the EEC was the dominant factor leading to the shift in U.S. trade policies witnessed in the passage of the RTAA of 1958 and the TEA in 1962. This narrative has challenged several alternative explanations, such as a geopolitical and a party politics explanation, for this move toward trade liberalization. These alternative arguments have difficulties in accounting for the timing of the shift in U.S. trade orientation, the debates within the U.S. administration, and the contents of the legislation. In contrast, the protection-for-exporters explanation accounts well for the trade policies chosen by the United States in response to the discrimination resulting from the creation of the EEC.

The European Reaction to the U.S. Initiative

The key question at this point was which balance of concessions would be attractive enough for the EEC to accept a reduction in its external trade barriers. As put by the *Economist* (22 September 1962, 1099), at the beginning the EEC showed little eagerness to engage in external trade liberalization: "It is questioned whether the prospect of lower American tariffs is so enticing that the common market will promptly throw open western Europe to American products." Whereas the experience of the Dillon round had revealed that the EEC would be unwilling to make unilateral concessions, trade policy episodes of the years 1962 and 1963 made clear that the EEC would even be prepared to risk conflict with trading partners before conceding on its trading interests. In 1962 the member countries of the EEC decided to use retaliatory measures in response to a U.S. increase in tariffs on glass and carpets (Alkema 1999). In this context, the Belgian minister for foreign commerce Maurice Brasseur told the U.S. ambassador in Brussels that "Europe was no longer a weak non-entity and had ability to retaliate."[26] In the Chicken War, the EEC member countries again assumed a tough line in their dealings with the United States. The president of the European Commission Walter Hallstein could thus observe a "strengthening of the European position as compared to the United States of America and the rest of the world that stands in fundamental contrast to the situation in the fifties."[27]

Societal Demands in the EEC

The expectation was for the EEC to take a similarly tough line in future trade negotiations with the United States and to accept an agreement only if it comprised major foreign concessions. Indeed, in the run-up to the Kennedy round, the expectation of substantial concessions led to the mobilization of some exporters in Europe. These exporters, however, were very explicit in pointing out that they would oppose a trade agreement that did not go a long way to satisfy their specific requests. Three demands were especially widespread.[28] First, European economic actors insisted on "reciprocity," meaning that they should receive what they considered a "fair" share of the concessions. The French automobile industry, for example, argued that automobiles should provisionally be included in the European list of exceptions from the 50 percent linear cuts as proposed by the United States, to be withdrawn from this list only after achieving "true reciprocity."[29] Second, European exporters demanded an overproportional lowering of high U.S. tariffs that would lead to the elimination of what was called "tariff disparities" between the United States and the EEC. Both the Federation of German Industry and the German section of the International Chamber of Commerce argued that the negotiations had to cut existing peaks in the U.S. tariff schedule.[30] The French Conseil national du patronat français (CNPF)

---

26. Telegram from the Embassy in Belgium to the Department of State, 22 March 1962, reprinted in U.S. Department of State, *Foreign Relations of the United States, 1961–63*, vol. 13, 71.

27. Reprint of a speech held by Hallstein before the European Parliament on 26 June 1963, in Siegler (1964, 374–75).

28. See, for example: *Economist,* 13 April 1963, 169; *Le Monde,* 2 May 1964, 1; "Note. Préparation de la Conférence Kennedy. Opinions des producteurs français," 5 February 1963, Service de Coopération Economique, no. 931, AD. See also the position taken by the European peak business association UNICE and the EEC Chambers of Commerce in Europäisches Parlament (1963a, 1963b).

29. Chambre Syndicale des Constructeurs d'Automobiles à Monsieur le Ministre des Affaires Etrangères Paris, 7 July 1964, Service de Coopération Economique, no. 932, AD.

30. Bundesverband der Deutschen Industrie 1963; "Stellungnahme der deutschen Landesgruppe der Internationalen Handelskammer zu den Dokumenten der IHK Nr. 102/20 betr. Zolldisparitäten und Nr. 102/21 betr. Nichttarifäre Handelshemmnisse," January 1964. B53-III-A2, no. 276, PA.

maintained that only the elimination of U.S. tariff disparities would allow for a balance of offers among developed countries.[31]

Finally, exporter interests in Europe argued that tariff reductions alone would not be able to resolve the problems that they experienced in access to the American market. Instead, tariff bargaining would have to be accompanied by negotiations concerning such diverse issues as customs valuation, the use of antidumping and countervailing duty instruments, and internal legislation. In particular, many European producers were interested in the abolition of the American selling price, a method used in the United States to evaluate the price of imported chemicals that inflated the tariffs that had to be paid. The German chemical industry highlighted the tariff peaks of up to 200 percent caused by this system.[32] Equally, the French chemical industry affirmed that in the case of abolition of the American selling price, it would be willing to accept a large reduction of European tariffs (*Le Monde*, 17 February 1967, 22). Moreover, the Americans were expected to agree to international rules for the use of the antidumping instrument and to abolish the escape clause introduced in the late 1940s.[33] The French Federation of Mechanical Industries, moreover, complained about the Buy America Act that allegedly disadvantaged European producers in American public procurement.[34] The Paris section of the French Chamber of Commerce went furthest when asking for negotiations on issues such as internal taxes and the Agricultural Adjustment Act that allowed the U.S. president to impose quotas on imports of agricultural products.[35]

European economic actors with exporting interests thus pushed their governments to drive a hard bargain and to use the propitious situation to gain concessions especially in the American market, which had been impossible to achieve in earlier negotiations. As *Le Monde* (30 April 1964, 20, my translation) put it, "Already, the most entrepreneurial among our industries think that we

---

31. The CNPF's position is cited in: "Note. Préparation de la Conférence Kennedy. Opinions des producteurs français," 5 February 1963, Service de Coopération Economique, no. 931, AD.

32. "Wirtschaftspolitik im Chemiebereich 1962/63," Verband der chemischen Industrie, 29 August 1963, B53-III-A2, no. 283, PA. See also "Trade Expansion Act…Yes. American Selling Price System…No," Verband der chemischen Industrie, 1962, B53-III-A2, no. 283, PA.

33. See, for example, "Note. Préparation de la Conférence Kennedy. Opinions des producteurs français," CNFP, 5 February 1963, Service de Coopération Economique, no. 931, AD; "Stellungnahme der deutschen Landesgruppe der Internationalen Handelskammer zu den Dokumenten der IHK Nr. 102/20 betr. Zolldisparitäten und Nr. 102/21 betr. Nichttarifäre Handelshemmnisse," January 1964, B53-III-A2, no. 276, PA. From 1947 onward the United States included escape clauses in its trade agreements that allowed for the withdrawal of specific concessions if they hurt domestic industries.

34. "Négociations tarifaires CEE/Etats-Unis au sein du GATT: Note complémentaire de la Fédération des Industries Mécaniques," FIMTM, August 1963, Service de Coopération Economique, no. 949, AD.

35. "Futures négociations commerciales en application du Trade Expansion Act," Chambre de Commerce et d'Industrie de Paris, 9 May 1963, Service de Coopération Economique, no. 930, AD.

absolutely have to seize this possibility to obtain from Washington the suppression of the most burdensome obstacles—this does not only concern the tariff peaks—that often interfere with the efforts undertaken to sell in the richest market of the world."[36] The German section of the Comité européen pour le progrès économique et social even argued:

> The EEC has now, as a result of its favorable position in the negotiations as the largest importer in the world, the chance to demand, as the price for an easier access to the most interesting market, that the trade barriers to the United States should be reduced or modified. If they miss this chance, the U.S. will, without outside pressure, probably never abolish these protectionist administrative practices. (CEPES-CED 1964, 30, my translation)

Not only exporting interests, however, engaged in lobbying activities; import-competing interests were even more vocal. In France, nearly all trade associations, whether broad, such as the Conseil national du patronat français, or sectoral, such as the automobile industry, asked for specific exceptions from the 50 percent linear tariff cuts that the United States and the EEC agreed on in the Kennedy round. The Paris section of the French Chamber of Commerce demanded the exclusion from tariff cuts of industrial machinery and electric and electronic material.[37] At the firm level, Renault opposed the opening of the French market for tractors, and Berliet, a French truck maker, opposed the liberalization of the market for trucks.[38] In Germany, two of the four largest industries, namely the textile and steel industries, supported protectionist policies. The steel industry even asked for an increase in the German steel tariff, while the textile industry insisted on a special treatment of textile trade because of the widespread praxis of what it called "abnormal prices."[39] Others, such as the aluminum, ceramic, coal, and glass producers, as well as the electrical sector, demanded exceptions for specific products from linear tariff cuts.[40]

---

36. For a similar appraisal of the French industry's position see also *Frankfurter Allgemeine Zeitung*, 4 May 1964, 14.

37. "Futures négociations commerciales en application du Trade Expansion Act," Chambre de Commerce et d'Industrie de Paris, 9 May 1963, Service de Coopération Economique, no. 930, AD.

38. Renault, le Président Directeur Général P. Dreyfus, à Monsieur Wormser, Directeur Général des Affaires Economiques et Financières, Ministère des Affaires Etrangères, 21 December 1961, Service de Coopération Economique, no. 2109, AD.

39. Letter of the Gesamtverband der Textilindustrie in der Bundesrepublik Deutschland [Association of German textile industries] to Legationsrat D. W. Keller (confidential), 11 November 1963, B53-III-A2, no. 107, PA. Tariffs in the steel sector, which was covered by the European Coal and Steel Community, were still under national control.

40. Internal memo of the German Federal Ministry for Economics, February 1964, B53-III-A2, no. 290, PA.

In all member countries of the EEC, moreover, the representatives of agricultural producers took a protectionist position. The French agricultural sector was mainly interested in the development of a European common agricultural policy protected from outside imports. The German agricultural association even feared French competition within the EEC, and was just as opposed to external liberalization as French farmers were (Neunreither 1968, 373). This lobbying activity by import competitors contradicts alternative arguments that predict a weakening of protectionist interests as a result of either "sectoral attrition" (for this term, see Hanson 1998) caused by increased competition in the EEC or the economic recovery that Europe experienced at that time.

From Societal Demands to the EEC's Position

The positions of the governments of the EEC member countries were largely in accordance with the demands voiced by the major interest groups, an observation that puts into doubt the "collusive delegation" hypothesis. According to this hypothesis, the delegation of trade-policy authority to the EU level, which was agreed on in the Treaty of Rome, insulated policymakers from protectionist pressures (Meunier 2005, 8–9; Woolcock 2005, 247). After gaining independence from specific economic interests, politicians supposedly used their autonomy to cut tariffs in international trade negotiations, a policy that is in the public interest but runs counter to the policies demanded by sectoral pressure groups. Illustratively, Sophie Meunier (2005, 8) posits that European policymakers "chose to centralize trade policymaking in order to insulate the process from protectionist pressures and, as a result, promote trade liberalization."

The empirical evidence, however, suggests a different story: the trade policies pursued mirrored the demands voiced by economic interests. In line with societal demands, EEC decision makers requested substantial U.S. concessions, or what the French foreign minister Maurice Couve de Murville called "complete" and "veritable" reciprocity (*New York Times,* 21 February 1962, 9; 26 March 1965, 47 and 55; *Economist,* 13 April 1963, 171). To achieve this aim, they called for the reduction of high U.S. tariffs without reciprocal European tariff cuts. The French delegation in Brussels, for example, maintained that for the negotiations to be interesting for European exporters, the United States would have to reduce the remaining extremely high duties because cutting solely already low duties would not lead to an increase in French exports to the United States.[41] In their view, U.S. concessions should be "double or treble those required of

---

41. "Aide—Mémoire à l'attention de M. le Secrétaire Général," Brussels, 22 October 1962, Service de Coopération Economique, no. 930, AD.

Europe" for "true equality" to be achieved (*Economist,* 13 April 1963, 171). The German position was slightly more upbeat about linear tariff cuts, but still insistent with respect to the need to reduce tariff disparities. European governments also asked for a series of exemptions from the linear tariff cuts to provide protection for import-competing industries in Europe. In addition, they demanded the extension of the negotiations to nontariff barriers, an area where they felt that European exporters suffered under U.S. regulations.[42] Illustratively, the French Foreign Ministry deemed necessary simultaneous negotiations in particular concerning the American selling price and the Buy American Act.[43] Equally, the Europeans insisted on negotiations concerning rules for the use of the antidumping instrument. Finally, and also in line with societal demands, all European governments concurred on the need to protect the agricultural sector from trade liberalization.

Despite the many similarities in the positions of the two dominant countries in the EEC, in several instances France and Germany disagreed over how to conduct the negotiations. Germany, in particular, was more eager to achieve a positive outcome in the negotiations than France.[44] This greater eagerness is not astonishing considering that Germany faced an increase in its external tariff as a result of the formation of a customs union; the Kennedy round thus was a welcome opportunity to bring this tariff back to its politically ideal level. To a certain extent, therefore, France could use its greater reluctance with respect to the reduction of industrial tariffs as a bargaining lever vis-à-vis Germany on other issues. Its strategy was to employ the Kennedy round as leverage to make Germany accept a common agricultural policy that was in line with the interests of the French agricultural sector. In the end, the two sides managed to find a major compromise that enabled progress both on the Kennedy round and on the implementation of the CAP (*Economist,* 30 July 1966, 432). Nevertheless, an account that tries to reduce the trade liberalization achieved in the Kennedy round to a simple package deal between France and Germany, with France conceding on the Kennedy round and Germany on the CAP, falls short of providing a comprehensive explanation. In particular, it fails to do justice to the fact that French industry was genuinely interested in using the EEC's bargaining power to gain concessions in the American market.

---

42. Ibid.

43. Memo, Ministère des Affaires Etrangères, Direction des Affaires Economiques et Financières, Service de Coopération Economique, 19 November 1962, Service de Coopération Economique, no. 930, AD.

44. Notes of a meeting in the economics ministry, Bonn, 11 June 1962, B53–401, no. 283, PA.

Building on these member-state positions, in February 1962 the EEC Council declared its willingness to negotiate for linear tariff cuts if the U.S. government was able to obtain a negotiating mandate. This occurred despite the concerns voiced by top officials of the European Commission about the possibility that further tariff cuts could undermine the identity of the EEC as a customs union. Interestingly, therefore, against frequent assertions to the contrary, the Commission initially took a more protectionist stance than the member states because it saw the existence of a common external tariff as the major unifying factor of the common market.[45] On 9 May 1963, the Council of Ministers formally resolved that the EEC would take part in the Kennedy round, enabling the GATT ministerial meeting one week later to settle on a date to commence the negotiations.

Several factors weigh against the contention that the European acceptance of the Kennedy round came about for geopolitical reasons. On the French side, the government challenged the United States in the 1950s when the security situation was even worse than in the 1960s, making it implausible to assume that concerns about American attitudes guided French foreign economic policies in the latter decade. According to most accounts, moreover, President Charles de Gaulle's foreign policy was aimed at challenging American hegemony (Lundestad 2003, chap. 4), and accepting trade negotiations with the United States was hardly a means to achieve this objective. Furthermore, the French acceptance of European participation in the Kennedy round was conditional on the defense of its trading interests in the negotiations. All internal memos insisted that France should push the other member countries to make the EEC's participation in the negotiations conditional on U.S. acceptance of specific European demands. There is little to suggest the importance of geopolitical considerations in shaping Germany's position in favor of trade negotiations.

Bargaining Power and the Kennedy Round

Can the EEC's increased bargaining power provide for a more satisfactory explanation of its trade policy stance? For U.S. decision makers, there was no doubt that the creation of the EEC had boosted the bargaining power of this entity in the trade field. Illustratively, G. Griffith Johnson, assistant secretary of state for economic affairs at that time, affirmed that the creation of the EEC had "greatly increased [its] bargaining power…in negotiations on trade matters in general and tariff matters in particular" (Johnson 1963, 114). An influential study for the

---

45. Frey and Buhofer (1986) provide a theoretical rationale for this stance.

Joint Economic Committee of Congress, moreover, maintained: "The real threat posed by the organization of the Common Market for the trade position of the United States is the greater concentration of economic and political power than had previously existed, particularly since there are built-in factors that may cause this power to be used in ways that will be harmful to American exports" (Kravis 1962, 97). Finally, the *New York Times* (31 October 1962, 67) stated: "The hard, or at least semi-hard, line that may be adopted by the community reflects in part its view of its strong bargaining position. In brief, this is that the United States needs European tariff cuts more than Europe needs American tariff cuts."

In fact, the EEC's increased bargaining power shaped the ensuing Kennedy round, allowing EEC negotiators to achieve a result that promised substantial gains for European exporters without imposing high costs on import-competing groups in the EEC (for detailed studies of the Kennedy round, see O'Halloran 1970; Preeg 1970; Evans 1971; Zeiler 1992). In the three major areas of negotiation, namely industrial tariffs, nontariff barriers, and agriculture, the outcomes achieved in the negotiations were far closer to the preferences of the EEC than the United States. Concerning industrial tariffs, for the first time the United States accepted the European demand for linear cuts, a request still objected to by the United States in the mid-1950s and early 1960s. Even more astonishingly, in the end higher U.S. tariffs were cut more than European ones, although the United States had resisted such an approach throughout the negotiations. The Kennedy round thus produced a drop in the average U.S. tariff level on manufactures of 38 percent. U.S. tariffs on chemicals even underwent a 50 percent reduction, and tariffs on machinery and equipment saw a 47 percent reduction (UNCTAD 1968, 63). European tariffs also went down, but less than American ones: chemical tariffs were cut by 20 percent, and tariffs on machinery and equipment by 40 percent. Overall, EEC tariffs on manufactures fell by 32 percent (UNCTAD 1968, 61).

Against American objections, the European side was also successful in its push for the inclusion of nontariff barriers in the negotiations (O'Halloran 1970, 235–48). The Europeans gained a first victory in this area when their demand for negotiations on nontariff barriers was incorporated in the GATT ministerial declaration agreed on in May 1963. In the ensuing negotiations, the United States accepted a deal outside of the main agreement of the Kennedy round that was to abolish the American selling price in return for some European concessions. Despite this success in the negotiations, however, the EEC could not take advantage of the agreement as the U.S. Congress failed to approve the deal. The two sides also agreed on an antidumping code, a further issue dear to the European negotiators. Again, Congress limited the extent of the U.S. concession by passing a resolution that stated that American antidumping laws should have precedence over the code signed in the Kennedy round. In this ambit, the Europeans were able to make some inroads, but in the end they did not get all that they wanted.

Finally, despite strong opposition from the United States, the EEC managed to exclude the agricultural sector from the negotiations and still achieve a liberalization of trade in industrial goods (O'Halloran 1970, 249–67; Meunier 2005, 74–101). From the beginning, the United States emphasized that a conclusion of the Kennedy round without a satisfactory solution of the agricultural issue would not be tolerable. As put by President Lyndon B. Johnson in 1964: "The United States will enter into no ultimate agreement unless progress is registered toward trade liberalization on the products of our farms as well as our factories" (quoted in the *Economist,* 2 May 1964, 482). The United States even hoped for a linear reduction of barriers to trade in agriculture, similar to what had been agreed on in the industrial field, and therefore pushed for a linkage between the negotiations in the two fields. Later, it downgraded its demands to a guarantee of access to European markets of a share at least as large as contemporary American exports. Yet, when the United States failed to attain even this objective, it only pushed for European participation in a food-aid program and a minimum price for wheat before agreeing to the conclusion of the Kennedy round, a demand that the EEC finally accepted.

One observer consequently stated that the U.S. negotiators tended to "overplay their hand":

> They made it sound as if they were doing the rest of the world a favour in coming to the negotiating table on industrial trade, and required a satisfactory agricultural agreement as a kind of sweetener. It was, however, clear that the United States had just as strong a motive as any other nation outside the EEC to arrive at an arrangement which would reduce the trade discrimination that would be introduced into the international system once the Community had established its customs union. (Shonfield 1976, 31)

The outcome of the Kennedy round thus confirms the expectation derived from Hypothesis 4 that the creation of the EEC should have strengthened the bargaining position of its members. In support of this view, the former director of the High Authority of the European Coal and Steel Community Pierre Uri (1969, 215) stated shortly after conclusion of the negotiations: "The establishment of the European Community gave the initial impetus to the Kennedy Round; its bargaining power has thawed American tariffs which had remained frozen for twenty years; and its existence induced some of its members to accept massive cuts in their previous levels of protection." The historian Thomas Zeiler (1992,

225n27) even referred to the "Common Market's ability to dictate terms at the Kennedy Round, to the detriment of U.S. interests."

To some extent, this European strength explains the fact that in 1972, the last year of the implementation of the Kennedy round results, for the first time after World War II the United States incurred a balance-of-trade deficit with the six member countries of the EEC. It also explains the change in the public perception of the EEC that took place in the United States in the late 1960s. In 1967, for example, the *Economist* (15 April 1967, 249) wrote that the Kennedy round had "made something very close to an enemy out of the European common market in many American minds; particularly in Congress but not only there. The effects of the experience will not soon be forgotten—and there will not be another American initiative toward freer trade in the near future." American economics reporter Edwin Dale expressed this opinion well when he wrote: "Of all the grand and sad dreams of American foreign policy in the past 20 years, one of the two or three grandest and saddest is 'European unity', as represented principally by the European Economic Community. We bought a pig in a poke. We have been taken" (*Times,* 24 September 1969, 25).

A prominent alternative explanation for this observation of asymmetric concessions is that the United States made greater concessions in trade negotiations in the GATT to strengthen the West in the face of the threat posed by the Soviet Union in the cold war. Yet, as pointed out above, this counterargument loses much of its plausibility once it is recognized that in the 1950s, when the perception of Western weakness was strongest, the United States failed to make concessions that were interesting enough to its trading partners to make GATT negotiations a success. In fact, some evidence even suggests that in the 1960s the United States tried to take advantage of its military power to gain leverage in trade negotiations. At least in one instance, President Kennedy proposed that the United States exploit their "military and political position to ensure that [their] economic interests [were] protected" in the emerging EEC (quoted in Winand 1999, 30). In short, the available evidence concurs best with the argument that European governments accepted trade liberalization in the Kennedy round because they managed to attain a balance of concessions that guaranteed them the support of export-oriented industries, while only marginally hurting import-competing ones (Hypothesis 5).

This chapter has provided additional support for the hypotheses set out in chapter 1 concerning the protection of exporters in response to foreign preferential trade policies. American exporters lobbied their government to react to the discriminatory effects of the establishment of the EEC, a lobbying effort that provides a rationale for the call by the United States for trade negotiations in the

Kennedy round. European governments, in turn, agreed to cut tariffs because they expected large concessions from the United States for a relatively small reduction in discrimination. In this chapter I have also offered an explanation of some substantively important events by filling the gap on trade policymaking in regard to the passage of the TEA in the United States and the EEC's trade policies immediately after the creation of this entity.

THE FIRST ENLARGEMENT OF THE EUROPEAN COMMUNITY AND THE U.S. REACTION

Most existing accounts of transatlantic trade relations in the 1970s are motivated by one of two puzzles: the "mercantilist" orientation of these trade policies as compared to the more liberal policies in the previous decade, or the maintenance of a principally liberal stance in the face of adverse developments. On the one hand, some authors stress that the 1970s were a decade in which the United States and the EC pursued trade policies characterized by sectoral protectionism and mercantilist competition (Bergsten 1971). In the United States, the administration negotiated voluntary export restrictions with foreign countries, such as for steel imports from Japan and the EC in December 1968, and threatened the imposition of quotas, such as in the textile sector, to satisfy import competitors. Similarly, the EC protected some import-competing interests in sectors such as agriculture, steel, and textiles.

For the case of the United States, I. M. Destler (2005, 65–71) explains these policies as a result of the breakdown of the committee system in the House of Representatives, which made the U.S. political system more open to interest-group influence. With Congress no longer protected from constituency pressures, it felt obliged to implement trade policies that were more in line with industry pressures. Others emphasize the erosion of the separation between trade policy and foreign policy, which had been achieved by establishing an international trade regime after World War II, as the main cause of the shift in U.S. trade policies (Cooper 1973). Lastly, studies that call attention to the role of a hegemonic power in providing an open international trading system contend that the decline of U.S. hegemony made American trade policies more vulnerable to particular interests (Krasner 1976 and 1979; Keohane 1980; Gilpin 1987).

For the case of Europe, existing studies refer to mounting competition from Japan and the newly industrializing countries, combined with increasing unemployment and a recession in the aftermath of the 1973 oil crisis as reasons for the shift toward greater protectionism in that decade (Farrands 1979; Strange 1979; Tsoukalis and da Silva Ferreira 1980; Page 1981; Dolan 1983; Schuknecht 1992). In addition, the European version of the "new protectionism" of the 1970s may have been a reaction to changes in attitudes concerning the role that governments should play in the economy, leading to the victory of the welfare state over the market economy (Krauss 1979).

On the other hand, for other authors the most puzzling aspect of the trade policies of the United States and the EC in the 1970s is their continued adherence to liberal principles, even in the face of the adverse factors just mentioned. Indeed, both trading entities agreed on trade liberalization in the Tokyo round of multilateral trade negotiations. One explanation for the continuation of transatlantic trade liberalization based on societal demands is that the rise in multinational and export-dependent companies may have biased the trade policies of developed countries in favor of freer trade (Milner 1988). The increasing interdependence that characterized the international political economy in the 1970s, according to this account, made firms more reluctant to push for the adoption of protectionist policies. Authors arguing within the institutionalist approach explain the persistence of relatively liberal trade policies in the 1970s with reference to the existence of an international regime (Lipson 1982; Keohane 1984; Keohane and Nye 1989). The international trade regime built around the GATT may have constrained national trade policies and helped developed countries avoid a protectionist backlash despite adverse international conditions. Finally, politicians in the United States and Europe may have defended liberal trade policies even in the face of strong protectionist lobbying because of their liberal ideas and values (Curzon and Curzon 1976, 195; Shonfield 1976, 95; Ruggie 1982; Goldstein 1993).

While all of these accounts contribute to our understanding of the trade policies pursued on the two sides of the Atlantic in the 1970s, they face difficulties in explaining the coexistence of liberal and protectionist elements. Drawing on the protection-for-exporters argument, I explain the dominance of import competitors in the United States in the aftermath of the Kennedy round with exporters' lack of incentive to mobilize at a time when they benefited from improved foreign market access during the implementation of the Kennedy round agreements. Only the impending accession of the United Kingdom to the EC, together with the accompanying free trade agreements between the EC and the remaining EFTA and some Mediterranean countries, led to a mobilization of American exporters. Facing a threat to their foreign market access, they lobbied Congress and the administration to pursue policies that protected their interests. This lobbying effort motivated decision makers in the United States to implement a mix of trade policies in support of exporting interests, which comprised a broader range of alternatives than in the previous decade, including retaliation and a call for multilateral trade liberalization. The EC, however, only accepted a move away from the protectionist trade policy status quo once it received a favorable balance of concessions in negotiations. At the same time as they negotiated with each other, both the United States and the EC also pursued trade policies that placated import-competing interests by restricting imports from the newly industrializing countries.

Enlargement and Discrimination against U.S. Exports

The first step toward an examination of the protection-for-exporters argument is to assess whether U.S. exporters' access to foreign market was threatened as a result of the trade policies pursued by foreign countries. Initially, the implementation of the trade agreements reached at the end of the Kennedy round actually improved U.S. exporters' export opportunities. The situation only changed in the early 1970s when the EC started to implement a series of discriminatory trade policies that threatened U.S. exporters' access to foreign markets. Three EC policies were particularly important in that respect: the accession of the United Kingdom, Denmark, and Ireland; the pursuit of preferential trade agreements with the remaining EFTA countries; and preferential trade agreements with the Mediterranean countries.

British accession to the EC ended a long struggle over membership that had started in the 1950s. Already in 1958, when the six members of the European Coal and Steel Community founded the EEC, British industry saw itself at a disadvantage, which could only be offset by better access to the EC markets. As the *Economist* (16 February 1963, 617) stated: "When British exporters start off at a tariff disadvantage in their largest market, the European Economic Community, a reduction in [the EEC's] tariffs is needed simply to help Britain's exporters to regain competitive parity." The British government, accordingly, tried to achieve a free trade area among all Western European countries that would have provided British industry with access to the continental markets. France's veto of this proposal compelled the British government to look for alternatives, which initially it found in the establishment of the European Free Trade Association. Unsatisfied with this alternative, however, already in July 1961 British prime minister Harold

Macmillan announced that the United Kingdom would apply for EEC membership. Nevertheless, with France continuing to block an accession agreement in the following years, the United Kingdom only formally acceded to the EC in January 1973, together with Denmark and Ireland. Over the following four years, these new members eliminated their tariffs on intra-EC trade and implemented the common external tariff of the EC.

The enlargement of the EC constituted a major threat to U.S. exporters' access to European markets. U.S. agricultural exports to Europe were seen to be most vulnerable, not least because they had already declined in absolute terms over the preceding years. It was widely feared that the expansion of the CAP to the United Kingdom, the fifth largest market for U.S. agricultural goods in 1970, and the other new member states would lead to further losses (Geiger 1970; Marsh 1971; Schmidt 1972; *Wall Street Journal*, 12 March 1973, 20–22). Enlargement would not only lead to discrimination but also increase the absolute level of trade barriers against U.S. exports of agricultural products. The guaranteed price in the United Kingdom for rye would even double as a result of accession (Schmidt 1972, 5). In the longer term, such price increases in a country with a relatively competitive agricultural sector would inevitably lead to an increase in production (by some 8 percent in 1977 according to one estimate), and in turn to greater exports that would threaten to displace U.S. exporters in third markets. Especially exporters of feed grains, rice, lard, meat, fruits and vegetables, and tobacco would be in a difficult situation (Schmidt 1972, 11). By contrast, exporters of soybeans and citrus fruits had little to fear from this step. The overall loss of U.S. agricultural exports from British accession was estimated to be between $20 and $100 million per year (Krause 1968, 220–21).

With respect to manufactured products, three factors alleviated the trade-diversionary consequences of enlargement. First, British industrial tariffs were on average slightly higher than EC tariffs (10 percent as compared to 8.5 percent for the EC after implementation of the Kennedy round agreements), and they had to be reduced to the level of the EC's common external tariff when entering the EC. Second, British accession to the EC led to the removal of discrimination in favor of some Commonwealth countries, that had lingered as a result of imperial preference. Third, since EC tariffs were reduced according to the schedule agreed on in the Kennedy round between 1968 and 1972, the benefits from these cuts offset at least some of the losses from trade diversion. Nevertheless, exports of some manufactured goods were likely to suffer from enlargement (Krause 1968). Contemporary studies even estimated losses of up to 22 percent of U.S. manufactured exports to the enlarged EC (Kreinin 1973, 563). More recent analyses also lead to the conclusion that at least some U.S. exporters suffered from trade diversion (Winters 1984; Yannopoulos 1988, 128; Bayoumi and Eichengreen 1997).

The conclusion of free trade agreements between the EC and the remaining EFTA members in July 1972 was the second EC trade policy of that time that had potential to hurt U.S. exporters. Western European countries excluded from the enlarged EC feared that British accession would further undermine their access to this market. The agreements that were designed to allay their fears foresaw the abolition of tariffs on industrial goods between the two groups of countries over a period of five years. For U.S. exporters, these agreements were a further step toward discrimination. As early as 1971, they feared a loss of up to $300 million of exports if these agreements were implemented (Scott 1971, 204).

The third EC trade policy that potentially caused injury for U.S. exporters was the conclusion of free trade agreements with some Mediterranean countries and with former colonies. The EEC had started this policy in the early 1960s, when it concluded association agreements with Greece (1961), Turkey (1963), and Israel (1964). In the late 1960s and early 1970s, the EC extended its Mediterranean agreements among others to Morocco (1969), Tunisia (1969), Spain (1970), and Egypt (1972). The EC also engaged in preferential trade policies with some former colonies. On 1 July 1964, the first Yaoundé association agreement came into existence, and in 1969 this agreement was extended to cover further countries. Both policies were particularly contentious in the United States because they included reverse preferences, that is, they not only granted preferential access for developing countries in the EC but also conceded EC producers preferential access to the markets of the developing countries. Whereas the losses for U.S. exports due to the EC's preferences for former colonies were estimated to be relatively small (Krause 1968, 186–88), the Mediterranean agreements were expected to be far less benign, with a substantial proportion of U.S. exports to Israel and Spain in danger of displacement (Kreinin 1976). Equally, some U.S. exports to the EC suffered from these agreements, not least because they were designed to be maximally trade diverting—to minimize the costs imposed on sectors within the EC (Hine 1985, 140). The anticipated losses had high political importance since they were concentrated on very specific producers, such as growers of citrus fruits.[1]

In conclusion, therefore, European discriminatory trade policies in the early 1970s had the potential to hurt a substantial number of U.S. exporters. The combined effects of enlargement and the free trade agreements with the remaining EFTA countries could have caused trade diversion of about $500 million

---

1. "The Preferential Agreements between the European Economic Community and Tunisia, Morocco, Spain, and Israel: Implications for U.S. Commodity Exports," Bureau of Intelligence and Research, 19 July 1971, State Department Records, Central Files, Record Group 59, Subject Numeric Files, 1970–73, NACP.

compared with the trade level in 1968 (Resnick and Truman 1975, 74). The exporters most threatened by these policies were the exporters of agricultural goods to the EC, whereas only a few manufactured products were thought to face trade diversion. The expectation derived from Hypothesis 1 is that this threat to foreign market access should have led to a mobilization of U.S. exporters.

The Mobilization of U.S. Exporters in the 1970s

In fact, such mobilization, especially of agricultural interests, did take place. In the late 1960s, as expected, import-competing interests dominated the policy-making process in the United States. In the hearings for the 1969 renewal of the RTAA, for example, import-competing interests made a very strong showing (Lindeen 1970). Even the Chamber of Commerce, although urging Congress to extend tariff-cutting authority for two years, stated that the president should not use this authority to engage in a trade round (*New York Times*, 10 July 1967, 43). Taking account of these protectionist tendencies, President Richard Nixon told reporters in March 1969: "We have to realize that we cannot anticipate in the near future another big round of reductions of tariff barriers. We are going to do well if we can digest what we have on the plate" (quoted in Eckes 1995, 212–13).

Soon thereafter, however, exporters started to voice concerns about the discriminatory effects of the enlargement of the EC and the EC's free trade agreements with the EFTA countries (*New York Times*, 9 November 1971, 69 and 74). Exporters were particularly wary about these developments as they only recently had experienced the negative consequences of the creation of the EEC. As one business executive put it:

> The European Common Market provides an excellent example of the possible effects [the] formation of a bloc can have upon U.S. trade. Business has been lost as low tariffs were raised, which has not been compensated for by high duties coming down as the Common Market achieves its common external tariff. Similarly, business has been lost to local competition as the internal duties have gone down. (quoted in Bivens 1968, 34)

When serious negotiations for EC enlargement started, the newly founded Emergency Committee for American Trade urged the Nixon administration to engage in "parallel negotiations" to prevent damage to American industry from this step. In defense of this position, it stated: "We do not want to sit on the sidelines while the Europeans and others go about making permanent arrangements affecting our interests" (*New York Times*, 25 February 1971, 53). The U.S.

Chamber of Commerce, in its recommendations on U.S.-EC relations, also pushed for an early resolution of the trade problems accompanying enlargement. It claimed that a possible trade conflict between the United States and the EC could have repercussions for the whole trading system. After complaining about the EC's discriminatory trade policies, it even contended that protectionist pressures in the United States were partly triggered by European trade policies that exposed European disregard for the existing multilateral trading system.[2]

Besides the broad business associations, some specific sectors were also active in lobbying the U.S. administration with regard to European discriminatory trade policies. The paper industry, for example, feared that its exports to the United Kingdom would suffer, since, as a result of the free trade agreements concluded between the EC and the remaining EFTA countries, the Scandinavian countries would benefit from a tariff advantage in the British market. Observing a "12-percent tariff disadvantage," a representative of this industry complained that some 80 percent of paper exports to the enlarged community would face discrimination.[3] The president of the American Paper Institute also made a visit to the German Foreign Ministry to present his concerns about the possibility that the EC's preferential agreements with Sweden and Finland could discriminate against American paper exports.[4] Other sectors, such as the semiconductor industry, complained about the new testing and certification requirements in the EC.[5] Multinational companies with a strong presence in the Common Market, by contrast, were largely indifferent to enlargement and the other discriminatory trade policies pursued by the EC, as they could service this market from within.[6]

Agricultural exporters lobbied even more than the producers of manufactured goods. This is in accordance with the expectations derived from the protection-for-exporters argument, given that the most significant trade diversion was anticipated for agricultural goods. In the 1973 hearings before the Committee on Ways and Means, among twenty-seven exporters testifying, no fewer than ten came from the agricultural sector.[7] Agricultural interests as diverse as

---

2. Letter to the President, Chamber of Commerce of the United States, 20 October 1970, State Department Records, Central Files, Record Group 59, Subject Numeric Files, 1970–73, NACP.

3. U.S. Congress, May–June 1973, Hearings before the House Committee on Ways and Means, *Trade Reform*, 3315.

4. Note concerning visit by Mr. Edwin A. Locke, President of the American Paper Institute, in the Foreign Office, 19 April 1972, B53-IIIA2, no. 329-E, PA.

5. U.S. Congress, May–June 1970, Hearings before the House Committee on Ways and Means, *Tariff and Trade Proposals*, 3000.

6. The position taken by Antonie Knoppers, the chairman of Merck pharmaceutical company, serves to illustrate this point. Knoppers stated: "I personally am not afraid of this greater industrial trading Europe. The multinational companies will love it" (*New York Times*, 8 August 1971, F3).

7. U.S. Congress, May–June 1973, Hearings before the House Committee on Ways and Means, *Trade Reform*. A similar lobbying pattern can also be observed in the 1970 Hearings of the Committee

the American Farm Bureau Federation (the largest farmers' organization in the United States), the National Farmers Union (which mainly represents family farms), the U.S. Feed Grains Council, the National Livestock Feeders Association, and the U.S. National Fruit Export Council spoke out against discrimination in the EC market. Although similar in theme, the statements varied highly in the way they attacked the CAP. On the more sober side, the National Farmers Union declared that the existence of the EC, and in particular of the CAP, increased the need for trade negotiations.[8] On the more impulsive side, Harold N. Williams, president of the Poultry and Egg Institute of America, in a letter to President Nixon, protested against the poultry industry's "disastrous experience with the Common Market these past nine or ten years" (quoted in Talbot 1978, 56).

Whereas many farm groups voiced general complaints against the CAP, others focused specifically on the issues of enlargement and the Mediterranean agreements. In a letter to the German foreign minister, the American ambassador complained: "U.S. farm groups...already are concerned about the effect of the enlargement of the Community on their traditional markets in the United Kingdom."[9] The California-Arizona Citrus League, moreover, objected to the preferential trade agreements that the EC had concluded with Israel, Morocco, Spain, and Tunisia, and estimated the costs of these agreements for U.S. citrus exports at $2 million (*National Journal*, 5 September 1970, 1941). This lobbying by agricultural-export interests continued into the mid-1970s when Congress even held hearings concerning the CAP that showed strong distress among American exporters concerning European trade policies.[10]

Import-competing producers also actively defended their interests throughout the 1970s. Indeed, according to one count, 67 percent of witnesses at the Committee on Ways and Means hearings concerning the Trade Act of 1974, which represented capital interests, favored protectionist policies (Magee 1978). Especially the steel (under the guidance of the American Iron and Steel Institute), textile, and shoe industries took protectionist positions. The chemical industry maintained its skeptical position with respect to trade liberalization (*New York Times*, 2 April 1978, F16). In addition, firms producing machines or machine tools complained about competition from cheaper imports. Finally, the consumer electronics industry, due to the rising competition from Japanese

---

on Ways and Means. See U.S. Congress, May–June 1970, Hearings before the House Committee on Ways and Means, *Tariff and Trade Proposals*.

8. U.S. Congress, May–June 1970, Hearings before the House Committee on Ways and Means, *Tariff and Trade Proposals*, 4237.

9. Letter to Walter Scheel, Kenneth Rush (Ambassador), 12 July 1971, B53-IIIA2, no. 329-B, PA.

10. U.S. Congress, 12 September 1977, Hearings before the House Committee on Ways and Means, *European Community Restrictions on Imports*.

Table 5.1 U.S. exporter lobbying, 1969–1974 (selection)

TYPE OF LOBBY	NAME
General business associations	Greater Detroit Chamber of Commerce
	Greater Minneapolis Chamber of Commerce
	International Trade Club of Chicago
	U.S. Chamber of Commerce
	U.S. Council of the International Chamber of Commerce
Exporter lobbies	Committee for a National Trade Policy
	Emergency Committee for American Trade
	National Foreign Trade Council
Sectoral associations	Aerospace Industries Association of America
	American Paper Institute
	Computer and Business Equipment Manufacturers Association
Individual companies	Boeing
	Caterpillar Tractor
	Fairchild
	Hewlett-Packard
	Intel
Agricultural interests	American Farm Bureau Federation
	California-Arizona Citrus League
	National Farmers Union
	National Grain and Feed Association
	Poultry and Egg Institute of America
	Tobacco Institute
	U.S. Feed Grains Council
	U.S. National Fruit Export Council

producers, turned protectionist at that time. These sectoral groups were supported by organized labor, signifying a radical change from the previous decade, when labor had supported trade liberalization (Helleiner 1977, 109–10).

At the beginning of the 1970s, therefore, U.S. exporters mobilized in reaction to foreign discrimination (see table 5.1). Reflecting on this mobilization of exporting interests, in an oral history, a former state department official observed that "a broad coalition of companies, industries, and agriculture—the major farm organizations—were supporters of trade."[11] The observation that exporters of agricultural goods were at the forefront of the resulting lobbying efforts is consistent with the expectations derived from the protection-for-exporters

---

11. See the oral history by Jules Katz, printed in Eckes (2000, 123).

argument, as they were the most likely losers from the various trade policies undertaken by the EC. At the same time, it poses a puzzle for arguments that stress the role of multinational firms, fearing foreign retaliation, in shaping U.S. trade policies in the 1970s (Milner 1988; see also Helleiner 1977). The arguments linking multinational companies to trade-policy outcomes in that decade also have difficulty explaining why, of the fifty largest multinational companies in existence at that time, only six appeared as witnesses in the hearings preceding the 1974 Trade Act, two of which (Dow Chemical and Monsanto) defended a protectionist position (Rode 1980, 50).

The U.S. Response to EC Enlargement

Did this mobilization of exporters have an effect on U.S. trade policies in the early 1970s? Hypothesis 2 of the protection-for-exporters argument leads to the expectation that U.S. decision makers should have taken measures to protect U.S. exporters against possible losses from European discriminatory trade policies. They should have chosen policies in response to the European threat that took account of the U.S. degree of vulnerability to changes in trade flows, as shaped by the balance of trade, the regional concentration of U.S. exports, and the general importance of external trade for the U.S. economy. As I demonstrate in the following narrative, historical developments largely confirm these predictions.

Immediately after the end of the Kennedy round, when import-competing interests dominated over exporting ones, the objective of protecting import-competing interests received increased attention. Two important examples are Congress's rejection of President Nixon's request for modest negotiating authority in 1969 and the following discussion about the imposition of mandatory quotas against steel and textile imports (Pastor 1980, 124–25). On 11 August 1970, the House Committee on Ways and Means reported a bill that, if enacted, would not only have established import quotas on shoes and textiles but also required the president to accept the recommendations for quotas made by the Tariff Commission. The Mills bill, named after the influential chairman of the Committee on Ways and Means, Wilbur Mills, passed the House of Representatives in November 1970 by a vote of 215–165, but never came to a vote in the Senate.

Mounting Concerns about Discrimination in Europe

From the early 1970s onward, and in parallel to the mobilization of exporters discussed previously, policymakers became increasingly attentive to the EC's discriminatory trade policies. What bothered U.S. policymakers most was the seemingly random spread of trade agreements concluded by the EC. As pointed out by one U.S. official: "It is disturbing that the Community appears to have no clear overall idea on what it wants to achieve. Each agreement is negotiated for its own political/economic reasons and represents a compromise among the member countries at the expense of the world trading rules."[12] The end result of the EC's policies, complained another, would be a "vast network discriminating against the United States."[13]

In October 1970, in an article with the title "Bigger Common Market Seen Posing Threat to American Exporters," the *Wall Street Journal* warned that the enlargement of the EC could lead to losses in such "key U.S. exports as crops and computers" (*Wall Street Journal*, 28 October 1970, 1). In addition, further European integration could stimulate the creation of larger, Europe-wide corporations that were more adept at competing with American companies in world markets. Finally, European integration could lead to the establishment of a common currency with the aim of challenging U.S. financial predominance. The piece concluded gloomily: "Since World War II, U.S. policy-makers have been promoting the dream of a united Europe. But now that an enlarging Common Market makes this much closer to reality, many officials are awakening to fears that the U.S. can ill afford the economic consequences" (*Wall Street Journal*, 28 October 1970, 1).

Two major reports on international trade policy published in 1971 by a presidential commission and a presidential council further illustrate the American distress with European preferential trade policies. The U.S. Commission on International Trade and Investment Policy, for one, predicted losses in U.S. nonagricultural exports of several hundred million dollars per year due to enlargement, and even more for agricultural goods (Commission on International Trade and Investment Policy 1971, 204). In addition, the commission criticized the extension of preferential agreements to the Mediterranean countries, since these agreements would endanger U.S. exports of citrus fruits. The United States, according to the commission's recommendations, should assert its agricultural interests and, in particular, the importance of grain exports in negotiations with the EC and its future new members. Furthermore, it recommended the start of multilateral trade negotiations with the objective of eliminating most tariffs over a period of ten years, and all tariffs over twenty-five years. This objective was important, given that it "would gradually eliminate the discriminatory effects on

---

12. "Memorandum for Mr. Henry A. Kissinger, The White House," 26 February 1970, State Department Records, Central Files, Record Group 59, Subject Numeric Files, 1970–73, NACP.

13. *Foreign Relations of the United States*, 1969–76, vol. 4, no. 221.

the United States and other nonmember countries of the European Community and its preferential trading arrangements" (14).

The second report strongly criticized the "trade-distorting practices" of the EC, and suggested a possible deviation of U.S. trade policies from the MFN rule as a consequence. It stated: "Discriminatory arrangements have proliferated in the last few years....The United States cannot for long be expected to adhere to the principle of non-discrimination when so large a breach in that principle has been made" (Peterson 1972, I:21). The report concentrated its criticisms on the CAP, a system that left outside producers only the role of "residual suppliers," but it also discussed the consequences of the evolving common industrial policy of the EC for U.S. trading interests. According to the report, U.S. exporters feared that the EC would not consider third-country concerns when harmonizing existing standards or establishing new ones, since the EC showed an "excessive preoccupation with the evolution of its internal policies and has not exhibited adequate regard for the effects of these policies on outsiders" (22). Following up on this analysis, the report concluded that the United States should try to influence the process of European integration to increase what its authors termed "external integration."

The future special trade representative Harald B. Malmgren (1973, 27) also heavily criticized the EC's agricultural policies, pointing to data that showed that there had been a 40 percent drop in U.S. exports to the EC of products covered by the CAP over the previous three years. The enlargement of the EC would aggravate the problem by providing new markets for the surpluses created by the CAP and thus easing internal pressure for reform of the EC's agricultural policy. In addition, the entry of Denmark, a country with a strong agricultural sector, would increase European exports to third markets. Malmgren also deplored the discriminatory trade agreements the EC had concluded with the Mediterranean countries, and in the future would perhaps conclude with the remaining EFTA and even with some Caribbean countries. In view of these policies, in March 1971 Senator Abraham Ribicoff (1971, 9) stated: "From an American point of view, the EEC appears to be looking after its own internal interests to an excessive degree and to the detriment of outside countries." The logical consequence for the United States was that it also had to take a tougher stance in its dealings with this entity.

Failed Strategies

The expectation derived from the protection-for-exporters argument is that these concerns should have translated into policies aimed at keeping open foreign markets. In fact, the U.S. administration was eager to react to the mobilization of exporters. It was recognized that failure to react to the negative effects of the CAP would lead to a loss of support for the administration in the Midwestern states of Indiana, Illinois, Ohio, and Missouri.[14] The administration's initial actions, however, were not very successful. Early on, for example, the United States complained about the Mediterranean agreements of the EC, and especially the discrimination that these agreements imposed on U.S. exports of citrus fruits. It instigated a GATT review of the agreements between the EC and Spain and Israel, respectively, that criticized the EC's rationale for the agreements. When the EC failed to react, in April 1971 the U.S. Senate called for retaliation within sixty days if the EC was not willing to eliminate the discrimination against lemons and oranges from Arizona and California.

The EC, however, proved a tough bargaining partner. Although it agreed in principle that all preferential trade agreements should be compatible with GATT regulations, it was not willing to make any changes to its trade agreements. Especially France resisted a compromise with the United States, pushing the EC Council of Ministers to demand concessions before a deal could be reached on citrus fruits. Among the concessions called for were a reduction of U.S. export subsidies and the abolition of the retaliatory measures that the United States had applied since the Chicken War.[15] A deal only became possible when the United States accepted these demands in July 1971. The EC, in turn, reduced tariffs on imports of citrus fruits, but only from June through September, during the peak season in the United States.

The United States also lodged formal protests with the EC member states concerning the EC's free trade agreements with the remaining EFTA countries. Again, however, the EC's position was intransigent, leading the *New York Times* (9 November 1971, 69) to refer to a "sharp dispute" between the United States and the EC over these agreements. The importance of exporter lobbying in stimulating the American reaction becomes evident when analyzing the specific demands made by the U.S. negotiators. In 1972, for example, the Embassy of the United States in Bonn composed an aide-mémoire in support of the paper industry in which it stressed its resolve to assist that industry's efforts to maintain access to the EC markets.[16] In this document, it directly referred to the American Paper Institute, the interest group representing the paper industry. The role of domestic interests in shaping U.S. policies is also recognized in a memorandum directed to the president's assistant for national security affairs, Henry Kissinger, that warned that the EC's discriminatory policies would "bring them into conflict with...potent U.S. economic interest groups."[17]

---

14. Ibid., no. 250.

15. Telegram from Brussels to the German Foreign Office, 28 May 1971, B53-IIIA2, no. 329-C, PA.

16. Embassy of the United States, Bonn, Aide-Mémoire, 22 March 1972, B53-IIIA2, no. 329-E, PA.

17. *Foreign Relations of the United States,* 1969–76, vol. 3, no. 104.

The United States further escalated its strategy when in August 1971 President Nixon announced a "new economic policy" that was intended to solve problems with respect to both trade policy and the U.S. current account. The backdrop to this policy was that, at that time, it had become clear that in 1971 the U.S. economy would incur its first trade deficit since 1893.[18] This was problematic in that until then the trade surplus had served to offset some of the net outflow of capital from the United States. The fear was that the enlargement of the EC would lead to a further worsening of the U.S. current account. It was clear to decision makers that a persistent deficit would make impossible the maintenance of the dollar-gold linkage, which was at the core of the Bretton Woods financial system.

As part of a larger package that included a wage-price freeze to counter inflation and the temporary suspension of the convertibility of paper dollars into gold to stop the outflow of dollars, Nixon also imposed a temporary 10 percent surcharge on all dutiable imports. The administration hoped that by imposing this surcharge, it could force other countries to revalue their currencies, provide (temporary) protection for import competitors, and protect the interests of exporters by asking foreign countries to offer concessions for a removal of the surcharge. Although the policy was not directly aimed at the EC, EC trade policy seems to have played a role in shaping it. The policy was largely designed by the secretary of the treasury John Connally, who repeatedly had complained about the economic costs that European integration had imposed on the United States. It seems likely that this conviction also shaped the specific policies implemented.

In fact, after presenting the new economic policy, the U.S. administration started bilateral consultations to gain concessions from the EC in return for a removal of the surcharge. It made clear that it expected the EC to end its negotiations for free trade agreements with EFTA members before the surcharge would be removed (Scott 1971; Shonfield 1976, 80). Moreover, the EC should halt the plan for the harmonization of the excise on tobacco that the United States believed would reduce American exports of tobacco to the United Kingdom. The EC, however, simply responded that the surcharge was illegal under the GATT (a position that was shared by all other members of a GATT working party, with the exception of the United States) and that it was not willing to compensate the United States for withdrawing an illegal trade measure. It even made implicit

---

18. The U.S. method of calculating exports and imports underestimates the amount of imports because import figures do not include insurance and freight costs. A trade deficit could, therefore, have existed from 1966 onward. See Commission on International Trade and Investment Policy (1971, 24n).

threats that it might consider retaliating against the United States (*New York Times*, 20 October 1971, 1).

In the end, the United States was forced to withdraw the surcharge in December 1971, without having received major concessions in exchange. On the question of currency revaluations, the developed countries found a compromise according to which the United States devalued the dollar by increasing the price of gold while other countries slightly raised the value of their currencies. On the trade issues, the settlement did not include any concessions by the EC (Scott 1971, 203) beyond a general agreement to engage in negotiations once the surcharge was removed. The EC, moreover, was very explicit that in these future negotiations, the United States would have to make concessions on antidumping policy and agricultural quotas, while any European concessions would be tightly restricted.[19] Compared to prior announcements that "tangible progress" on trade was needed before the surcharge could be removed (U.S. Special Representative for Trade William Eberle, as quoted in Shonfield 1976, 81), this outcome was a clear failure. It is no wonder, then, that in 1972 officials in the United States had to concede that American opposition to the EC's pursuit of preferential trade agreements had "so far done little good."[20]

This failure of the more aggressive strategies finally induced the U.S. administration to change its strategy, making it willing to make concessions to the EC for a reduction in the discrimination that U.S. exporters faced in foreign markets. The agreement reached in December 1971 among the United States, the EC members, and Japan, which is known as the Smithsonian agreement, also included a proposal for the start of a new multilateral trade round. In a joint U.S.-EC declaration on 11 February 1972, the two sides announced the start of preparations for future trade negotiations, which, as both delegations confirmed, should cover tariffs as well as nontariff barriers, and industrial as well as agricultural goods. In November 1972, the other contracting parties of the GATT also accepted the start of preparations for what originally was called the Nixon round.

Toward the Trade Act of 1974

The prospect of a new multilateral trade round made it necessary for the U.S. administration to seek trade legislation from Congress. President Nixon hoped that he would be able to receive authority from Congress to abolish all tariffs and to conclude agreements on nontariff barriers without further vote by Congress. The policy of eliminating all tariffs was pushed by officials in the U.S. administration

---

19. *Foreign Relations of the United States,* 1969–76, vol. 4, no. 259.

20. Ibid., no. 281.

who reckoned that by doing so they would also undermine all foreign discrimination. In the ensuing discussions over the Trade Reform Act (later renamed the Trade Act of 1974), which the administration sent to Congress on 10 April 1973, the trade policies of the EC were a major issue.[21] Indeed, President Nixon explicitly mentioned the EC's pursuit of preferential trade agreements as one of the reasons for his request for trade authority when presenting draft legislation for the Trade Reform Act to Congress.[22]

In the Congressional debates, the EC also played a major role. The mood in Congress was that the United States should take strong measures in reaction to the discriminatory trade policies of the EC. In the hearings for the Trade Reform Act, for example, Senator Russell Long (D-LA), chairman of the Senate Finance Committee, stated:

> The bloom is off the rose of "Atlantic partnership," as our friends in Europe concentrate on bilateral deals....I'm not at all sure they want to negotiate on a basis of fairness and reciprocity. If they were sincere, they would offer us fair compensation for the $1 billion trade loss that we will suffer from the enlargement of the European Common market....I am tired of the United States being the "least favored nation" in a world which is full of discrimination.[23]

On 11 December 1973, the House passed the Trade Reform Act with 272 votes for and 140 against the bill. The vote signaled a reversal of the traditional party positions on trade, as for the first time a slight majority of Democrats took a protectionist stance (for this reversal in party positions, see Keech and Pak 1995; Karol 2000). After being bogged down in the Senate for nearly a year over an amendment concerning emigration of Jews from the Soviet Union, the final bill was passed in December 1974 and entered into force in early 1975.

Despite some concessions to import-competing interests, especially the textile and steel industries, the Trade Act of 1974 turned out to be a remarkably far-reaching trade bill, leading to the conclusion that "the protectionist forces essentially lost the battle" (*New York Times,* 23 May 1976, F17). Nevertheless, Congress imposed several limits on the president's negotiating authority. First, the House of Representatives limited tariff cuts to 60 percent of existing duties. Rates of 5 percent or less could be eliminated. Second, the Senate Finance Committee

---

21. Ibid., no. 286.

22. "Special Message to the Congress Proposing Trade Reform Legislation," 10 April 1973, available at http://www.presidency.ucsb.edu/ws/index.php?pid=3800 (accessed 1 April 2009).

23. U.S. Congress, March–April 1974, Hearings before the Senate Committee on Finance, *Trade Reform Act of 1973,* 2.

insisted that ratification of any agreements covering nontariff barriers would require congressional approval. The administration had to accept this change, but it was successful in imposing a time limit for the congressional vote. The resulting procedures for nontariff barrier negotiations, which have become known as "fast-track authority," required the consultation of Congress ninety days before the administration entered into an international agreement. If Congress decided to oppose the international agreement at that stage, the administration could not sign it. Otherwise, Congress had only ninety days' time after the signature of the agreement to make an up-or-down vote, meaning that there was no possibility of amending the agreement at this stage.

While other authors have interpreted the Trade Act of 1974 as an act of congressional abdication (Destler 1978), the protection-for-exporters argument sees the passage of this bill as evidence of the strong pressure that exporting interests, keen to preserve foreign market access in the face of discrimination, exerted on legislators. The existing literature also stresses the fact that the trade act had the objective of making U.S. trade policy compatible with GATT obligations (Chorev 2007), for example by channeling protectionist pressures to administrative trade instruments such as antidumping duties. The bill for the first time even authorized the president to pay the U.S. share of the expenses of the GATT. The protection-for-exporters argument explains this eagerness to bring U.S. policy in line with the GATT with exporters' concerns about the violation of the GATT's nondiscrimination principle by European trade policies. In this view, the GATT gained special value as a tool to restrain foreign trade policies, an objective that could only be achieved by restraining U.S. trade policies.

From the perspective of the protection-for-exporters argument, what is most interesting about this bill is the inclusion of fundamentally different provisions to protect exporter interests. In particular, the 1974 Trade Act saw the introduction of what is known as Section 301 procedures.[24] This section enabled the president to use a broad array of measures to retaliate against foreign countries that, in the terminology of the legislation, maintained "unjustifiable or unreasonable" trade barriers that injured U.S. exports. Considering the fact that, of the first ten proceedings initiated under this section, seven were directed at the EC, it seems plausible to suggest that Congress's preoccupation with the protection of exporters was a response to the EC's discriminatory trade policies.[25] Alternative

---

24. Section 301 was not completely new since it was based on Section 252 of the Trade Expansion Act, but the 1974 Trade Act substantially increased the significance of this provision by giving private parties the right to initiate proceedings.

25. All but one of these cases directed at the EC concerned agricultural products. A further early case, initiated in November 1976, condemned the EC's citrus tariff preferences for some Mediterranean countries. See the list in Destler (1992, app. C).

explanations, by contrast, generally fail to account for this mix of measures in support of exporter interests. Following Helen Milner's (1988) argument, the rise in export-dependent and multinational companies should have made the United States more worried about the possibility of foreign retaliation. Why then would it have dared to use threats in an effort to pry open foreign markets?

In addition to the presidential authority to engage in trade negotiations and to impose retaliatory trade barriers, the bill that was discussed in Congress also included provisions for a generalized system of preferences (GSP). GSP was supposed to offer developing countries better access to the U.S. market, without requiring reciprocal concessions from them. Already in 1971, GATT contracting parties had agreed on a waiver from GATT obligations for such one-sided preferences. The inclusion of GSP provisions in the 1974 Trade Act can be seen as a strategy aimed at presenting an alternative to the EC's reverse preferences with developing countries, which the United States had been criticizing since the 1960s. In fact, Congress legitimized the GSP as "an alternative to the proliferation of special preferential trading arrangements between the European Community and the developing countries of Africa and around the Mediterranean."[26] The analysis of this trade legislation thus largely supports the protection-for-exporters argument by demonstrating that countries that are excluded from preferential trade agreements react to protect their exporters against the negative consequences of discrimination.

Explaining the Choice of Strategy

The U.S. administration used a combination of retaliation and bilateral and multilateral negotiations to react to European discriminatory trade policies in the early 1970s. This differs from the strategy chosen one decade earlier, when these options had been considered but immediately discarded. The protection-for-exporters argument explains this change mainly with reference to the U.S. balance of trade with the largest member countries of the EC, which turned negative in the early 1970s (for the trade data, see Carter et al. 2005, tables Ee376–84, Ee533–50, and Ee551–68). The negative trade balance reduced the vulnerability of the United States to changes in trade flows and made sure that the U.S. negotiators could use continued openness of the American market as a bargaining lever in international trade talks. In turn, this expanded the range of options available to the United States.

Nevertheless, the threat of retaliation remained largely ineffective, and not only because there were good foreign policy reasons for not escalating the

---

26. *Congressional Quarterly. Weekly Report,* vol. 31, no. 42, 20 October 1973, 2794.

confrontation between the United States and the EC. The United States continued to rely on the European market for about a third of its exports. In addition, the increasing importance of trade for the U.S. economy (Shonfield 1976, 59) made sure that the United States could not respond with retaliation to the discriminatory trade policies pursued by the EC. Recognizing these constraints, President Nixon stated that the threat of "foreign reaction against our own exports" made an increase in U.S. trade barriers impossible.[27] The continued dispersion of U.S. exports across many markets, moreover, did not make the pursuit of a rival regional trade agreement very attractive. In short, in line with Hypothesis 3, the degree of vulnerability resulting from the trade flows at that time explains why the United States felt more confident in using threats, why these threats mostly did not achieve their stated aims, and why the United States finally settled for multilateral trade negotiations.

Geopolitics, or Protection for Exporters?

When analyzing these trade policy episodes, several authors have stressed the role of the cold war in shaping U.S. trade policies (Eckes 1995). Indeed, the available evidence suggests that in the 1970s geopolitical considerations were more important in shaping U.S. trade policies than in the 1960s. This is probably a consequence of the strong role that Henry Kissinger played as an adviser to the president on national security and later as secretary of state, which meant that many trade issues were decided at the level of the National Security Council. The "overriding importance of [the U.S.'s] political relationship with Europe" was thus emphasized quite frequently in internal documents.[28]

Nevertheless, the impact of geopolitics should not be overestimated, either. References to geopolitics were at least partly used in a strategic manner to achieve other objectives. For one, to administration officials it was clear that the trade-security linkage could serve as further incentive for Congress to pass trade legislation.[29] Moreover, they realized that given the Europeans' "security dependency" on the United States this linkage could be used as a "lever or carrot" to gain concessions from the EC concerning trade issues.[30] The latter objective is also visible in debates in Congress about the withdrawal of U.S. troops from Europe, which were kept alive by the periodic reintroduction of the Mansfield Resolution to the Senate after August 1966. Some advocates of this resolution hoped that the

---

27. "Special Message to the Congress on United States Trade Policy," 18 November 1969, available at http://www.presidency.ucsb.edu/ws/index.php?pid=2325 (accessed 1 April 2009).
28. *Foreign Relations of the United States, 1969–76,* vol. 4, no. 277.
29. Ibid., no. 287.
30. Ibid., no. 286.

threat of troop withdrawal would make the Europeans more willing to concede on trade issues (Bergsten 1971, 633; Shonfield 1976, 74).

The content of the Trade Act of 1974 also casts some doubt on a geopolitical interpretation. Congress feared that the executive could use trade-negotiating authority to pursue geopolitical interests, and so introduced new control mechanisms that limited the leeway of the president in trade negotiations.[31] One such control mechanism was the creation of the Advisory Committee for Trade Negotiations, a committee of industry, labor, and consumer representatives, that was intended to give the administration an advisory opinion on the results of the negotiations. It was instructed to report at the conclusion of the negotiations "as to whether and to what extent the Agreement promotes the economic interests of the United States and…provides for equity and reciprocity" (Trade Act of 1974, as quoted in Winham 1986, 135). An explanation of American trade policies in the early 1970s that mainly relies on geopolitics thus faces severe challenges. By contrast, the available evidence largely supports the protection-for-exporters argument and provides further plausibility for Hypothesis 2, which links a mobilization of U.S. exporters to trade policies aimed at the protection of exporter interests.

European Trade Policies in the 1970s

What explains the trade policies chosen by the EC in response to the American initiatives? In the 1970s, European exporting interests were more concerned about maintaining access to the U.S. market than they had been one decade earlier. Nevertheless, they fell far short of asking their governments to make unilateral concessions; rather, their hope was to exploit the American eagerness for a reduction of European trade barriers to gain concessions in the U.S. market. As long as the United States requested unilateral concessions from the EC, consequently, the Europeans simply rejected these demands. They also countered U.S. claims that European trade policies caused harm to American exporters by arguing that the U.S. economy suffered from ill-conceived monetary policies and domestic inflation caused by the costs of the Vietnam War. Only when the United States became willing to make concessions, did the European stance change, allowing for an agreement that further liberalized transatlantic trade relations.

---

31. That Congress was critical of the link between geopolitics and trade is also supported by an interview with Robert C. Cassidy Jr., senior staff member in the Subcommittee on Trade, Senate Committee on Finance, during the final phase of the Tokyo round, printed in Twiggs (1987, 111).

Interest-Group Demands and the EC Position

European domestic interests had changed in the decade since the creation of the EEC. Due to their higher export dependence, many firms had become increasingly vulnerable to the trade policies of foreign countries. For Germany, for example, exports to the U.S. market became substantially more important, accounting for nearly 11 percent of total German exports in 1968. Although this percentage slightly declined over the following years, it was still consistently higher than in the early 1960s (for example, 7.3 percent in 1962). In the late 1960s, the rising protectionist pressures in the United States threatened these growing exports to the U.S. market. Interest groups, consequently, expressed their concerns about the protectionist bills discussed in the U.S. Congress. The Permanent Conference of the EC's Chambers of Commerce, in October 1970, for example, denounced the protectionist Mills bill that was being considered at that time in Congress.[32] One year later, the European steel industry was considerably upset about the surcharge that was part of Nixon's "new economic policy" (*Guardian*, 9 September 1971, 17). For European exporters, the U.S. surcharge effectively meant a doubling of the tariff barriers that they encountered when exporting to the United States (Commission of the European Communities 1971, 11).

Nevertheless, European exporters were also aware of the fact that the U.S. administration's eagerness to avoid the imposition of losses on U.S. exporting interests increased the EC's bargaining power. At no point, therefore, did they exhibit a willingness to support unilateral concessions by the EC to the United States. Rather, European exporters requested the harmonization of tariff levels and the abolition of the American selling price and the Buy America Act as preconditions for an accommodation of U.S. interests. Beyond the common aim of getting concessions in the U.S. market, however, British, French, and German domestic interests diverged on several issues. In West Germany, business associations were least willing to risk a trade war with the United States, and therefore they took the least confrontational position. Fritz Berg, president of the Bundesverband der Deutschen Industrie, for example, early on expressed concerns about the mounting trade conflicts between the EC and the United States.[33] He suggested the creation of a commission, consisting of representatives of the industries of the United States and the EC, which should try to find solutions to

---

32. "The Protectionist Trends in the United States. Resolution," Permanent Conference of the European Economic Community's Chambers of Commerce, 15 October 1970, State Department Records, Central Files, Record Group 59, Subject Numeric Files, 1970–73, NACP. Early on, the broad European-level business association UNICE also attacked U.S. trade policies. See UNICE, "Mitteilung an die Presse," 25 October 1967, B53-IIIA2, no. 329-A, PA.

33. Letter to Economics Minister Karl Schiller, Fritz Berg, 28 July 1970, B53-IIIA2, no. 177, PA.

the existing trade problems. The other major German business association, the Deutsche Industrie und Handelstag, demanded that the EC not take measures that could result in a further burden on agricultural imports, and that the EC should restrain its subsidization of exports of agricultural goods.[34] In addition, the German group of the International Chamber of Commerce proposed multilateral trade negotiations to tackle the existing trade conflicts.[35] This was the only European exporter association that favored an elimination of industrial tariffs among all countries willing to participate in such an undertaking.[36]

In the United Kingdom, as well, exporters were worried about the possibility of an escalation of trade conflicts between the two sides of the Atlantic. Consequently, by September 1970 the Association of British Chambers of Commerce asked the British government to work toward a resolution of these conflicts (*Times*, 28 September 1970, 17). The Confederation of British Industry published a pamphlet on its "objectives in Europe," arguing that "the enlarged EEC should try to ensure that the forthcoming multilateral negotiations to liberalise world trade further produce substantial and fair results as quickly as possible."[37] Nevertheless, it made progress on the trade issue dependent on the creation of a viable international monetary system. In addition, it was skeptical with regard to the U.S. proposal to eliminate all tariffs on industrial goods (*Times*, 12 September 1973, 17). By the mid-1970s, moreover, it asked for import controls on a series of manufactured goods, such as cars and paper.

French domestic interests were least accommodating vis-à-vis the U.S. demands. Some French business associations even called for retaliation against unilateral U.S. policies. In October 1971, for example, the president of the French Aerospace Industry Association suggested that the EC should impose higher barriers to aircraft imports as a reaction to the U.S. surcharge.[38] Moreover, agricultural interests, such as the National Confederation of Cooperatives and Agricultural Credit, opposed further trade liberalization and, instead, defended the unchanged continuation of the CAP. In short, while European exporting interests were concerned about a deterioration of transatlantic trade relations in the early 1970s, they did not push their governments to make unilateral concessions

---

34. Telegram to Foreign Minister Walter Scheel, DIHT, 24 July 1970, B53-IIIA2, no. 177, PA.

35. Letter to Foreign Minister Walter Scheel, Deutsche Gruppe der Internationalen Handelskammer, 24 July 1970, B53-IIIA2, no. 177, PA.

36. "Die Wiederherstellung des multilateralen Handelssystems. Stellungnahme," annexed to a letter by the German section of the International Chamber of Commerce addressed to Foreign Minister Walter Scheel, 29 May 1972, B53-IIIA3, no. 231, PA.

37. "Objectives in Europe," Confederation of British Industries, 6 June 1972, State Department Records, Central Files, Record Group 59, Subject Numeric Files, 1970–73, NACP.

38. Memo, State Department Records, Central Files, Record Group 59, Subject Numeric Files, 1970–73, NACP.

to the United States to ease these conflicts. Rather, their position can be summarized as cautiously embracing negotiations with the hope of gaining concessions in the U.S. market without having to give in too much with respect to European trade policies favoring their interests.

Consistent with these interest-group demands, EC member countries early on declared a willingness to engage in negotiations with the United States, but only on the basis of reciprocal concessions. The French government's stance was the most confrontational, insisting that the EC should not give in to U.S. demands for compensation. It threatened counterretaliation if the United States implemented its threats of raising some tariffs to compel the EC to give in (*Wall Street Journal*, 16 April 1973, 13). France even opposed the U.S. proposal for regular bilateral economic consultations, since in the opinion of the French government this would give the United States too much influence over European policies. It did, however, support the start of a multilateral trade round. Such a round should lower (high) U.S. tariffs more than European ones, but it should not lead to a complete abolition of all tariffs, as initially suggested by the Nixon administration. The reason that it gave for this position was that both the CAP and the common external tariff were important for "Community solidarity."[39] France also defended a linkage between trade and monetary issues, to make sure that a devaluation of the dollar, as had happened in 1971, would not make all U.S. concessions on trade worthless (Louis 1984, 25).

By contrast, West Germany was far more concerned about the possibility that the United States might retaliate against European trade policies. Internal papers in the German administration thus stressed the importance of considering American interests when formulating European trade policies, and of designing trade agreements and European integration more generally, in a way that would create rather than divert trade.[40] Moreover, the EC's trade policies should comply with GATT rules. The reverse preferences with developing countries, for example, should be abolished, since these preferences were of low economic value. Nevertheless, there was no mention of unilateral commercial disarmament. In multilateral trade negotiations, it hoped to achieve a linear reduction of tariffs

---

39. It does not seem plausible that the French government was really driven by an abstract concept such as "Community solidarity." As put in a U.S. document: "A more obvious cause of the hard French position is French self-interest in preserving the CAP, and particularly the principle of community preference." Telegram from Paris, 1 April 1972, State Department Records, Central Files, Record Group 59, Subject Numeric Files, 1970–73, NACP. This American skepticism concerning French appeals to "Community solidarity" is supported by the fact that after a devaluation of the franc in the late 1960s, France simply suspended the CAP (without concern for Community solidarity) to allow for a new alignment of agricultural prices.

40. "Handelspolitische Probleme zwischen den USA und den EG (Gefahren für den Welthandel)," German Federal Ministry of Economics, 17 January 1969, B53-IIIA2, no. 329-A, PA.

and negotiations on a variety of nontariff barriers. The EC, however, should make only minor concessions on agriculture, leaving the general features of the CAP of the EC untouched.[41]

The EC's trade policy preference was largely driven by these two countries, and in particular by France (see Louis 1984, 25), with the United Kingdom—which only acceded to the EC in the middle of these developments—playing a minor role. In essence, the mandate given to the European Commission in its talks with the United States from 1971 onward was that in the absence of broader negotiations it should make only minor concessions, and even these should be conditional on reciprocity from the United States. The expectation derived from the protection-for-exporters argument is that this lower eagerness as compared to the United States to achieve a trade agreement should have increased the EC's bargaining power. Such a boost in the EC's bargaining power in the aftermath of enlargement was also predicted by a series of observers. As early as 1962, a study for the U.S. Congress maintained: "The bargaining power of the Common Market, already substantial, will of course be further increased if Great Britain and other new members and associates are admitted" (Kravis 1962, 99). Similarly, in 1971 the report of the Williams Commission concluded that enlargement "would, of course, further enhance the Community's bargaining power" (Commission on International Trade and Investment Policy 1971, 205–6).

Staying Put in the Bilateral Negotiations

Indeed, in the initial bilateral negotiations, the EC did not give in to U.S. demands for unilateral concessions. This was the case, as shown above, before the United States imposed the surcharge in August 1971. It is equally true, however, for the situation after that event. At that stage, the United States demanded a "standstill agreement," which would stop the "proliferation" of preferential trade agreements beyond Europe, and informal consultations concerning the EC's negotiations with the EFTA countries. The United States seemed to be in a good position to achieve its aims, as some of the agreements concluded by the EC were in clear violation of the GATT. The agreements with Spain and Israel, for example, only foresaw tariff reductions on some products, and on those, for which reductions were made, they did not eliminate tariffs. This clearly fell short of the conditions spelled out in article 24 of the GATT, namely that free trade agreements have to cover substantially all trade and should eliminate tariffs between the participating countries. Nevertheless, the United States had to scrap the surcharge under the threat of foreign retaliation before it could accomplish its objectives.

---

41. "Vorstellungen über ein handelspolitisches Gesamtkonzept für multilaterale Handelsverhandlungen im GATT ab 1973," 14 November 1972, B54-IIIA3, no. 231, PA.

When the United States failed to achieve a standstill agreement, it demanded specific concessions for losses incurred due to discrimination, as for example with respect to citrus fruits. Initial talks between the United States and the EC took place at the end of December 1971 and in January 1972, immediately after the American removal of the surcharge. Again, however, the United States was able to secure only minor concessions, and those in exchange for some concessions of its own. Basically, the EC's position was that it would accept negotiations on these issues, but only in the context of a broader round, where other countries would have to make concessions as well. The concessions that the EC did make were to increase the stockpiling of grains, to submit the enlargement treaties to the GATT when signed, and to engage in negotiations with third countries for possible compensation. Concerning the last of these issues, on 31 May 1974 the EC and the United States reached an agreement that—despite threats of retaliation by the United States (*New York Times,* 24 June 1973, 139)—only envisaged minor reductions of the EC tariffs on tobacco, citrus, paper, and some other products.

What the United States also achieved was a commitment by the EC to abolish reverse preferences in trade agreements with developing countries, excluding, however, the Mediterranean countries. In exchange, in the informal Casey-Soames understanding (1974), the United States agreed to end its legal challenge of the EC's preferential agreements in the GATT (Luyten 1989, 273). This understanding paved the way for the EC's Lomé agreements, which granted one-sided preferences to former European colonies in Africa, the Caribbean, and the Pacific area.[42] Again, however, the U.S. success was far from complete, as the understanding excluded countries such as Israel and Spain, which were far more important to European and U.S. trading interests than the ones covered by the Lomé agreements. What is more, it seems actually plausible that the EC did not give in to U.S. pressure but rather satisfied a demand voiced by the African, Caribbean, and Pacific countries themselves when accepting nonreciprocity (Coffey 1976, 76). Overall, therefore, the available evidence confirms the expectation derived from the protection-for-exporters argument that discrimination should have increased the EC's bargaining power (Hypothesis 4).

Asymmetric Concessions in the Tokyo Round?

A major move away from the protectionist status quo only became possible when the United States and the EC engaged in negotiations across many trade policy issues, a condition achieved as part of the Tokyo round—initially known

---

42. Ironically, since 2002 the EU has engaged in negotiations with African, Caribbean, and Pacific states to conclude agreements with reverse preferences (called European partnership agreements), as the prior nonreciprocal trade agreements are now considered to be in violation of WTO law.

as the Nixon round—negotiations that started in 1973 (Kakabadse 1980; Winham 1986; Grieco 1990). As expected by the protection-for-exporters argument, the analysis of these negotiations reveals that the United States both wanted and needed a substantial agreement, while the EC took a relaxed attitude, waiting for the Americans to offer concessions for a reduction of discrimination (Golt 1978, 12). The prediction thus is for the EC to have won asymmetric concessions. I examine this prediction by comparing the preferences of the two actors to the outcomes reached at the end of the negotiations.

On many issues, it was the United States that preferred a move away from the status quo. It hoped for a substantial agreement on industrial tariffs, expecting that this would alleviate the negative consequences of discriminatory trade policies. Even more important for the United States was a liberalization of trade in agricultural goods, to satisfy American exporters of farm products who suffered from the CAP. The Trade Act of 1974, therefore, includes a provision that states that agricultural trade liberalization "shall be undertaken in conjunction with" industrial trade liberalization "to the maximum extent feasible" (quoted in Destler 1978, 47). EC trade policies also stimulated U.S. interest in a series of nontariff barriers. Concern about European moves to harmonize standard setting, for example, motivated the United States to seek negotiations on this issue. It hoped to achieve an agreement that would allow it to monitor standard setting in the EC (Winham 1986, 103). Greater limitations on the use of subsidies were expected to help U.S. exporters of both agricultural and manufactured goods. In the final phase of the negotiations, the United States also sought a code on trade in civil aircraft, which would impose limits on European moves to bolster its aircraft industry.

The EC's position was that a further lowering of industrial tariffs was desirable; a total elimination of tariffs, however, was not (Commission of the European Communities 1973). It demanded that tariffs should be reduced using a formula approach, which would harmonize rather than linearly cut industrial tariffs. In essence, this meant that U.S. tariffs should be cut more than European ones. The EC was also insistent on the point that reciprocity should be achieved within all areas of the negotiations, thus forestalling U.S. demands for larger EC concessions on agriculture in exchange for U.S. concessions on industrial goods. The initial negotiation position concerning nontariff barriers was not very precise, but it soon became clear in which areas the EC hoped for U.S. concessions: customs valuation (in particular the removal of the American selling price system), public procurement (a repeal of the Buy America Act), international standard setting (American acceptance of international standards), and countervailing duty procedures (the introduction of material injury requirements in U.S. countervailing procedures). The EC also stood behind its strong defensive interests with respect to the agricultural sector. Instead of accepting a liberalization of this sector, the EC pushed for commodity agreements establishing maximum and minimum prices on a series of agricultural products, such as wheat, flour, feed grains, rice, sugar, and some dairy products. Indeed, it insisted that it would not be willing to engage in negotiations on the principles or even the "mechanisms" of the CAP (Louis 1984, 26).

In the ensuing negotiations, in accordance with the expectation set out above, the EC managed to gain asymmetric concessions. As put by the author of a book about the EC's engagement in the Tokyo round, "the United States gave way on almost every major European Communities' claim" (Taylor 1983, 141; see also Kakabadse 1980). Most important, the EC managed to uphold agricultural protection (and make only minor concessions in that area) despite initial American pledges that the United States would not accept an agreement without a substantial agricultural package. At the same time, the EC succeeded in gaining important concessions in the American market, among them a further asymmetric cut of tariffs (following the "Swiss formula") that favored the EC. The United States subjected its industrial tariffs to an average cut of 42 percent, substantially larger than the 31 percent cut accepted by the EC (Corbet 1979, 328). Weighted by imports, the U.S. reduction of 30 percent was still larger than the EC reduction of 27 percent.

A further important result of the Tokyo round was the conclusion of a series of codes on nontariff barriers, covering issues such as customs valuation, subsidies and countervailing measures, and technical barriers to trade. On these, again, the EC received major concessions. The United States agreed to the abolition of the American selling price system and to the introduction into U.S. countervailing duty law of a clause stipulating that "material" injury had to be given for the United States to impose countervailing duties. Concerning government procurement, the United States opened its purchases to foreign bidding slightly more than the EC, namely $11 billion versus $10 billion (Krasner 1979, 614). The U.S. administration also agreed to change the taxation of spirits, a move that offered major gains to EC producers (Winham 1986, 280–302). By contrast, the attempt by the United States to limit the European use of subsidies in the agricultural sector was not successful, as the final code on that topic explicitly excluded raw materials, and thus agricultural products (although it stated that subsidies on these products should not lead to a displacement of the exports of other countries on world markets). In short, the balance of concessions exchanged in the Tokyo round favored the EC, providing a rationale for the EC's acceptance of trade liberalization as hoped for by the United States (Hypothesis 5).

In this chapter I have outlined transatlantic trade relations in the wake of the first EC enlargement in the early 1970s. I have shown how concerns among American exporters about discriminatory European trade policies contributed to their mobilization. This lobbying, in turn, motivated the United States to engage in policies intended to protect the interests of U.S. exporters. Initially, the U.S. administration used unilateral and sector-based bilateral strategies in reaction to foreign discrimination, but it failed to achieve its aim of reestablishing foreign market access before showing a willingness to make concessions in broad negotiations. Once American concessions were forthcoming, the European position also changed, enabling the two sides to conclude a major deal at the end of the Tokyo round.

The narrative, beyond establishing the explanatory power of the protection-for-exporters argument for these developments, casts further doubt on the validity of those versions of the hegemonic stability theory that expect trade liberalization to be dependent on the presence of a hegemonic power (Krasner 1976). Despite a decline in U.S. hegemony, the two sides of the Atlantic managed to achieve a liberalizing agreement.[43] Neither do geopolitical considerations provide for a comprehensive explanation of U.S. trade policy choices, although foreign policy concerns evidently played a role in shaping them. Quite obviously, then, trade policies in the 1970s can be better explained with reference to domestic interests than to the distribution of power in the international system or geopolitical objectives (see also Keohane 1980).

---

43. There are also aspects of the Tokyo round that are in line with the same interpretation of hegemonic stability theory, especially the United States insisting on extending the benefits of the subsidies and antidumping codes only to signatories.

6

THE SINGLE MARKET PROGRAMME AND TRANSATLANTIC TRADE POLICIES IN THE 1980s

Transatlantic trade policies in the 1980s were characterized by an increasing U.S. reliance on offensive trade instruments to open European markets without providing major concessions in return. This aggressive stance, which is often summarized as the pursuit of "fair" rather than free trade policies (Goldstein 1993, 176–80; Nollen and Quinn 1994), was very prominent in the U.S. reaction to the southern enlargement of the EC and the implementation of the single market programme (SMP, also known as EC-92 because it was supposed to be completed in 1992) from the mid-1980s onward. While the United States managed to attain its objectives on some issues using that strategy, on others it had to be more conciliatory and engage in bilateral negotiations with the EC. The two sides also were the key actors in the multilateral trade negotiations known as the Uruguay round that started in 1986. The protection-for-exporters argument set out in chapter 1 is of major use in explaining these developments. It correctly predicts the prevalence of essentially protectionist U.S. trade policies in the early 1980s, when, in the absence of a threat to their foreign market access, only a limited number of exporters tried to influence trade policies in their favor. The result was "the period of greatest congressional trade intensity since the 1930s" (Destler 2005, 88). The argument can also provide an explanation for the U.S. choice of more aggressive trade policies in response to discrimination abroad than in past decades. With the United States incurring a trade deficit in its trade with most foreign countries, its vulnerability to changes in foreign trade policies was relatively low.

The argument fares particularly well in explaining the interaction between U.S. and European trade policies in the aftermath of the European decision to

159

create a single European market. This step toward abolishing the remaining barriers to intra-EC trade led to a short but intensive reaction by U.S. exporters in 1988 and 1989, who complained about the potentially negative effects of the SMP for their access to European markets. The main criticisms were directed at the reciprocity provisions attached to some of the internal liberalization measures, the exclusion of U.S. interests from the European standard-setting process, rules of origin, and the public procurement provisions. Given its low degree of vulnerability to changes in foreign trade policies, the United States could react to these policies with threats of retaliation. European policies, by contrast, were heavily influenced by a perception of vulnerability to these American threats. Although the EC tried to use the SMP to gain concessions in the U.S. market, because of fear of American retaliation it could never make credible its threat to establish a Fortress Europe. Instead, on most of the controversial issues, the EC adopted a conciliatory position and tried to avoid a direct confrontation with the United States.

This reading of the evidence challenges a series of alternative explanations. It suggests, for example, that the more aggressive U.S. stance was not so much a consequence of the breakdown of the system that protected Congress from the influence of domestic interests (Destler 2005), a change in the geopolitical situation of the United States (Gilpin 1987; Verdier 1994), or a shift in the beliefs of the main decision makers (Goldstein 1993, 176–80). Rather, it reflects changes in trade flows that lowered the U.S. degree of vulnerability in the face of European trade policies: a large trade deficit and a greater concentration of exports outside of the EC.

In this chapter I also provide an alternative to the dominant explanations for why the EC did not establish a Fortress Europe in the aftermath of the move toward a single European market. While Brian Hanson (1998) rightly points out that the requirement of supermajorities in the EC Council of Ministers hindered the imposition of nontariff barriers at the level of the EC, he cannot explain the concurrent decisions to remove some trade barriers. In addition, Kerry Chase's (2005) focus on companies benefiting from economies of scale can explain protectionist pressures better than incentives for liberalization. In the interpretation that emerges from the application of the protection-for-exporters argument to this case, exporting interests and decision makers in Europe recognized the strong bargaining position of the United States and opted to make concessions to avoid retaliation.

The explanatory power of the protection-for-exporters argument for this case of transatlantic trade relations, however, is not as high as for the other cases discussed in this book. In particular, the argument fails to provide an explanation for the start of the Uruguay round of world trade negotiations in the framework of the GATT. The mobilization of U.S. exporters in support of a liberal trade policy in the mid-1980s exceeds the level expected by the protection-for-exporters argument in the absence of a threat to exporters' foreign market access. This is partly a result of changes in the world trading system, which meant that trading entities other than the EC became increasingly important in shaping U.S. external trade policies (and vice versa for the EC). While in the previous chapters the focus on transatlantic trade relations covered most of what happened in the international trading system, from the 1980s and beyond other countries' policies create noise in the narrative provided here.

The failure of the argument is limited, though, by the fact that it can explain several other aspects of the Uruguay round. For one, partly the round had the purpose of protecting the interests of American agricultural exporting interests that mobilized in response to the discrimination they suffered from the EC's common agricultural policy. Second, the GATT negotiations served to resolve some of the issues emanating from the SMP that could not be settled by way of bilateral negotiations. In fact, in 1988 the deputy United States trade representative, Michael Samuels, stressed: "More and more we see the influence of 1992 on this round [the Uruguay round]. That's why we want to get these talks finished by 1990" (quoted in *Journal of Commerce*, 6 December 1988, 4). Finally, the objective of protection for European exporters contributed to the conclusion of the round. There is some evidence to suggest that the American pursuit of discriminatory trade policies in the early 1990s provided the final stimulus for the EU to accept a major trade agreement. In particular, the first summit of the Asia-Pacific Economic Cooperation (APEC) group in Seattle in 1993 influenced EU trade policies (Bergsten 1996). As stated by Lorenz Schomerus, a European trade negotiator: "The chief determination of the successful conclusion of the Uruguay Round was the APEC summit in Seattle; they sent us a clear message. You [North America] had an alternative, and we did not" (quoted in Gruber 2000, 166).

The SMP and Discrimination against U.S. Exports

In the early 1980s, U.S. exporters had little reason for concern about discrimination in Europe. Since the first enlargement in the early 1970s, European countries had made little progress in advancing European integration, whether by deepening or by widening the existing agreement. In this situation, U.S. exports to the EC doubled between 1977 and 1980 (Gianaris 1991, 115), but the following appreciation of the dollar made sure that U.S. exports to all markets—including the

EC—stagnated in the first half of the 1980s. European trade policies only became more discriminatory once the EC member countries started to implement the SMP. Already in 1983, the governments of the EC members had agreed on a Solemn Declaration on European Union that demanded the creation of a single market to improve the competitiveness of European companies (see Moravcsik 1998, 314–78). The objective was to establish an area in which capital, goods, persons, and services could freely circulate. At that time, frontier formalities and legal trade restrictions such as technical standards, freight-transport regulations, state subsidies, and public-procurement policies still hindered the movement of goods and services within the EC.

In 1985 the EC Commission published a white paper entitled "Completing the Internal Market" that contained some three hundred proposals for the abolition of these remaining barriers to trade in the EC. The proposals envisaged the elimination of physical (border formalities, quotas), technical (standards, public procurement rules), and fiscal (taxation) barriers within the EC. Starting in 1987, and gathering speed in 1988 and 1989, the EC implemented the recommendations of the white paper with the aim of establishing a single market in Europe by 31 December 1992. The removal of some of the existing barriers required agreement on common regulations, or at least minimum and maximum margins, that would apply to all EC members. The completion of the SMP, for example, entailed a tighter competition policy and stricter subsidy rules within the EC. With regard to standards, both mutual recognition and harmonization were used to eliminate their trade-restraining consequences. Furthermore, the SMP demanded that the remaining quantitative restrictions on extra-EC imports sustained at the member-state level had to be abolished. This concerned the quotas maintained under article 115 of the Treaty of Rome, which allowed for the limitation of third-country imports to specific countries despite these goods already circulating within the EC, and bilateral voluntary export restraints agreed on with third countries. The member countries had the possibility of simply abolishing these restrictions, which mainly affected textile and automobile imports, or to extend them to the EC level by finding EC-wide regulations.

The implementation of the SMP had the potential to hurt exporters in excluded countries through two channels. On the one hand, by increasing the preferences that producers from within the EC enjoyed vis-à-vis exporters from third countries, the single market could intensify trade diversion (Balassa 1989, 311). Indeed, one study found that trade diversion resulting from the SMP would reduce imports from third countries by 2.2 percent (Venables 1991, 60). In some industries imports from the rest of the world could drop by up to 8.5 percent. More recent studies also come to the conclusion that the SMP led to a decline in EC imports from third countries (Soloaga and Winters 2001,

19). On the other hand, there was the possibility that the restructuring process required by the SMP would increase protectionist pressures within the EC member countries (Kreinin 1991, 65; Nedergaard 1993, 59). This could lead to the imposition of novel restrictions at the EC level. The SMP was also expected to have some positive consequences for exporters from third countries, however. Most important, the SMP would lead to the removal of some barriers to imports from third countries. The harmonization of standards, moreover, could make it easier for them to supply all EC markets. Finally, higher growth rates in the EC could stimulate imports from third countries. In fact, some studies suggest that on average non-EU producers may have gained from the SMP (European Commission 1997; Buigues and Martinez-Mongay 1999).

For the United States, these potential consequences of the SMP were of major importance, since, by 1987, 24 percent of U.S. exports went to the EC (see table 6.1), as compared to 11 percent that went to Japan. U.S. exports to the EC amounted to nearly $60 billion in the same year, and mainly consisted of aircraft, data-processing equipment, electronics components, machinery, organic chemicals, and transport equipment. Some 10 percent of total U.S. exports to the EC were in the agricultural sector, including oilseeds and feedstuffs in particular (Woolcock 1991, 8). The United States also exported $17 billion of services to the EC in 1987 (29 percent of total U.S. service exports). With U.S. exporters thus having a major stake in the EC, the SMP had the potential to impose considerable costs on them.

Four features of the SMP were particularly threatening for U.S. exporters: the demand for reciprocity in the service sector, new rules of origin in some

Table 6.1 U.S. trade with the EC, 1980–1990 (in billion dollars and percent)

	EXPORTS TO THE EC	PERCENT OF TOTAL	IMPORTS FROM THE EC	PERCENT OF TOTAL	BALANCE
1980	52.5	26.2	38.0	15.8	14.5
1981	50.0	23.5	43.6	16.8	6.4
1982	50.8	24.1	46.4	18.3	4.4
1983	47.4	23.8	47.8	17.8	−0.4
1984	49.0	22.7	63.0	18.6	−14.0
1985	48.1	22.7	71.3	19.9	−23.2
1986	52.1	24.6	78.7	20.6	−26.0
1987	59.4	23.5	84.6	20.0	−25.2
1988	74.8	23.2	84.9	19.2	−10.3
1989	87.0	23.8	85.1	18.0	1.5
1990	98.0	24.9	91.9	18.5	6.2

Sources: Data 1980–87 from Gianaris (1991, 115); data 1988–90 from Schott (1998, 39).

sectors, the harmonization of standards and certification, and public procurement rules.[1] First, with regard to reciprocity in the service sector, the Second Banking Directive created a single banking license (a "single passport") for European banks, allowing them to operate throughout the EC and to provide a wide range of financial services. Of concern to U.S. banks, the draft directive that was published in 1988 included a clause that asked for reciprocity from third countries before third-country banks could avail themselves of the single passport. While the directive was not very precise with regard to the reciprocity provision, it was interpreted as demanding mirror rather than solely national treatment. In the United States, the McFadden Act (1927) prohibited interstate branching and thus restricted access to the national market for all banks, European as well as American. In addition, the Glass-Steagall Act (1933) limited the range of financial services that a bank could provide in the United States, and the International Banking Act of 1978 extended these restrictions to non-U.S. banks. The liberalization of the EC banking sector thus made banking regulations in Europe significantly more liberal than in the United States. Consequently, if the EC had insisted on mirror treatment, the United States would have had to liberalize its own financial market to maintain its access to the European market. The fact that initially it was not clear in which other sectors the EC would apply a reciprocity provision aggravated this issue even further.

A second area of concern was the inclusion of rules of origin in some of the directives linked to the SMP. This mainly affected computer chips and the broadcasting sector. With regard to computer chips, in 1988 a European directive stated that only chips that were diffused in Europe would be considered to be of EC origin. Diffusion is the most complex process in the manufacturing of a chip, thus imposing difficulties for American producers who before had assembled (but not diffused) their chips in Europe to avoid the EC's 14 percent tariff on chips (Kreinin 1991, 64). With regard to the broadcasting sector, the October 1989 broadcasting directive demanded that broadcasters reserve transmission time for European works. The provision stated that, "where practicable," a majority of programs (excluding news, sports, and game shows) had to be European, and foreign films (and series) should be limited to less than 50 percent of the market (Calingaert 1996, 155).

On standards and certification, the third issue of contention, it appeared possible that the process of harmonizing standards across Europe would put American companies at a disadvantage. In addition, it was not clear whether the agreements that the United States had with individual member states about the mutual recognition of certification would be extended to the EC level. Another

---

1. See, for example, Calingaert (1988); Balassa (1989); U.S. International Trade Commission (1989); Hufbauer (1990); Cooney (1991); Venables (1991).

uncertainty was whether U.S. companies could continue to get their products certified in the United States, or whether they would have to do this in the EC. The move toward standardization across Europe thus had the potential to impose major costs on U.S. exporters.

Finally, new rules for public procurement also could be used to discriminate against American companies. In 1987 the European Commission published a "green paper," an informal discussion paper, on the telecommunications sector, which formulated the objective of deregulating national markets but restricted the opening of procurement policies to EC suppliers (Graham 1991, 189). Later, the same principle was applied to other sectors, such as energy, transport, and water. The draft directives for these sectors foresaw a 50 percent EC-content rule and a 3 percent price preference for EC companies (Woolcock 1991, 78; Hocking and Smith 1997, 154). Since for many products research and development are extremely important, such a content provision can be difficult to satisfy even for foreign companies with production facilities in Europe.

Several aspects of the SMP thus had the potential to discriminate against U.S. exporters. The SMP, however, was not the only contentious European trade policy at that time. The accession of Spain and Portugal to the EC in 1986 endangered U.S. agricultural exports of fruits and vegetables to the old member states of the EC (Sarris 1983). By extending the CAP to these countries, the enlargement also hurt U.S. exporters of grains to Spain and Portugal (Yannopoulos 1988). According to one estimate, the U.S. faced losses of grain exports to Spain as high as $400 million a year (*Time,* 9 February 1987). Overall, the expectation was that the United States could lose $900 million in agricultural exports to Portugal and Spain (*Washington Post,* 18 March 1986, E1). Furthermore, the accession of these two countries to the EC imposed some trade diversionary costs on U.S. exporters of manufactured goods (Glejser and Moro 1996). Beyond southern enlargement, the strengthening of preferential ties with the EFTA countries that resulted from the plans for a European Economic Area (EEA) was also expected to lead to some trade diversion. The EEA, which was signed in 1992 and entered into force in 1994, extended the SMP's objectives of free movement of capital, goods, people, and services to the six remaining members of the European Free Trade Association. By widening the zone of preferential trading, the EEA created the opportunity for the EC to export Fortress Europe to the EFTA countries.

The Mobilization of U.S. Exporters in the 1980s

Based on this discussion, the expectation derived from Hypothesis 1 of the protection-for-exporters argument is that U.S. exporters should have remained largely absent from the political process until the mid-1980s. Agricultural interests should have mobilized against the EC's southern enlargement around 1985–86, and then service providers and some manufacturing interests in response to the SMP in the years 1987–88. This expectation is largely borne out by the available evidence. Nevertheless, the relatively high level of political activity of exporting interests in the early to mid-1980s, in the absence of a threat to their foreign market access, is surprising from the perspective of the protection-for-exporters argument. In 1986 broad trade associations such as the American Association of Exporters and Importers, the Business Roundtable, the Emergency Committee for American Trade, the National Association of Manufacturers, and the National Foreign Trade Council supported the start of a new multilateral trade round in the framework of the GATT.[2] At the sectoral level, financial services providers demanded the liberalization of trade in services in the ensuing Uruguay round (Freeman 1998). This lobbying effort indicates that by that time a series of export interests had managed to become proactive in their lobbying effort.

A mobilization against losses, as expected by the protection-for-exporters argument, is observable in the agricultural sector. Agricultural interests engaged in a major lobbying effort to push the U.S. administration to protect their market access in Spain and Portugal after EC enlargement (Odell 1993, 241–43). The National Grange, for example, asked for the protection of farmers' interests in the face of the negative impact of the accession of these two countries to the EC on U.S. agricultural exports.[3] Equally, the American Soybean Association engaged in a major lobbying effort as it feared that enlargement would lead to restrictions on U.S. soybean exports (*Washington Post*, 18 March 1986, E1). Once the U.S. government threatened with retaliation against the EC's trade policies, it showed itself "pleased" with the government's actions (*Agra Europe*, 4 April 1986, 2).

The SMP and U.S. Exporters

The response by U.S. exporters to the implementation of the SMP from the mid-1980s on is also in line with Hypothesis 1. One of the first trade associations to show some disconcert was the Business Roundtable that, in 1987, warned of the possibility that the EC could become inward oriented owing to the SMP.[4]

---

2. U.S. Congress, March–April 1986, Hearings before the House Committee on Ways and Means, Subcommittee on Trade, *Trade Reform Legislation*.

3. Ibid., 281.

4. U.S. Congress, February 1987, Hearings before the House Committee on Ways and Means, *Comprehensive Trade Legislation*, 217.

In the following year, the issue experienced a boom in public attention, and many U.S. exporters expressed their alarm about the consequences of the internal market for their business interests. A statement by the European Commission indicating that the SMP would mainly profit European business interests was particularly important in triggering this boom. The *New York Times* (23 October 1988, III:1), therefore, under the title "The Growing Fear of Fortress Europe," wrote: "[Exporters from third countries] fear that as Europe tears down its internal barriers to form a single, unified market of 320 million people, it might erect higher protective walls to keep competitors out." For a while, the issue was so salient in the United States that even firms in sectors that were not or only slightly affected by the EC-92 program used the opportunity to direct attention to their long-standing trade conflicts with the EC. Boeing, for example, took advantage of the issue to repeat its complaints about subsidies for Airbus.

Nevertheless, many exporters were genuinely concerned about the effects of the SMP and, therefore, mobilized to avoid the possible negative consequences. The first action of most major trade associations in response to these concerns was to set up task forces studying the consequences of EC-1992. After these task forces produced their reports, associations such as the Business Roundtable, the National Association of Manufacturers, the U.S. Chamber of Commerce, and the U.S. Council for International Business welcomed the general objectives of the SMP, but criticized a series of features that were likely to harm U.S. exporters. This led to a more specific debate, during which only sectors that felt directly affected by one of these issues continued the lobbying effort.

In the manufacturing sector of the U.S. economy, the semiconductor industry, represented by the American Electronics Association and the Semiconductor Industry Association, heavily lobbied the U.S. government to avert the imposition of rules of origin in the EC for computer chips.[5] The industry also pushed U.S. negotiators to insist on an elimination of EC tariffs on this product during the Uruguay round of trade talks (*New York Times,* 29 November 1990, D1). At the same time, however, firms in this sector engaged in foreign direct investment in the EC to safeguard their access to this market. The automobile and electrical industries were active in publicizing the issue of standard setting in the EC. The Motor and Equipment Manufacturers Association voiced concern that the "harmonization of European Community Industrial Standards and of their testing may well facilitate internal EC trade but could discourage imports

---

5. U.S. Congress, 20 March 1989, Hearings before the House Committee on Ways and Means, Subcommittee on Trade, *Europe 1992*.

from non-member countries such as the United States."[6] In addition, the health industry and electrical manufacturers feared the possible negative effects of protectionist standards.[7] Finally, producers of telecommunications equipment stressed the changes in European procurement policies resulting from the SMP. At the same time as they lobbied the U.S. government to protect their market access in Europe, they also strove to avoid discrimination by other means. In 1989, for example, AT&T, as the main exporter of telecommunication products from the United States, set up a joint venture with Italtel to respond to this challenge (Graham 1991, 190).

In the services sector of the U.S. economy, banks and other financial institutions such as American Express lobbied their government to engage in negotiations with the EC to avoid being disadvantaged in that market.[8] The American banks, however, were also eager to use this issue to influence U.S. policymaking more broadly, since they were eager to achieve repeal of the Glass-Steagall Act, with the aim of extending their services to the insurance sector (Hocking and Smith 1997, 87). Finally, the U.S. film industry, which made about two-thirds of its total foreign sales in the EC, mobilized against the EC's rules of origin in the broadcasting sector. Especially the Motion Picture Association of America lobbied the administration with the aim of averting the implementation of the broadcasting directive (*Financial Times,* 1 August 1989, 2).

In short, as expected by the protection-for-exporters argument, the mobilization of exporters was strongest in the sectors that anticipated negative consequences from the implementation of the SMP. This mobilization in response to the deepening of European integration continued until late 1989 (*Journal of Commerce,* 30 November 1989, 1). By this date, interest started to fade because a vigorous U.S. reaction led to a resolution of most of the issues early on. Nevertheless, some exporters persisted in expressing their fears about the establishment of a Fortress Europe, and as late as 1990, the U.S. International Trade Commission perceived concerns, especially among service providers such as insurance companies and television show producers (*Wall Street Journal,* 17 April 1990, 19).

Even within the sectors affected by the SMP, however, a marked difference existed between smaller companies that exported from the United States and U.S. firms with European subsidiaries (*Economist,* 13 May 1989, 92; Woolcock

---

6. U.S. Congress, February–May 1989, Hearings before the House Committee on Foreign Affairs, Subcommittee on Europe and the Middle East, *Europe 1992,* 55.

7. Ibid.

8. U.S. Congress, 20 March 1989, Hearings before the House Committee on Ways and Means, Subcommittee on Trade, *Europe 1992.*

1991, 13; Calingaert 1996, 204). For one, U.S. multinationals, whose sales in Europe were six times higher than direct exports from the United States to the EC, consistently drew attention to the gains they could derive from the SMP (Hocking and Smith 1997, 88). Realizing that their subsidiaries in Europe were well placed to serve the whole market of the EC, they expected to be among the main winners of the SMP, and thus they welcomed the reduction of internal barriers. Some U.S. companies with production facilities in more than one EC member country also expected to be able to rationalize their investments in the EC by concentrating production within one EC member country. The *Financial Times* (8 May 1989, 3) thus concluded: "Many U.S. businessmen have told the administration that, while they have a number of specific concerns, they see great opportunities within an enlarged market with fewer internal regulations."

Second, U.S. companies with subsidiaries in the EC could rely on their own contacts in Europe to influence the various provisions of the SMP. The EC Committee of the American Chamber of Commerce in Brussels, which included well-known companies such as American Express, AT&T, Caterpillar, Coca-Cola, General Electric, General Motors, IBM, Intel, Texaco, and Texas Instruments, sharply increased its lobbying activities in Brussels in the wake of the SMP (Cowles 1996, 348–49). In addition, the United States Industry Coordinating Group's exclusive purpose was to influence policymaking in Brussels. A final difference between exporters and companies with subsidiaries in the EC was that some of the latter supported higher European barriers to imports. General Motors and Ford, in particular, concentrated on maintaining their market share in the EC vis-à-vis rising Japanese imports (Graham 1991, 198).[9] The fact that Japanese companies (Honda, Nissan, and Toyota) with production facilities in the U.S. tried to export cars manufactured in the United States to the EC complicated the situation. Ford and General Motors, therefore, had to compete with these Japanese companies for influence on the position of the U.S. government.[10]

The Persistence of Import-Competing Interests

Protectionist interests—in particular from the automobile, steel, and textile and apparel industries, organized in the Trade Reform Action Coalition—remained

---

9. This runs counter to Milner's (1988) hypothesis that multinational companies should be more free trade oriented than other companies.

10. The question was whether the EC would consider the cars produced in the United States by Japanese subsidiaries as Japanese cars, and thus limit their importation, or as American cars. The U.S. administration was in doubt as to whether it should push for an opening of the EC market for Japanese cars manufactured in the United States, or rather protect the subsidiaries of General Motors and Ford that produced inside the EC.

vocal (Cohen 1994, 138–39), casting doubt on arguments predicting their disappearance as a result of the process of liberalization (Bailey, Goldstein, and Weingast 1997). In response to the trade deficit that the United States incurred at that time, they asked for "fair" rather than free trade (Nollen and Quinn 1994). The Labor-Industry Coalition for International Trade, representing import-competing companies such as Motorola and National Steel and labor unions, even introduced its own—highly protectionist—version of a trade bill in 1985. In the view of at least one author, consequently, the import-competing camp appeared "to span a broader array of interests" at that time than had been the case since World War II (Nivola 1986, 599). The protectionist lobbying effort by the Labor-Industry Coalition for International Trade and by textile manufacturers continued throughout the Uruguay round (*New York Times,* 29 November 1990, D1).

In short, the mobilization of U.S. agricultural interests in response to the southern enlargement of the EC, and the increase in lobbying activity among American exporters with interests in the European market in response to the SMP, support Hypothesis 1 of the protection-for-exporters argument. Although some major U.S. multinationals were little concerned about the impact of the SMP, exporters as the potential victims of Fortress Europe reacted with a major lobbying effort. (For an overview of the composition of the exporter group at that time, see table 6.2.) Lacking other appropriate means to influence decision making in the EC more directly, they supported intergovernmental contacts to defend their cause. Support for the protection-for-exporters argument is, in this instance, diminished by U.S. exporters' high level of political activity in the mid-1980s, however. An—admittedly ad hoc—explanation for this deviant observation is that the institutionalization of exporter groups as a result of the earlier lobbying efforts during the 1960s and 1970s allowed them to overcome some of the problems that generally inhibit proactive lobbying.

U.S. Trade Politics in the 1980s

Did the balance of domestic interests influence U.S. trade policies, as expected by Hypothesis 2? Several observations suggest a positive response to this question. As discussed above, the trade deficit incurred by the United States from the early 1980s onward intensified protectionist demands. One response to these pressures was the negotiation of voluntary export restraints, a feature of the so-called new protectionism. In October 1982, for example, the United States negotiated a voluntary export restraint with the EC for steel. The trade legislation

Table 6.2   U.S. exporter lobbying in the 1980s (selection)

TYPE OF LOBBY	NAME
General business associations	National Association of Manufacturers
	U.S. Chamber of Commerce
	U.S. Council of the International Chamber of Commerce
Exporter lobbies	American Association of Exporters and Importers
	Business Roundtable
	Committee for a National Trade Policy
	Emergency Committee for American Trade
	National Foreign Trade Council
	U.S. Council for International Business
Sectoral associations	American Electronics Association
	Computer and Business Equipment Manufacturers Association
	Computer and Communications Industry Association
	Health Industry Manufacturers Association
	International Intellectual Property Alliance
	Motion Picture Association of America
	Semiconductor Industry Association
Individual companies	American Express
	AT&T
	Hewlett-Packard
	IBM
	Motorola
	Texas Instruments
Agricultural interests	American Farm Bureau Federation
	American Soybean Association
	National Grange

that passed Congress in 1984 also took account of protectionist pressures when strengthening the trade-remedy statutes and providing relief for steel producers (although the relevant provision was nonbinding for the administration). In the following year, the salience of the trade issue further increased, pressuring President Ronald Reagan to announce a comprehensive action plan to reduce the U.S. trade deficit in September. This plan, among other measures, proposed the increased use of Section 301 of the Trade Act of 1974, which allowed retaliation against countries that use unfair trade practices to bring down foreign barriers. While intended to appease domestic interests, the plan was subject to being superseded by a 1986 protectionist House bill that, if enacted, would have made it easier for firms to qualify for import relief (Shoch 2001, 108). The measure did not come to a vote in the Senate, however.

In this heated climate, Congress and the administration were very receptive to complaints by agricultural exporters about losses incurred as a result of the accession of Spain and Portugal to the EC (Odell 1993). In early 1986, the U.S. administration threatened to impose retaliatory duties for white wines, gin, brandy, cheese, endives, and other products if the EC failed to compensate the United States for the negative consequences of the extension of the Common Agricultural Policy to these two countries. When announcing U.S. measures, President Reagan declared that the United States could not "allow the American farmer, once again, to pay the price for the European Community's enlargement" (quoted in *Agra Europe,* 11 April 1986, 3). The menace was backed up by a Senate concurrent resolution asking for retaliation in the absence of full compensation. After initially threatening with counterretaliation (*Agra Europe,* 4 April 1986, 1–3), then agreeing on a truce with the United States, the EC finally agreed to partly compensate the United States for its loss of market access in February 1987, and thus averted a trade war.

The U.S. administration, however, also engaged in two liberalizing initiatives at that time. On the one hand, in February 1984 it started negotiations with Canada concerning a bilateral free trade agreement. On the other hand, in 1985 it agreed with other GATT contracting parties on the start of a new multilateral round of trade negotiations. As suggested above, some support for these initiatives was forthcoming from U.S. exporters. Nevertheless, in the absence of a fully fledged exporter mobilization as in the early 1960s and early 1970s, an explanation of these initiatives is likely incomplete without consideration of decision makers implementing trade policies following their preferences.

Reacting to the SMP

As the Uruguay round hardly made any progress in the following years, another trade issue was able to dominate transatlantic trade relations, namely the U.S. reaction to the SMP. The mobilization of U.S. exporters in opposition to the expected negative consequences of the SMP put substantial pressure on U.S. decision makers to deal with this issue. As the *Economist* (8 July 1989, 20) wrote: "American businessmen became alert first, then parts of Washington's bureaucracy and then Congress." From 1987 on, both Congress and the administration closely observed European steps toward establishing the internal market, and in more than one case they demanded changes in European directives.

Initially, exporter lobbying in response to the SMP had an impact on the trade legislation that was discussed in Congress at that time. From 1986 on,

Democratic members of Congress, in particular, tried to pass a fairly protectionist trade bill, which among other features included an amendment that would have imposed a 25 percent surcharge on imports from countries that had a large bilateral trade surplus with the United States and where U.S. exports faced unfair barriers (Schwab 1994, 69). After a first version of the bill was vetoed by President Reagan because of a section granting workers sixty days' notice before plant closings or layoffs, Congress enacted a slightly changed bill, called the Omnibus Trade and Competitiveness Act, in August 1988. The legislation renewed the presidential fast-track authority, which had expired in 1987, strengthened the unilateral trade instruments, and moved the authority to initiate Section 301 cases from the president to the United States trade representative (USTR), thus making the use of this instrument more probable.[11] A new section, commonly called Super 301, requested the USTR to identify trade liberalization priorities and countries that should be asked to reduce trade barriers.

One link between the SMP and the Omnibus Trade and Competitiveness Act resulted from U.S. exporters' complaints about the European Commission's 1987 green paper on the telecommunications sector. As discussed, this green paper raised the prospect of the EC establishing preferences concerning public procurement in that sector. In response to exporters' concerns, Congress instituted a review mechanism for foreign compliance with the procurement code signed at the end of the Tokyo round. If a signatory of the code did not comply with its provisions, it would face a 6 percent disadvantage concerning public procurement in the United States.[12] In addition, Section 1374 of the act concerned telecommunication products and services and demanded the completion of negotiations with third countries concerning this sector within eighteen months. If a foreign country was not willing to give in, it was confronted with the threat of being excluded from all government procurement bids in the United States. The EC was named as priority entity for negotiations in this sector in January 1989.

After the passage of the Omnibus Trade and Competitiveness Act, Congress continued monitoring the SMP, with several committees asking for studies on the subject and holding oversight hearings with regard to EC-92.[13] In one of

---

11. The office of the USTR was created in 1979, building on the position of special representative for trade negotiations that had been established by the TEA of 1962.

12. The Buy America Act of 1933 established a 6 percent preference for U.S. companies in federal purchases. Under the 1979 Trade Agreements Act, however, the U.S. president could waive this provision for countries that had signed the public procurement code agreed on in the Tokyo round.

13. See, for example, U.S. Congress, 18 November 1988, Hearings before the Joint Economic Committee, *Europe, 1992;* U.S. Congress, February–May 1989, Hearings before the House Committee on Foreign Affairs, Subcommittee on Europe and the Middle East, *Europe 1992;* U.S. Congress, 20 February 1990, Hearings before the House Committee on Foreign Affairs, Subcommittee on International Economic Policy and Trade, *Europe 1992.*

these hearings, USTR Carla Hills threatened that the United States would not accept the establishment of new barriers at the EC level: "Our position is that the 1992 package cannot be an excuse for new external trade barriers, and we have repeatedly made known our intention to challenge any new barriers in the GATT should they be introduced by the Community."[14] The Senate set up a task force on EC-92, comprising some thirty senators, to act as a point of access for industry interests. Moreover, it passed a resolution that called on the president to establish a bicontinental dialogue to discuss the implications of European integration. On the issue of rules of origin in the broadcasting services, Congress passed a resolution condemning the broadcasting directive.

The U.S. administration's reaction to the SMP entailed the setting up, in February 1988, of an interagency task force focusing on the external effects of this move toward deeper integration in Europe. This task force, under the coordination of the USTR, included representatives from various departments and agencies, such as the Departments of State, Agriculture, and Commerce, the Council of Economic Advisers, and the National Security Council (Hocking and Smith 1997, 60). Members of the administration also publicly voiced their concerns about European trade policies. In a speech in August 1988, for example, the deputy treasury secretary M. Peter McPherson showed distress about the possibility of discrimination, the extension of voluntary export restraints from the member-state level to the European level, the EC's internal preoccupation that made it unable to negotiate in the GATT, and the request for reciprocity as a price to gain access to the single market. McPherson affirmed that the United States could not accept further discrimination resulting from deeper European integration: "We would find unacceptable measures that would limit market access for third countries and discriminate against foreign companies already established in the Community" (quoted in *National Journal*, 29 October 1988, 2729).

Whereas in early 1988 there was a lot of talk about a "Fortress Europe," soon the assessment became more nuanced. By mid-1988 most decision makers accepted that only a few issues were of real concern for U.S. exporters. USTR Hills described the resulting U.S. stance toward the SMP as "optimism tempered with vigilance" (quoted in the *Economist*, 8 July 1989, 20). In line with this assessment, the administration concentrated its efforts on resolving the issues that were of particular concern to U.S. exporters rather than trying to oppose the SMP as such. Each of these issues required a different response, but in general the position of the United States was characterized by the use of a wide range of

---

14. U.S. Congress, 10 May 1989, Hearings before the Senate Committee on Finance, *Europe-92 Trade Program*.

instruments in response to perceived discriminatory measures by the EC. Illustratively, the United States employed threats of retaliation with respect to reciprocity in financial services and public procurement, and offered concessions in the Uruguay round to avoid discrimination as a result of the EC's moves toward standardization.

Explaining the Choice of Strategy

The choice of strategy in response to discrimination in Europe was discussed in great depth in Congress and the administration. Again, there were calls to use multilateral trade negotiations to reduce discrimination. The former deputy assistant secretary of state for international finance and development Sidney Weintraub (1986, 366), for example, suggested: "This may be a propitious moment for a round of trade negotiations having as one objective tariff-free industrial trade among the leading industrial countries. This would…remove the effects of discrimination in the trade of all [countries excluded from the EC] with Western Europe." Others, such as Representative Richard Gephardt, a major figure in trade policy debates in Congress in the 1980s and a contender for the Democratic presidential nomination in 1988, even proposed the creation of an "economic NATO" (*Washington Post,* 13 October 1988, C3), that is, the establishment of some kind of transatlantic preferential trade agreement.

Nevertheless, in the end advocates of a strategy of prying open foreign markets prevailed. Explanations for this choice of strategy abound. Some authors in the line of the hegemonic stability theory argue that the United States adopted a more mercantilist strategy because its power started to wane in the 1970s and 1980s (Gilpin 1987). As a weaker power, according to this view, the United States no longer had an incentive to pay the price for the public good of an open-and-stable trading system. The perception of a weakening of American hegemony may also have influenced trade-policy choices by giving rise to a "diminished giant syndrome" in the United States (Bhagwati 1988). According to this argument, psychological factors push a hegemon in decline to respond to the rise of rival powers with protectionism and fair trade policies. Common to both of these explanations is that they start from the assumption of a fundamental shift in U.S. trade policies, away from more liberal policies pursued in earlier years.

The protection-for-exporters argument, by contrast, sees the policies implemented in the 1980s as a continuation of earlier policies aimed at the protection of exporters' foreign market access. Only the strategies chosen to achieve this objective were different, a shift explained by changes in trade flows that lowered U.S. vulnerability in its relations with the EC (Hypothesis 3). Three factors converged in producing this outcome. First, and most important, changes in trade patterns reduced American reliance on European markets and thus opened up the possibility for the United States to pursue a "rival agreement" strategy in response to European discrimination.[15] Realizing this opportunity, early on President Reagan asserted that in the absence of progress in multilateral negotiations, his administration would pursue regional and bilateral agreements.[16] The *Financial Times* (17 November 1988, Survey:3), consequently, suggested that "the U.S. disposition to view Europe as its most natural economic ally seems to be diminishing." In fact, the United States concluded a free trade agreement with Israel in 1985, which was explicitly portrayed as a reaction to the preferential agreement the EC had signed with that country in 1975 (Aminoff 1991, 15). The U.S. share of total Israeli imports had declined from 35 percent in 1950 to 16 percent in 1987, partly as a result of European exporters' preferential access to that market. In February 1984, moreover, the United States started talks with Canada, which led to the establishment of a U.S.-Canadian free trade agreement in 1989.

Second, the United States incurred a substantial trade deficit with the EC between 1983 and 1988 ($25 billion, or 18 percent of total transatlantic trade, in 1987; see table 6.1 above) and thus could make retaliation credible. The deputy secretary of state John C. Whitehead, consequently, claimed: "I believe that our policy of keeping the European markets open will be successful because we have some potent retaliation ability" (quoted in the *National Journal*, 29 October 1988, 2729). Finally, the early realization that the threats emanating from the SMP were not as serious as initially believed strengthened the American position. Together, these factors allowed the United States to follow a more aggressive strategy in response to foreign discrimination. The U.S. pursuit of fair trade policies, therefore, rather than reflecting a revival of fair trade ideas (Goldstein 1993, 176–80), may simply have resulted from changes in trade flows. The European position should, however, have improved in the late 1980s, as U.S. exports to the EC grew at a staggering rate of 25 percent in 1988, leading to the disappearance of the EC's trade surplus with the United States in 1989.

In short, the protection-for-exporters argument could shed light on a series of major developments in U.S. trade politics in the 1980s. Domestic interests continued to have a major influence on policy outcomes, as witnessed both with respect to import-competing pressures in the early to mid-1980s and the U.S.

---

15. The share of U.S. exports going to Europe had fallen by 6 percent between 1970 and 1988, from 34.3 percent to 28.4 percent (calculated from data in Carter et al., 2005, table 5–538).

16. *Europe Documents,* no. 1372, 27 September 1985, 4.

response to the SMP in the late 1980s. The protection-for-exporters argument also provides a plausible explanation for the changed U.S. strategy in response to discrimination abroad.

European Trade Policies in the 1980s

How did these American trade policies interact with European ones? In the early 1980s, just as in the United States, import-competing interests dominated EC trade policymaking, demanding limits on imports from Japan and other emerging economies of goods such as automobiles, color televisions, steel, textiles, and videocassette recorders. Mostly, decision makers satisfied these pressures with voluntary export restraint agreements negotiated by individual member states with exporting countries (Schuknecht 1992). Protectionist trade policies were not the only response to the rise of competitive pressures, however. There was also a drive to reestablish the competitiveness of European goods by deepening European integration. Large parts of the European private sector supported a step toward eliminating barriers to intra-European trade, with the hope that this would boost European competitiveness worldwide (Sandholtz and Zysman 1989, 116–17; Moravcsik 1998, 318). The implementation of the Single Market Programme was partly a response to these pressures.[17]

In addition, in 1985 the EC agreed to participate in the Uruguay round of world trade negotiations. It remains unclear why the EC changed its position on this issue after having rejected the start of a new round in 1982. Few economic interests outside of the service sector actively supported new trade negotiations in Europe, while substantial opposition existed, especially among agricultural interests. The most plausible explanation is that the EC felt strong enough to avoid the imposition of costs on import-competing interests in such a round. In fact, very early it became clear that developing countries in particular would have to make concessions on issues such as intellectual property rights, trade-related investment measures, and trade in services. With respect to agriculture, the agreement reached at the beginning of the round gave equal weight to the EC objective of bringing "more discipline and predictability" to agricultural trade and to agricultural exporters' goal of liberalizing trade

---

17. An extensive literature discusses the relative importance of leadership by the European Commission and pressures by domestic and transnational economic interests for the launch of the SMP. While the present account favors the role of interest groups, it cannot resolve the debate between the two opposing positions.

in that sector.[18] While the protection-for-exporters argument has little to say about these developments, it can explain some further developments in the Uruguay round.

The Foreign Reaction to the SMP and European Trade Policies

The SMP, and the foreign reaction to it, had two distinct effects on European trade policies: boosting protectionist pressures and raising demands for foreign concessions. On the one hand, the single market required the abolition of some national barriers to imports, both from within and from without the EC. This led to more intensive competitive pressures, attempts at restructuring, and a rapid increase in mergers. In this situation, some EC firms—although supporting intra-European liberalization—hoped for an increase of protection accompanying the SMP to ease their adjustment process. One demand voiced was that the benefits of the SMP "should be reserved first and foremost to European firms" (a representative of Elf Aquitaine, quoted in Calingaert 1988, 93). The textile industry lobbied for a slowdown of the move from national to an EC-wide quota to avoid increased pressures from imports. The electronics industry also asked for protectionist measures at the level of the EC, including antidumping rules, rules of origin, and standards (*National Journal*, 13 May 1989, 1180).

Similarly, the European automobile industry, with the exception of the German producers, took a protectionist position. The chairman of Fiat, Umberto Agnelli, declared that "the single market must first offer an advantage to European companies," before these benefits could be extended to foreign competitors (quoted in Calingaert 1988, 93). The chairman of Peugeot, Jacques Calvet, was actually calling for import barriers when he declared that Europe should "develop a trade policy based not on outdated notions or old habits of free trade or protectionism but on modern realities and reciprocity" (quoted in the *New York Times*, 30 April 1989, III:1). In particular, European car producers pushed for a limit on car imports from Japan, by replacing existing national quotas with a Community-wide voluntary export restraint (*New York Times*, 23 October 1988, III:1; Mason 1994). As the SMP also attracted Japanese investments in Europe, the French car industry even tried to obtain limits on Japanese cars produced in Europe. Raymond Levy, the chairman of Renault, for example, called for the limitation of imports to France of Japanese cars produced in Great Britain,

---

18. The ministerial declaration launching the Uruguay round can be found at http://www.sice.oas.org/trade/Punta_e.asp (accessed 1 April 2009).

unless they reached a minimum local content of 80 percent (*Financial Times,* 29 September 1988, 6).

On the other hand, the concerns voiced by U.S. exporters and the U.S. administration had an influence on European trade policies by raising hopes that the EC would be able to use the discrimination created by the SMP to gain concessions abroad. Already in 1985 the Commission white paper had stated that trading partners should "not be given the benefit of a wider market without themselves making similar concessions" (Commission of the European Communities 1985, 8). In line with this statement, in December 1988 the heads of the main European employers' associations agreed on a charter in support of the SMP, which included a demand for "equality and reciprocity" in GATT trade negotiations (*Financial Times,* 14 December 1988, 2). Similarly, the Dutch company Philips, together with other European technology firms, such as AEG, Alcatel, Siemens, and Thomson, which were organized in a "Group of 12," maintained that access to the European procurement market for foreign telecommunications companies should be tied to reciprocal concessions (Hufbauer 1990, 36n69).

Nevertheless, the vulnerability of the EC trading position to potential U.S. retaliation did not escape the European exporting interests. The Federation of German Industry, for example, feared that the imposition of Community-wide voluntary export restraints could stimulate retaliation from the EC's major trading partners (Bundesverband der Deutschen Industrie 1989). Due to the export dependence of German industry, but also industry in other EC countries, such retaliation was to be avoided. In fact, already in the 1986–87 trade conflict over Spanish and Portuguese accession to the EC, the U.S. threat with retaliatory duties had been perceived as very credible in Europe (Odell 1993, 243). In that earlier trade-policy episode, European export interests threatened by American retaliatory duties lobbied European governments to give in to U.S. demands.

The EC's vulnerability was a result of the trade surplus that it had with the United States in the mid-1980s. In addition, the United States was the largest export market for the EC, with EC exports to the United States significantly increasing over these years (Cooney 1991, 108). In some sectors, such as chemicals, instruments, nonelectrical machinery, and pharmaceuticals, EC exports accounted for up to 40 percent of total U.S. imports (Hine 1985, 234). Also German producers of luxury cars, such as Mercedes and Porsche, were heavily dependent on continued access to the American market. In this situation, as put by the CEO of an American company, "a European-initiated duty war would be suicidal" (quoted in the *Wall Street Journal,* 11 September 1989, A18).

The European perception of vulnerability was further reinforced by the U.S. initiative to establish a Canada-U.S. free trade agreement, starting in 1984. In effect, U.S. decision makers openly alluded to the possibility of using talks for preferential agreements as bargaining chip in negotiations with the EC (*New York Times,* 4 December 1990, D7; Feinberg 2003, 1024). During the U.S.-Canada free trade agreement negotiations, for example, USTR Clayton Yeutter stated:

> There is a bit of leverage here, in that it indicates to the rest of the world that we, the United States, can make progress in opening up borders and confronting trade barriers either bilaterally or multilaterally. Our preference is the multilateral route…but if the multilateral route should prove fruitless for any one of a variety of reasons, this certainly indicates that we are prepared to pursue these basic objectives on a bilateral basis should that become essential. (quoted in Fishlow and Haggard 1992, 20)

In 1989, moreover, the establishment of APEC that involved the U.S. and several Pacific countries created fears in Europe that the United States was moving away from its transatlantic orientation (*Wall Street Journal,* 12 July 1989, A14; Luyten 1989, 275–76). The June 1990 launch of the Enterprise for the Americas initiative by President George Bush, which aimed at regional integration in the Americas, further reinforced these worries.

As a result, the range of trade policies that the EC could pursue was heavily constrained. William de Clercq, commissioner for external trade relations, stressed that for Europe it was not feasible to turn protectionist: "When you're the biggest exporter in the world, you don't turn protectionist. That would be shooting yourself in the foot" (quoted in the *New York Times,* 23 October 1988, III:1). Nevertheless, he insisted on the aim of achieving reciprocal trade agreements. In a speech in July 1988, he stated: "We shall be ready and willing to negotiate reciprocal concessions with third countries, preferably in [a] multilateral context but also bilaterally. We want to open our borders, but on the basis of a mutual balance of advantages in the Gatt" (quoted in the *Financial Times,* 14 July 1988, 4). In the same speech, he suggested that the single market might give the EC "the negotiating leverage to obtain a worldwide liberalisation of markets" (quoted in Henderson 1989, 11).

The European Commission also stressed the importance of international trade for the EC, and promised that the EC would fulfill its GATT obligations (Commission of the European Communities 1988). In the same spirit, the European Council in Hanover in July 1988 agreed on a common declaration that tried to reduce the fears existing among excluded countries. It called for negotiations with third countries to guarantee access to the single market. The declaration, however, remained ambiguous since it also stressed the necessity to preserve the internal market's identity. In December 1988 the declaration of the European Council in Rhodes stated that the single market would "not close in on itself": "1992 Europe will be a partner and not a 'fortress Europe'. The internal market will be a decisive factor contributing to greater liberalization in international trade on the basis of the GATT principles of reciprocal and mutually advantageous arrangements" (European Council 1988).

Issue-Specific Solutions

Apart from these general statements, the European reaction differed from one issue to the next. Concerning banking, France and Italy initially demanded that reciprocal treatment should signify identical rather than only national treatment. France even wanted to limit the rights of existing European subsidiaries of U.S. banks if the United States did not grant identical treatment (*New York Times*, 10 February 1989, IV:2). These demands were based on a hope for concessions in the U.S. market. As stated by an observer, "The movement towards a single EC banking market provides the EC with considerable leverage to seek changes in the more restrictive U.S. financial services market" (Ahearn 1992, 189). In the end, however, facing stern U.S. criticism, the EC largely gave in on this issue. Early on, the European side conceded that it would not apply the reciprocity provision retroactively to U.S. banks already established in the EC, and offered to negotiate a bilateral agreement (Calingaert 1988, 88–89). Moreover, in April 1989, Sir Leon Brittan, then EC commissioner for competition policy, announced that the final Second Banking Directive would include a national treatment test, thus making clear that there would be no requirement for mirror legislation. The Council of Ministers approved this decision when adopting the Second Banking Directive on 15 December 1989. The European side made it explicit that, since EC banks received national treatment in the United States, U.S. banks would receive national treatment in the EC. Although several observers saw good chances for successfully pressuring the United States into changing its banking provisions (Golembe and Holland 1990, 93), recognizing its own vulnerability in the case of a trade conflict with the United States, the EC thus decided not to push the case for mirror legislation.[19]

---

19. It did not back down completely, however. The Commission was charged with drawing up periodic reports on the treatment that EC banks received abroad. If EC banks faced major barriers in another country, the final legislation retained the possibility for some punitive action. Soon after, moreover, the United States relaxed its domestic legislation: it allowed interstate banking in late 1994 (Riegle-Neal Act) and banks to offer investment and insurance services in 1999 (Gramm-Leach-Bliley Act).

With respect to the harmonization of standards, in January 1989, the U.S. secretary of commerce Robert Mosbacher asked to have a "seat at the table" of EC standard setting. The EC rejected this request and, instead, tried to convince the United States to accept international standard setting. International standard-setting bodies were (and still are) largely controlled by the EC, since the EFTA and the central and eastern European countries adopt most EC standards. Together, these countries have many more voices in the standard-setting bodies than the United States, and consequently substantial influence over their decisions. This gives EC producers a major advantage in international standard setting. The EC hoped to use the leverage gained by international standard setting to get some control over the decentralized process of standard setting in the United States, where many standards are not set at the federal but at the state level. In the end, the United States and the EC found an agreement on standardization in the Uruguay round. The resulting Agreement on Technical Barriers to Trade outlines transparency and national treatment as major objectives in standard setting, but it also calls for international standard setting in such agencies as the International Electrotechnical Commission, the International Standards Organization, and the International Telecommunications Union.

In the context of the SMP, the EC also decided to regulate procurement policies in the member countries. The resulting directives required public authorities to follow specific procedures when advertising and awarding contracts above a certain threshold level. The EC members, however, disagreed over the extent to which they should open public procurement to international competition. The German and British governments wanted liberal provisions, whereas the governments of France and Italy supported the inclusion of preferences for European producers and providers. Initially, it seemed as if third-country bidders would face discrimination in all areas of public procurement. In the end, however, the preference and local-content provisions only applied to the Utilities Directive that regulated public procurement for energy, telecommunications, transport, and water. Article 29 of the directive determined that EC producers would receive a 3 percent price preference and that contracting authorities could exclude offers with less than 50 percent European content.

The German government, however, was concerned that the EC-content provision could hurt its industry, as German electronics products included a large share of foreign components. Therefore, the EC member countries agreed that the clause would be used as a bargaining chip in the Uruguay round negotiations. The EC offer was to drop it if the United States agreed to abolish its own preferential-procurement legislation both at the federal and at the state level. The United States, by contrast, demanded the inclusion in any international agreement of entities, which, although not owned by governments, benefited from special rights, a demand that would have affected many entities, especially in the EC (Woolcock 1991, 88). In February 1992, with the two positions still far apart and the implementation of the directives pending, the U.S. government threatened to impose sanctions if the Utilities Directive entered into force without changes. It was not until a year later that the two sides could agree on a memorandum of understanding. The compromise was that the EC would not apply the reciprocity clause with regard to electrical equipment. The United States, in turn, would eliminate discrimination against EC bids in relation to federally owned electrical utilities. The United States still imposed sanctions in the telecommunications sector, and the EC retaliated. Although the two parties were able to reach an agreement on procurement rules in the Uruguay round, the issue was not completely resolved, and negotiations in the telecommunications sector continued until the late 1990s.

Alternative Explanations

In the 1980s, the EC thus had only limited success in using foreign concerns about discrimination to gain concessions abroad. It was weakest between 1985 and 1987, when it made unilateral concessions with respect to the consequences of southern enlargement. Its position improved slightly in the late 1980s, when it achieved some U.S. concessions with respect to the issues of standard setting and public procurement. In this view, Fortress Europe did not materialize because the EC recognized its vulnerability to foreign retaliation, and because it managed to get some concessions in exchange for guaranteeing market access. This argument runs counter to two prominent explanations for the same developments. Kerry Chase (2005), for one, suggests that companies benefiting from economies of scale after the creation of a larger market may start to lobby for external trade liberalization. When discussing the case of the SMP, however, his evidence suggests that practically all sectors demanded protectionist policies. In view of this evidence, he explains the persistence of relatively liberal policies after the implementation of the SMP with foreign direct investments that made protectionism ineffective, as well as factors that are exogenous to his theoretical framework such as poor organization of economic interests.

Brian Hanson (1998) argues that institutional rules that require supermajorities for the imposition of trade barriers at the European level made the achievement of Fortress Europe impossible. Again, this argument falls short of providing a completely comprehensive account. For one, if Hanson's analysis of a strong status quo bias were correct, the EC should have moved in neither a liberal nor a protectionist direction but simply retained its existing policies. As has been demonstrated above, however, the member states of the EC agreed on some steps toward liberalizing their external trade relations. Hanson's interpretation also has difficulty accounting for the fact that in some cases the EC reached agreement on a common stance, but then was forced to abandon this stance because of strong U.S. pressure. Finally, concerning some issues, Japan and the United States received differential treatment. As put by John Conybeare (1993, 153), the SMP measures were "crafted so as to impose most of the burden on Japan and to avoid angering the United States." Since the same institutional rules apply to negotiations with both countries, such differential treatment is inconsistent with Hanson's institutionalist argument. By contrast, the protection-for-exporters argument, with its emphasis on the degree of vulnerability, can explain this differential treatment, as Japan had a major trade surplus with the EC at that time and thus was less capable of using threat in response to European trade measures.

In conclusion, despite hopes that "the establishment of a powerful European trading bloc may well give the EC greater clout to exert pressure for reform of various aspects of the U.S. legal and regulatory structures" (Ahearn 1992, 189), in the end the EC largely had to concede to American pressures. On most of the controversial issues, the EC backtracked in the face of U.S. opposition. This observation explains why, in the end, the Fortress Europe outcome—which had been predicted by many observers in 1987 and 1988—was avoided.

In this chapter I have outlined the interaction between U.S. and European trade policies in the 1980s. The main argument has been that the deepening and widening of European integration in that decade created fears among American exporters, which in turn made the U.S. government pursue policies to protect exporter interests. The U.S. response to European preferential policies included various strategies, from threats to bilateral deals to negotiations in the GATT. This broad range of strategies was a result of the relatively low degree of vulnerability of the United States in these years, which resulted from changes in trade flows that lowered U.S. exporters' dependence on the European market. The analysis of the response of the EC to the U.S. initiatives has provided further illustration of this argument. The EC's reaction was again shaped by the attempt to make use of the external impact of intra-European integration to gain concessions in the U.S. market. Nevertheless, the strength of the American position, and the recognition that the European threat to establish a Fortress Europe was not credible, undermined the European strategy and made the EC adopt an accommodating stance.

COMPETITION BETWEEN THE EUROPEAN UNION AND THE UNITED STATES FOR MARKETS, 1995–2010

Transatlantic trade relations in the 1990s and early 2000s were characterized by competition over access to the markets of emerging countries. Initially, it was mainly the EU that partly reacted to and partly anticipated U.S. initiatives when concluding preferential trade agreements with a series of countries in Latin America and Africa. At the same time, the U.S. Congress failed to pass trade legislation, making William J. Clinton the first American president since the introduction of fast-track legislation in 1974 who never managed to obtain fast-track authority. Congress finally passed a trade bill in 2002, which was immediately used by the U.S. administration under George W. Bush to pursue preferential trade agreements. In parallel, the EU pushed for the start of a new trade round, called the Doha Development Agenda (2001 onward).

Several explanations have been provided for these developments. On the U.S. side, an influential argument stresses the role of party politics in shaping trade policymaking (Shoch 2001). From the 1980s on, according to this account, trade increasingly became an issue of party competition. The leadership of the Democratic Party, as the minority party in the House of Representatives between 1995 and 2006, used the trade issue to mobilize its electorate, in particular organized labor, which opposed further trade liberalization. In this view, only after unified government was in place in 2001 did a Republican-controlled Congress delegate trade authority to a Republican president. Other observers draw attention to the end of the cold war, which supposedly reduced the utility of the multilateral trading system for the only remaining hegemon (Schwok 1991; Kerremans 1999). They suggest that in the absence of an obvious challenger, the United

States became free to follow predatory policies, allowing Congress to block the delegation of trade-negotiating authority to the president for a considerable period.

On the European side, importance has been given to the EU's pursuit of geopolitical interests in concluding preferential trade agreements with emerging economies (Sapir 1998, 726–27; Messerlin 2001, 226; Maur 2005, 1578). Since the EU's foreign policy instruments are weak, EU member states may employ the more developed Common Commercial Policy to achieve foreign policy aims. For example, preferential trade agreements may serve to balance the influence of the United States in Latin America and other regions of the world. The EU may also use trade agreements to stabilize adjacent regions, such as the Balkans and the Mediterranean. Alternatively, the European Commission's bureaucratic interest may drive the EU's foreign trade policies (Woll 2008). The Commission may gain in status within the EU's institutional framework as it engages in an increasing number of foreign trade negotiations, especially since these negotiations tend to cover a broad array of topics. It therefore has an incentive to lure member states into the negotiation of preferential trade agreements with emerging economies.

All of these explanations have the potential to clarify some important aspects of the puzzle at hand. Nevertheless, the variables stressed by these studies fall short of providing a comprehensive view of transatlantic trade relations from the mid-1990s into the first decade of the twenty-first century. On the U.S. side, for example, the party politics approach correctly predicts party struggles over trade policy, but has little to say about the American pursuit of preferential agreements. The geopolitical argument can explain the turn toward preferential agreements, but it fails to account well for the contents of Congressional debates when passing trade legislation. Similarly, for European trade policies, the bureaucratic interest explanation is weak in explaining the choice of specific partners for preferential agreements. The foreign policy argument, by contrast, fails to offer a reason why from the late 1990s until about 2006 the European focus shifted to multilateral negotiations in the WTO. In short, there is space for a novel interpretation of these various developments.

The protection-for-exporters argument can provide such an interpretation. In accordance with this argument, I propose that U.S. exporters mobilized when they felt the negative consequences of the EU's (and other countries') pursuit of bilateral trade agreements. The spread of preferential trade agreements excluding the United States incited American exporters to push Congress to delegate authority to the president. I demonstrate that both the timing of the mobilization of exporters and the contents of the statements they made support this argument. In 2002 Congress acceded to the demands voiced by exporters and passed the Trade Act of 2002, claiming that this bill was necessary to protect

U.S. exporters from the negative consequences of the trade policies of foreign countries. The ensuing American trade policies interacted heavily with European trade policies: while on some occasions the Europeans felt excluded from the preferential agreements concluded by the United States, in other cases European trade policies created fears of exclusion in the United States. At the same time, the spread of discriminatory trade agreements across the world convinced European societal interests and decision makers that European exporters' foreign market access was best protected by way of a multilateral agreement in the WTO.

Before examining the plausibility of this argument, it is important to stress that in the period covered in this chapter, even more strongly than in the case of the 1980s, transatlantic trade relations have been heavily influenced by developments in the international trading system more generally. U.S. exporters have mobilized, not only in response to the preferential trade agreements signed by the EU (and vice versa for European exporters), but also in response to the general proliferation of preferential trade agreements across the globe. Moreover, the choice of strategy by the United States and the EU has been partly shaped by the increasing clout of emerging countries in WTO negotiations, which has contributed to the stalemate of multilateral negotiations. With the rise of emerging countries having made the world more complex, current U.S. and EU trade policies are exposed to often contradictory influences, making it more difficult to examine the protection-for-exporters argument. The greater complexity, however, is by itself confirmation of the argument, which is built on the premise that a country's trade policies cannot be studied in isolation from the trade policies of other countries.

Threats to U.S. Exporters' Foreign Market Access in the 1990s and 2000s

Did U.S. exporters face a threat to their foreign market access in the 1990s? Initially, American exporters had little reason for concern. The conclusion of the Uruguay round led to a worldwide liberalization of trade barriers. The only major discriminatory trade initiative undertaken by the EU at that time was the conclusion of the Europe agreements with ten central and eastern European countries, which entered into force beginning in 1994. The agreements, however, had little impact on U.S. exports, because European exporters already dominated these markets. Neither did the exports of the central and eastern European countries to the EU compete with U.S. exports, especially because certain sensitive products were excluded from the agreements. The situation changed in the late 1990s and early 2000s, however, when the EU started to negotiate a series of preferential agreements with emerging economies. In early 2009, the EU was party to free trade agreements (FTAs) or customs unions in all areas of the world other than Asia, and was in the course of negotiating a number of additional agreements (see table 7.1). Among the existing agreements, the ones with the Mediterranean countries, Chile, and South Africa were most likely to threaten U.S. exports.

The EU's agreements with Mediterranean countries were largely a response to their demand for additional ties with Europe in the aftermath of the closer integration within Europe resulting from the single market programme (Sapir 1998, 726). The EU concluded association agreements with Algeria, Egypt, Israel, Jordan, Lebanon, Morocco, the Palestinian Authority, Syria, and Tunisia. While

Table 7.1   The EU's network of preferential trade agreements, 2009

EUROPE	MEDITERRANEAN	AMERICAS	AFRICA/ASIA
Customs unions with Andorra (1990) and San Marino (1991)	Customs union with Turkey (1995)	Free trade agreements (FTAs) with Chile (2002) and Mexico (2000)	FTA with South Africa (1999)
EEA (1992; Iceland, Liechtenstein, Norway)	Association agreement with Israel (1995)	Economic partnership agreement with the Caribbean countries (2008)	FTA negotiations with ASEAN (since 2007), the Gulf Cooperation Council (since 2002), India and South Korea (both since 2007)
FTAs with Albania (2006), Bosnia and Herzegovina (2008), Croatia (2001), the Faroe Islands (1996), the former Yugoslav Republic of Macedonia (2001), Montenegro (2007) and Switzerland (1972)	Euro-Mediterranean agreements with Algeria (2002), Egypt (2001), Jordan (1997), Lebanon (2002), Morocco (1996), the Palestinian Authority (1997), Syria (2004), and Tunisia (1995)	FTA negotiations with the Andean Community (since 2007), Canada (since 2009), Central America (since 2007), and Mercosur (since 1999)	Interim economic partnership agreements with a series of African and Pacific countries (2008)

Note: Years in parentheses refer to the year of signing. Some of these agreements were preceded by earlier agreements. The agreements with South Africa and Syria were concluded but have not yet been signed. The one with South Africa is being provisionally applied. Trade with Syria is still regulated by an agreement from 1977.

in the past the EU granted one-way preferences to most of the Mediterranean countries, the new agreements introduced reciprocity, thus ensuring that the EU could export tariff-free to these countries. The effect of these agreements on U.S. exporters was notable, especially because countries such as Egypt, Jordan, Morocco, and Tunisia had unweighted average tariffs of around 30 percent in the 1990s (Pelkmans and Brenton 1999, 106). The agreements, however, hardly led to trade diversion in the EU's market, where the Mediterranean countries have enjoyed preferential access since the 1970s.

In the Western Hemisphere, the EU signed free trade agreements with Mexico (2000) and Chile (2002). While U.S. exporters already benefited from preferential access to Mexico, the EU-Chile agreement had the potential to impose some costs on U.S. exporters. Although Chilean tariffs were on average quite low (a uniform 6 percent tariff across all products in 2003), the fact that the EU and the United States exported similar goods to Chile made some trade diversion probable. Indeed, the United States had nearly the same share of Chilean imports in 2000 as the EU, namely 19.7 percent compared to 19 percent (Schiff 2002, 975), but lost significantly in 2003, after the EU concluded its preferential agreement with Chile. The EU has also been engaging in negotiations with the Mercado Común del Sur (Mercosur), which integrates South America's major economies. For the United States, a future EU agreement with Mercosur would be quite threatening since the exports of the EU and the United States are highly competitive in this market. In 1995 the export shares of the United States and the EU in major sectors were practically the same (Thorstensen and Peña 1999, 242). In addition, the average MFN tariff of Mercosur remains very high. A preferential EU-Mercosur agreement would thus impose considerable costs on U.S. exporters. The pending conclusion of a free trade agreement between the EU and the Andean Community (Comunidad Andina, comprising Bolivia, Colombia, Ecuador, and Peru) will not cause losses for U.S. exporters, as the United States signed its own agreements with these countries.

Furthermore, the EU concluded a trade, development, and co-operation agreement with South Africa in 1999, which will establish bilateral free trade by 2012. The trade-related aspects of the agreement provisionally entered into force in 2000, although ratification of the agreement is still pending. The agreement has the potential to introduce substantial discrimination in favor of the EU as a result of South Africa's high MFN tariffs. Nevertheless, initially the agreement has scarcely boosted EU exports to South Africa. This may be a result of the features of the agreement that allow South Africa to make most of its liberalizing moves late in the twelve-year transition period.

Finally, a series of further initiatives may impose some costs on U.S. exporters. The EU is in the process of transforming the formerly nonreciprocal preferential agreements with the African, Caribbean, and Pacific (ACP) countries under the Cotonou Partnership Agreement into reciprocal economic partnership agreements. In Asia the EU is engaging in negotiations with the Gulf Cooperation Council, India, and South Korea for the establishment of free trade arrangements. The completion of the agreement with South Korea was imminent in early 2009. In 2007, moreover, the EU started negotiations for a free trade agreement with the ten member countries of the Association of South East Asian Nations (ASEAN).

In short, U.S. exporters faced several new preferential agreements concluded by the EU with emerging markets in Latin American and the Mediterranean. These agreements not only threatened trade in goods but, owing to the broad agenda of some of the agreements, also trade in services. In addition, the investment provisions included in many agreements may offer European competitors privileged access to these emerging markets. Finally, the export of standards from the EU to the partner countries may put U.S. exporters at a disadvantage. The expectation derived from this discussion is that U.S. exporters should have mobilized in response to these preferential trade policies. The spread of preferential trade agreements among other countries, especially in Asia, which has accelerated since about 2000, should have further intensified this mobilization.

The Mobilization of U.S. Exporters

In the mid-1990s, in the wake of the NAFTA agreement, U.S. exporters reduced their lobbying effort. Only a few leaders of associations demanded additional bilateral agreements to gain preferential access to some important markets. Among them, in 1995, the chairman of the National Foreign Trade Council defended an extension of NAFTA to include Chile by directly alluding to the benefits of trade diversion:

> By obligating Chile to eliminate its current 11 percent duty on manufactured goods, the United States has an opportunity to not only gain better market access in Chile, but preferential market access....That means companies like Caterpillar will be able to sell virtually their entire product lines in Chile duty free, while our European and Japanese competitors will continue to be subject to Chile's high tariffs.[1]

Nevertheless, as an EU free trade agreement with Chile was still considered highly improbable at that time, this lobbying effort by exporters remained weak

---

1. U.S. Congress, 11 May 1995, Hearings before the House Committee on Ways and Means, *Fast Track Issues,* 84.

and was clearly overshadowed by strong lobbying from labor unions for import protection.

From 1997 on, the preferential liberalization of trade within Mercosur and the EU's involvement in Latin America slightly increased concerns among U.S. exporters (*Wall Street Journal,* 12 September 1997, 23). The Business Roundtable thus invested in a campaign to secure fast-track legislation in 1997 and supported the formation of a coalition of fast-track supporters called America Leads on Trade that comprised around 550 trade associations (*National Journal,* 5 July 1997, 1379; Shoch 2001, 214). As stated by a lobbyist for America Leads on Trade, however, the exporter lobbying still was not very effective: "There was generally poor coordination between lobbying groups and many companies assumed that others in the coalition would do the work" (quoted in Schnietz and Nieman 1999, 247). As a result, America Leads on Trade spent around $600,000 to $800,000 on television advertising between September and October 1997, but the labor union AFL-CIO spent at least a million dollars on its campaign opposing fast-track legislation (*National Journal,* 18 September 1997). Since the extent of discrimination that U.S. exporters faced at this time was still modest, this relatively low level of mobilization is in line with the protection-for-exporters argument.

The Exporter Lobbying Effort Takes Off

It was only in the following years, when facing growing discrimination abroad, that U.S. exporters became increasingly anxious about their foreign market access and started to lobby in defense of their interests. Most statements made to back exporters' pleas for government help concentrated on the issue of foreign discrimination. In 1999, for example, the Emergency Committee for American Trade argued that "regional preferential trade arrangements among our competitors in Europe, Latin America, and Asia have mushroomed, putting U.S. products at an increasing disadvantage."[2]

In the following years, exporter lobbying substantially increased. In 2001 the Business Roundtable spent $1 million on a campaign in favor of fast-track legislation. In that context, it published a pamphlet that argued that the United States was falling behind in negotiating preferential agreements. The pamphlet concluded: "U.S. companies, workers and farmers are being surrounded by preferential trade and investment agreements negotiated by their foreign competitors' governments. Time is running out for the United States to get back into

---

2. U.S. Congress, 11 February 1999, Hearings before the House Committee on Ways and Means, Subcommittee on Trade, *The Importance of Trade Negotiations.*

the game."[3] In 2002 the same group spent more than $500,000 on television and radio advertisements that announced: "Our foreign competitors have 190 international trade agreements that give their products and workers a better deal. These agreements are squeezing the goods and services produced by American workers out of the global marketplace....If Congress doesn't act, we will only fall further behind" (*National Journal,* 26 July 2002). The Roundtable also emphasized the common product standards and investment regulations included in preferential agreements that discriminate against U.S. firms.[4] While supporting a new trade round within the WTO, this business association mainly pushed for various bilateral trade agreements with, among others, Chile, Morocco, and the members of the South African customs union, countries with which the EU also negotiated or had concluded free trade agreements.

A second major actor in the exporter camp was the U.S. Chamber of Commerce. It aired a radio spot in which it clearly alluded to the need for protection of exporters: "Other countries have the flexibility to negotiate trade agreements that cut barriers and tariffs—giving their businesses a big advantage. The U.S. is, well, sitting on the sidelines watching other countries make those deals" (*National Journal,* 7 November 2001). Congress, according to the Chamber of Commerce, had to pass trade legislation to change this situation. In hearings in Congress, the representative of the Chamber of Commerce made a similar statement: "Only 11 percent of the world's exports are covered by U.S. free trade agreements, compared with 33 percent of the European Union's. I came back just last night from a four-day visit with the European Union and find them aggressively pursuing further discussions around the world."[5] The Chamber of Commerce was particularly eager to see an agreement with Chile to eliminate discrimination against U.S. exporters:

> Many of you know that Chile's free trade agreement with the European Union came into force on February 1. On that day, tariffs on nearly 92% of Chilean imports from the EU were eliminated. Consequently, it is not surprising to note that Chilean imports from the EU expanded by 30% in the year ending in February 2003, whereas Chilean imports from the United States grew by less than 6%. Chilean imports from Germany grew by 47% and those from France grew by 41% in the same period.[6]

---

3. "The Case for U.S. Trade Leadership: The United States Is Falling Behind," 2001, available at http://web.archive.org/web/20021030045704/http://www.brtable.org/pdf/498.pdf (accessed 1 April 2009).

4. U.S. Congress, 29 March 2001, Hearings before the House Committee on Ways and Means, Subcommittee for Trade, *Free Trade Deals,* 22.

5. Ibid.

6. U.S. Congress, 10 June 2003, Hearings before the House Committee on Ways and Means, Subcommittee on Trade, *Implementation of U.S. Bilateral Free Trade Agreements.*

Several other business groups also came out in favor of trade-negotiating authority—by that time called trade promotion authority—and organized such activities as telephone and letter campaigns (*National Journal,* 28 July 2001). Together with the Business Roundtable and the Chamber of Commerce, they launched a coalition to push for trade-negotiating authority called USTrade. Again, these groups showed similar concerns. The representative of the National Association of Manufacturers, for example, warned that the tariff preferences that the EU received in its agreements would "put U.S. companies at a disadvantage."[7] The association was particularly concerned about the EU's agreements in South America:

> There is a real urgency to negotiating the FTAA [Free Trade Area of the Americas], for the European Union (EU) is also negotiating free trade agreements with key South American countries. This is no trivial matter, for the European Union currently sells about as much to South America as we do. The consequences for U.S. exports would be severe if the EU were to obtain duty-free access to these markets while U.S. exports continued to face duties that could be 20 or 30 percent. A huge shift away from U.S. products to European products would result.[8]

In 2003 it published a detailed analysis of the export losses that U.S. exporters faced in the Chilean market, putting major pressure on Congress to approve the U.S. agreement with that country.[9]

Equally, before the Senate Committee on Finance, the representative of the Emergency Committee for American Trade argued:

> Free trade agreements with preferential rules that exclude the United States have sprung up throughout Latin America and in Europe and elsewhere. U.S. exporters are severely disadvantaged because their products are now subject to higher relative tariffs and other barriers, which their competitors' governments have been able to negotiate away.[10]

In response to this challenge, the association called for both a new WTO trade round and further preferential trade agreements. Moreover, the Council of the

---

7. U.S. Congress, 29 March 2001, Hearings before the House Committee on Ways and Means, Subcommittee for Trade, *Free Trade Deals.*

8. U.S. Congress, 8 May 2001, Hearings before the House Committee on Ways and Means, Subcommittee on Trade, *Outcome of Summit of the Americas and Prospects for Free Trade in the Hemisphere.*

9. "Absence of Chilean Trade Agreement Costing U.S. over $1 Billion per Year," 2003, available at http://www.nam.org/s_nam/bin.asp?CID=201738&DID=225837&DOC=FILE.PDF (accessed 1 April 2009).

10. U.S. Congress, 20–21 June 2001, Hearings before the Senate Committee on Finance, *Trade Promotion Authority.*

Americas, an organization for companies doing business in Latin America, stated: "There are real costs to the United States when our hemispheric trading partners conclude trade agreements without our participation."[11] The National Foreign Trade Council lobbied for an agreement with Morocco, arguing that it was needed to reestablish a level playing field for U.S. exporters after the creation of the EU-Morocco free trade agreement.[12] Finally, the Brazil-U.S. Business Council maintained that the negotiations between Mercosur and Europe over a free trade agreement increased the need for a Free Trade Area of the Americas (FTAA) that had been proposed in 1994 with the aim of establishing free trade among thirty-four countries of the Western Hemisphere.[13]

By the late 1990s and early 2000s a large number of sectoral associations also supported the granting of trade authority to the president. The U.S. High-Tech Coalition on Trade Promotion Authority, for example, invested in pushing for fast-track legislation (*National Journal,* 8 April 2002). Its major initiatives were CEO visits to members of Congress, news releases, and letters. The American Forest and Paper Association complained about discrimination in the markets of South America due to Mercosur and the preferential trade agreement that Canada had concluded with Chile granting it preferential access to this important market.[14] The National Electrical Manufacturers Association supported global as well as regional initiatives toward trade liberalization. The Business Software Alliance and the Entertainment Industry Coalition for Free Trade, including among many other members the Motion Picture Association of America, Time Warner, Universal Studios, and the Walt Disney Company, supported the conclusion of free trade agreements with Chile and Singapore.[15] With regard to individual firms, the chairman of Purafil, a manufacturer of air-purification systems, complained about the possible negative effects of the EU-Egypt association agreement and the EU–South Africa agreement.[16] In Egypt, he argued, his products faced a 13 percent tariff, while after implementation of the EU-Egypt free trade agreement European producers would enjoy tariff-free entry.

---

11. U.S. Congress, 29 March 2001, Hearings before the House Committee on Ways and Means, Subcommittee for Trade, *Free Trade Deals.*

12. "U.S.-Morocco FTA Coalition, Letter to Robert B. Zoellick," 2003, available at http://www.nftc.org/default/021803%20Zoellick%20ltr1.pdf (accessed 1 April 2009).

13. U.S. Congress, 7 February 2002, Hearings before the House Committee on Ways and Means, *President Bush's Trade Agenda for 2002,* 85.

14. U.S. Congress, 7 March 2001, Hearings before the House Committee on Ways and Means, *President Bush's Trade Agenda,* 51–53.

15. U.S. Congress, 10 June 2003, Hearings before the House Committee on Ways and Means, Subcommittee on Trade, *Implementation of U.S. Bilateral Free Trade Agreements.*

16. U.S. Congress, 29 March 2001, Hearings before the House Committee on Ways and Means, Subcommittee for Trade, *Free Trade Deals.*

Import-Competing Lobbying

While most of the opposition to further trade liberalization came from labor unions and environmentalists, a few business groups engaged in protectionist lobbying throughout the late 1990s and early 2000s.[17] One of the more important of these was the U.S. Business and Industry Council, which represented small manufacturing and textile companies in its campaign to stop the passage of trade legislation (*National Journal,* 28 February 2002). Some import-competing companies—such as the glassware producer Corning and Milacron, which focused on plastics technology—also used the Labor-Industry Coalition for International Trade to get their voices heard. This coalition sponsored trade legislation in 1997 that would have allowed the administration to impose sanctions against countries that keep their markets closed. In addition, the steel industry, led by companies such as Bethlehem Steel (which ended up being dissolved in 2003), lobbied for protection and opposed the passage of new trade legislation. Finally, a series of smaller manufacturing companies also came out in favor of protectionist policies (*Financial Times,* 1 February 2005, 10).

Most important, however, a variety of agricultural interests opposed trade promotion authority and later tried to block the passage of bills implementing bilateral trade agreements with Australia and the Central American countries. The Florida Fruit and Vegetable Association, for example, strongly opposed the plans for the Free Trade Area of the Americas. The growers of fruits, vegetables, and sugar mobilized so heavily in response to the Central American free trade agreement, which the United States and five Central American countries signed in 2003, that they made the American Farm Bureau release a statement opposing further trade agreements that worked to the detriment of American farmers (*Financial Times,* 16 January 2004, 4). This episode also reveals the weakness of exporting interests in the U.S. farm sector in the period covered in this chapter: a weakness that the protection-for-exporters argument explains with reference to the fact that U.S. agricultural exporters faced little threat to their foreign market access as a result of the discriminatory trade policies pursued by different countries at the time (Vollrath 1998). Only the enlargement of the EU, which was costly for some U.S. agricultural interests, should have motivated agricultural exporters to become politically active. Indeed, this was the case: the National Pork Producers Council, for example, complained about the agreements between

---

17. Among the labor unions and environmental groups that opposed further trade liberalization were the Communications Workers of America, Friends of the Earth, the Sierra Club, and the United Steelworkers. Many of them joined the Citizens Trade Campaign, which was created in 1992 to lobby for changes to the NAFTA agreement and which continues to oppose U.S. trade agreements concluded with countries such as Colombia and South Korea.

Table 7.2 U.S. exporter lobbying in the 1990s and 2000s (selection)

TYPE OF LOBBY	NAME
General business associations	Business Roundtable
	National Association of Manufacturers
	U.S. Chamber of Commerce
	U.S. Council of the International Chamber of Commerce
Exporter lobbies	America Leads on Trade
	Emergency Committee for American Trade
	National Foreign Trade Council
	U.S. Council for International Business
	USTrade
Sectoral associations	Advanced Medical Technology Association
	American Forest and Paper Association
	Business Software Alliance
	Chemical Manufacturers Association
	Coalition of Service Industries
	Information Technology Industry Council
	National Electrical Manufacturers Association
	Society of the Plastics Industry
Individual companies	Boeing
	Caterpillar
	General Electric
	Monsanto (chemicals)
	Purafil (air-purification systems)
	Warner Lambert (pharmaceuticals)
Agricultural interests	American Farm Bureau Federation
	Chiquita Brands International
	National Pork Producers Council
	U.S. Dairy Export Council

the EU and the central and eastern European countries, in which the two sides granted each other duty-free quotas for specific agricultural products.[18]

This discussion, even if only a rough overview of the lobbying activity in the 1990s and early 2000s, has several implications. On the one hand, it provides substantial support for Hypothesis 1 of the protection-for-exporters argument. The analysis revealed that exporter lobbying became stronger in response to increasing foreign discrimination. (See table 7.2 for a summary of exporter

---

18. U.S. Congress, 29 March 2001, Hearings before the House Committee on Ways and Means, Subcommittee for Trade, *Free Trade Deals.*

lobbying.) The contents of the statements made by exporters indicate that foreign discrimination really was a cause of this increased lobbying activity. What the protection-for-exporters argument fails to explain, however, is the strong lobbying effort by labor unions and environmentalists, groups that would be expected to suffer from collective-action problems. On the other hand, some observations cast doubt on alternative theories of interest-group activity. In particular, the continued lobbying by import-competing industries indicates that trade liberalization, at least as practiced by the United States over the last decades, does not necessarily undermine future protectionist lobbying (Hathaway 1998). Neither was there particularly strong exporter lobbying in the mid-1990s, suggesting the need to revise the explanations focusing solely on reciprocal trade agreements as the basis for the empowering of exporters (Gilligan 1997a). Exporters become politically active mostly to forestall losses, and only rarely to achieve gains.

The Pursuit of Preferential Trade Agreements by the United States

The conclusion of the Uruguay round, the establishment of NAFTA, and the Bogor Declaration (1994) calling for free trade in the Pacific region by 2020 indicate that President Clinton started his presidency with an impressive trade agenda. The Clinton administration tried to build on the momentum created by these initiatives and advance with plans for the Free Trade Area of the Americas, a scheme that was partly a response to fears voiced by Latin American and Caribbean countries about trade diversion resulting from NAFTA. At the Summit of the Americas in Miami in December 1994, the United States and thirty-three countries of the Western Hemisphere agreed to establish a regional free trade area by 2005. The administration's plans were short-lived however, as Congress failed to renew the president's fast-track authority that had expired in 1994. USTR Mickey Kantor wanted to include the renewal of fast-track legislation in the bill implementing the results of the Uruguay round. As the proposed language of the legislation gave too much weight to labor and environmental issues, though, most Republican members of Congress opposed it, and the administration, fearing that the conflict could threaten the implementation of the Uruguay round agreements, removed the provision from the bill. In the absence of a major mobilization of exporters, this setback is consistent with Hypothesis 2 of the protection-for-exporters argument.

During the rest of his presidency, President Clinton failed to secure fast-track authority. The divide between Republicans, who wanted to pass a narrow trade bill, and many Democrats, who demanded the inclusion of environmental and labor issues, was difficult to bridge.[19] In 1997 Democratic members of Congress opposed a bill that was introduced by the Clinton administration, which they believed accepted too much of the language for trade legislation proposed by the Republicans (*Economist,* 27 September 1997, Special:23; Schnietz and Nieman 1999). In 1998, by contrast, the Republican Speaker of the House, Newt Gingrich, pushed for a vote on fast-track legislation without support from the Clinton administration, leading to a clear defeat for the bill. Party politics clearly played a major role in these developments (Shoch 2001). Nevertheless, party politics does not provide a sufficient explanation of U.S. trade politics at that time. In particular, if exporters had been very concerned about losses of foreign market access, they probably would have pushed representatives of both parties to reach a compromise solution, even if this implied the acceptance of labor and environmental clauses in an international agreement. Precedents for such compromises are not difficult to find in the history of U.S. trade politics.

Although failing to secure fast-track legislation, the U.S. administration still tried to conclude bilateral trade agreements over the course of these years. In 1997 Vice President Al Gore and Egyptian president Hosny Mubarak agreed to explore the possibility of establishing a U.S.-Egypt trade agreement. In July 1999, the two nations concluded the Trade and Investment Framework Agreement, which did not include any concrete steps toward trade liberalization, however. Of greater relevance, the United States and the Kingdom of Jordan entered into a free trade agreement in October 2000, which had the objective of eliminating duties and other barriers to bilateral trade in goods and services within ten years. Although the agreement included provisions for labor and environmental standards, Congress ratified it in 2001, and thus enabled its entry into force in December 2001 (demonstrating that, as suggested above, a compromise between the positions of Democrats and Republicans was indeed possible). To some extent, these agreements can be understood as a response to preferential trade agreements concluded between the EU and these two countries some years earlier. Nevertheless, geopolitics clearly also played a role (Rosen 2004).

Passing Trade Promotion Authority

When entering office in early 2001, President George W. Bush immediately pushed for the passage of fast-track legislation—or "trade promotion authority"

---

19. The Democrats' position is not astonishing considering the strong lobbying effort by environmental and labor groups; what is an anomaly from the perspective of the protection-for-exporters argument, as pointed out above, is that these groups managed to overcome collective-action problems and engage in lobbying.

as USTR Robert Zoellick called it during his confirmation hearing. As expected by the protection-for-exporters argument, the impression that the United States was lagging behind in the negotiation of trade agreements strongly influenced the resulting debate. In the hearings for a new trade bill, USTR Zoellick directly alluded to the negative consequences for American exporters of the spread of preferential trade agreements excluding the United States when he stated: "There are approximately 130 free trade agreements in the world globally, but the United States is party to only two. Our deadlock hurts American businesses, workers and farmers, and they are going to find themselves shut out of many preferential trade agreements and investment agreements negotiated by others."[20]

Similarly, President Bush proclaimed that it was important for the United States to counter foreign discrimination and to establish a level playing field by concluding preferential agreements. He stated:

> More than 150 regional free trade and customs agreements exist throughout the world; the European Union is party to 31 of them; Mexico is party to 10; the world's largest economy is party to three. While we've been marking time, our competitors have been working, and they've been signing agreements.... What we need to do is to engage in competition ourselves.[21]

Several legislators echoed this language. As put by the chairman of the House Ways and Means Subcommittee on Trade: "During the 7 years since the president's trade authority expired, America's exporters and workers have faced higher tariff differentials, and more and more discriminatory rules, unfamiliar product standards, and unnecessary threats to their investments."[22]

With labor unions and some import-competing industries engaging in a major lobbying effort, however, opposition to a new trade bill remained strong, especially in the House of Representatives. Consequently, when in December 2001 the Bipartisan Trade Promotion Authority Act passed the House of Representatives, it did so with only a one-vote margin (215:214).[23] In this instance, pressure by exporting interests was strong enough for the Bush administration to be willing to make concessions to some members of Congress to attain passage

---

20. U.S. Congress, 7 March 2001, Hearings before the House Committee on Ways and Means, *President Bush's Trade Agenda*.

21. "President Calls on Senate to Pass Trade Promotion Authority," speech held on 4 April 2002, available at http://georgewbush-whitehouse.archives.gov (accessed 1 April 2009).

22. Philip M. Crane, U.S. Congress, 29 March 2001, Hearings before the House Committee on Ways and Means, Subcommittee for Trade, *Free Trade Deals*.

23. The narrow result was also a consequence of the strongly partisan stance adopted by the then chairman of the House Committee on Ways and Means, Republican William Thomas.

of the bill. For example, the administration placated the steel industry by initiating a safeguard investigation in June 2001.[24] The objective of protecting U.S. exporters was even more present in debates in the Senate, as by that time the EU had concluded its free trade negotiations with Chile. A comfortable majority supported passage of the bill in the Senate in May 2002.

In the following House and Senate Conference on the Trade Act of 2002, the leading Republican member on the Senate Committee on Finance, Senator Chuck Grassley, again complained about the inability of the United States to penetrate foreign markets, while "other nations have engaged in preferential trade agreements to our detriment."[25] On 27 July 2002, the House of Representatives passed the conference version of the bill by a vote of 215 to 212, and in August 2002 the Senate followed suit. As was the case for the trade bills in the second half of the 1990s, the voting in the House was strongly along party lines, with Republicans voting in favor and Democrats overwhelmingly voting against the legislation. Although this voting behavior supports a party-politics argument (Shoch 2001), it is interesting to see that quite a few Republicans voted against the passage of one of the priority bills of the Bush administration, knowing that their votes could severely hurt Bush's political standing, while some Democrats supported it. This suggests that party politics alone is not sufficient for an explanation of the Trade Act of 2002.

In the debate leading up to the Trade Act of 2002, the Bush administration also stressed the importance of trade agreements for its strategy of fighting terrorism in the aftermath of the attack on the World Trade Center on September 11, 2001. USTR Zoellick, for example, argued that new trade negotiations were necessary to "counter the revulsive destructionism of terrorism" (quoted in the *Economist*, 3 November 2001). The text of the bill also mentions the importance of trade expansion for the security of the United States.[26] What was the importance of geopolitical objectives in securing passage of the trade legislation? I argue that although they had some influence on the debate, the objective of protecting U.S. exporters was more important. The perception that the United States had to pursue preferential agreements to counter the agreements concluded by other countries, mainly the EU, has persistently influenced U.S. trade policies since the late 1990s. Given the persistence of this argument for a long period, it is difficult to claim that this was no more than rhetoric. Even in an article on "countering

---

24. A more far-reaching concession that would have substantially increased support for the bill would have been stronger language with respect to labor standards and environmental protection. Beyond party politics, such a move was made difficult by the fact that developing countries had strictly opposed negotiating on these issues in the Seattle ministerial meeting of the WTO in 1999.

25. "Trade Act of 2002," press release by Senator Chuck Grassley, 23 July 2002.

26. *Congressional Record. Proceedings and Debates*, 107th Congress, 2nd session (vol. 148), PH5904.

terror with trade," USTR Zoellick actually stressed the negative consequences of foreign preferential trade agreements for the United States (*Washington Post,* 20 September 2001, A35). Moreover, the support by business lobbies for the Trade Act of 2002 outlined in the previous section is a strong indication of the importance of the motive of protecting U.S. exporters for U.S. decision makers.

Pursuing Preferential Trade Agreements

The Bush administration pledged to use the trade legislation both for the conclusion of preferential agreements and for the conduct of multilateral negotiations in the framework of the WTO. It constantly indicated that it perceived these two aims of global and regional trade liberalization, not as contradictory, but rather as complementary. Former USTR Zoellick, in particular, claimed that he defended a strategy called "competitive liberalization" that aims at increasing pressure on other countries to accept trade liberalization by concluding bilateral and regional preferential agreements. In practice, however, U.S. trade policies were hardly ever proactive. Decision makers required support from exporting interests for their policies, and such support was strongest when exporters faced a threat to their foreign market access. After the partial failure of the Doha Development Agenda in the Cancún ministerial meeting in late 2003, the United States put even more emphasis on the pursuit of preferential agreements. At this stage, the "need to counter FTAs that place U.S. commercial interests at a disadvantage" was explicitly mentioned as a factor in the selection of partners for preferential trade agreements (U.S. General Accounting Office 2004, 8). As a result of the ensuing negotiations, in early 2009 the United States had a network of preferential agreements with a substantial number of countries on nearly all continents (see table 7.3).

The first agreement concluded under the provisions of the Trade Act of 2002 was with Chile in April 2003. As Chile had negotiated bilateral agreements with Canada, the EU, Mercosur, and Mexico, the issue of trade discrimination loomed large in the rationale given for the agreement. In May 2003, assistant USTR for the Americas Regina Vargo claimed that Chile's preferential agreements with other countries cost U.S. companies around $1 billion annually in lost exports (a number previously floated by the National Association of Manufacturers), and concluded: "The United States needs an FTA with Chile to ensure that we enjoy market access, treatment, prices and protection at least as good as our competitors."[27] Similarly, President Bush affirmed: "United States workers and

---

27. Regina Vargo, U.S. Congress, 8 May 2003, Hearings before the House Committee on Energy and Commerce, Subcommittee on Commerce, Trade and Consumer Protection, *Trade in Services and E-Commerce.*

Table 7.3 The U.S. network of preferential trade agreements, 2009

AMERICAS	MIDDLE EAST	AFRICA, ASIA, AND OCEANIA
NAFTA (1988–92)	Free trade agreements (FTAs) with Bahrain (2004), Israel (1985), Jordan (2000), Morocco (2004), and Oman (2006)	FTAs with Australia (2004), Singapore (2003), and South Korea (2007)
FTAs with the Central American countries and the Dominican Republic (2004), Chile (2003), Colombia (2006), Panama (2007), and Peru (2006)	FTA negotiations with the United Arab Emirates (since 2005)	FTA negotiations with Malaysia (since 2006), the Southern African Customs Union (suspended in 2006), and Thailand (suspended in 2006)
Plans for Free Trade Agreement of the Americas (currently suspended)	Middle East Free Trade Initiative (2003)	Plans for an FTA with APEC member countries (by 2010-20)

Note: Years in parentheses refer to the year of signing. Not all of the signed agreements have entered into force.

businesses are currently at a competitive disadvantage in the Chilean market. Chile is an associate member in Mercosur and has FTAs with many other countries, including Canada, Mexico, and the 15 members of the European Union. Securing an FTA with Chile will ensure that U.S. workers and businesses will receive treatment in the Chilean market that is as good as or better than their competitors."[28] On 1 August 2003, the Senate approved the agreement, which immediately liberalized around 85 percent of the trade between the two countries, and which aims at achieving free trade before 2015. USTR Zoellick greeted the agreement saying that it "levels the playing fields" with the EU and Canada (quoted in the *New York Times,* 7 June 2003, C3).

In addition to this agreement with Chile, the U.S. administration announced the start of negotiations with five Central American countries in January 2003 (Costa Rica, El Salvador, Guatemala, Honduras, and Nicaragua). Again, this step followed earlier actions taken by the EU establishing closer trading relations with the Central American region. Between December 2003 and January 2004, the United States concluded negotiations with these countries, thereby creating the Central American Free Trade Agreement (CAFTA). In March 2004, the U.S.

---

28. "Message from the President of the United States, transmitting a draft of proposed legislation and supporting documents to implement the United States-Chile Free Trade Agreement (FTA)," 16 July 2003, available at http://www.gpo.gov/fdsys/pkg/WCPD-2003-07-21/pdf/WCPD-2003-07-21-Pg918.pdf (accessed 1 April 2009).

administration also concluded negotiations with the Dominican Republic for the latter country's accession to the CAFTA. The U.S. administration sold these free trade agreements as building blocks toward the creation of the FTAA, which would comprise thirty-four countries of the Western Hemisphere. In April 2001, a Summit of the Americas meeting of the potential FTAA member countries set deadlines of January 2005 for the conclusion of the FTAA negotiations, and of December 2005 for the entry into force of the resulting agreement. The EU's negotiations with Mercosur that started in 1999 gave particular urgency to the creation of the FTAA. Since January 2004, however, the talks have been deadlocked, as are the negotiations between the EU and Mercosur.

Outside of the Americas, the EU's conclusion of trade agreements with all Mediterranean countries and negotiations for a free trade agreement with the Gulf Cooperation Council influenced the decision by the United States to propose the creation of a U.S.–Middle East free trade agreement in 2003.[29] When the United States started negotiations with Morocco, for example, USTR Zoellick clearly stated that one of the reasons for an agreement with Morocco was the preferential access to this market that the EU had gained.[30] In southern Africa, the United States started negotiations with the five members of the Southern African Customs Union in June 2003, a move that was a response to the EU's free trade agreement with South Africa (Leith and Whalley 2004). In 2006, however, these negotiations stalled over U.S. demands to include intellectual property rights, government procurement, and investments in an agreement. The U.S. negotiations with Australia and Singapore (agreements were concluded in 2004 and 2003 respectively) were not a response to European trade policies but still linked to discrimination: both of these countries had concluded (or engaged in negotiating) a series of agreements with potential competitors of the United States.

The U.S. choice of preferential agreements in response to discrimination abroad has been legitimized by the apparent stagnation of the multilateral approach. The former USTR Zoellick, for example, declared: "As WTO members ponder the future, the U.S. will not wait: we will move towards free trade with can-do countries" (*Financial Times,* 22 September 2003, 23). Nevertheless, for two reasons this stagnation of the multilateral approach is only part of a comprehensive explanation of the U.S. pursuit of bilateral agreements. First, the United States itself partly inhibited progress in the multilateral negotiations. In the WTO ministerial meeting in Seattle in 1999, for example, it was the position of the U.S. negotiators with regard to labor and environmental clauses that impeded an

---

29. The U.S. agreements with Bahrain and Oman, in turn, caused concern among European exporters about exclusion (*AME Info,* 26 July 2007).

30. U.S. Congress, 7 February 2002, Hearings before the House Committee on Ways and Means, *President Bush's Trade Agenda for 2002,* 43.

agreement. In Cancún in 2003, the unwillingness of U.S. negotiators to concede on the issue of export subsidies to cotton farmers made an agreement more difficult (*Economist*, 20 September 2003, Special Report). Second, the multilateral approach had stagnated before (for example in the mid-1960s), but the United States had not chosen preferential trade policies at that time.

I suggest, instead, that the recent emphasis on preferential trading should be seen as a continuation of a trend started in the 1980s, which was made possible by changes in trade flows. In particular, with 37.1 percent of U.S. exports covered by NAFTA in 2000 (as compared to 28.4 percent in 1990), the United States had become less dependent on multilateral trade negotiations than in previous decades. Moreover, the United States has developed a large trade deficit, making many countries dependent on continued access to the U.S. market. Consequently, the United States accounted for a striking 18 percent of world imports in 2002 ($1,202.5 billion), but only for 10.8 percent of world exports ($693.5 billion) (World Trade Organization 2003, 68).[31] The regional concentration of exports within NAFTA combined with the trade deficit has lowered U.S. vulnerability to changes in the trade policies of foreign countries, suggesting that for the United States the pursuit of bilateral agreements has become a credible alternative to the multilateral approach (Hypothesis 3).

The EU's Position Weakened

The U.S. trade policies just outlined interacted with European trade policies in several ways. On the one hand, and as argued above, U.S. trade policies were partly a response to European ones. On the other hand, American trade policies also shaped European trade policies. What is interesting about the European strategy in this period is the preference for multilateral trade negotiations that the EU developed. The multilateral strategy was expected to have the advantage of protecting European exporters across a series of different countries without having to negotiate with all of them individually. In addition, it was the most viable strategy, as it had become clear that many potential partners for preferential agreements made liberalization in the European agricultural sector a precondition for the conclusion of a trade agreement. Concessions in the agricultural sector, in turn, were best made in broad multilateral negotiations, where the EU could get most in return. After 2005, however, deadlock in the Doha Development Agenda forced the EU to revive its preferential approach.

---

31. The percentage values include intra-EU trade. Excluding intra-EU trade, the United States accounted for nearly a quarter of world imports in 2003.

Competing for Market Access

In the early 1990s, the EU found itself in a situation in which the United States was pushing for preferential trade agreements with a series of emerging economies. Especially the establishment of NAFTA and the signing of the Bogor Declaration in November 1994 that set out the aim of achieving free trade and investment flows by 2010 for the industrial members of APEC (Australia, Canada, Japan, New Zealand, and the United States) and by 2020 for the other members caused concerns in Europe (*Wall Street Journal,* 6 May 1994, 10). The *Financial Times* (6 August 1996, 5) thus could observe "growing complaints in Brussels that European exporters have been put at a disadvantage by the North American Free Trade Agreement and fears that they will face discrimination from other emerging trade groupings, above all in Asia." In 1997 the European Commission adopted a communication in which it maintained that other countries' preferential agreements were a cause for concern (Nagarajan 1998, 5).

An initial response to U.S. preferential trade policies, at least partly driven by exporter demands (*Süddeutsche Zeitung,* 18 May 1995), was a proposal for a preferential trade agreement with the United States. In 1995 the EU commissioner for external affairs Sir Leon Brittan, the British prime minister John Major, and the German foreign minister Klaus Kinkel all spoke out in support of a North Atlantic free trade agreement (Barfield 1996, 152). In the words of one observer, the EU's fondness for these transatlantic initiatives was "also motivated in part by concern over U.S. efforts to engage in competitive liberalization of trade, i.e., working toward free trade areas in the Asia-Pacific area and in Latin America" (Calingaert 1996, 201). The threat resulting from APEC for European trading interests soon turned out to be less severe than originally imagined, however. Japan and South Korea, in particular, showed no willingness to engage in preferential liberalization as proposed by the United States, leading to a deadlock in these talks. It is quite ironic that the U.S. administration then tried to use the plans for establishing a transatlantic free trade area to push APEC into accepting its design of a preferential trade agreement in the Pacific region (Saxonhouse 1996, 120).

In the end, neither in the Pacific nor across the Atlantic did the plans for closer economic integration work out. In Europe, France slowed further progress on transatlantic trade liberalization because of opposition from French business interests (*Le Monde,* 4 December 1995). The New Transatlantic Agenda on which the EU and the United States finally agreed in December 1995 did not even come close to establishing preferential trading relations. In 1998 Commissioner for External Affairs Brittan tried to resuscitate this idea by advancing a proposal for a "new transatlantic marketplace" that entailed the elimination of industrial tariffs by 2010 and the extension of the negotiations for a mutual recognition agreement to a larger number of sectors. In March 1998, the European Commission gave its support to this plan, but only one month later the EU Council dropped it, as France again objected to negotiations that were likely to entail U.S. demands for a liberalization of the agricultural and audiovisual services sectors. Instead, the 1998 U.S.-EU summit agreed on the establishment of a Transatlantic Economic Partnership, which again was a very modest agreement. The episode thus illustrates the limits to Commission entrepreneurship in the absence of support from exporting interests.

The parallel spread of bilateral and regional agreements across the world made the EU concentrate on the pursuit of preferential trade agreements with countries where it saw European exporters' interests at risk (Barfield 1996, 152). The European Commission (1995, 6) clearly stated that the EU should use preferential trade agreements "to attenuate the potential threat of others establishing privileged relations with countries which are economically important to us." This defensive component is most obvious in the case of the EU-Mexican free trade agreement (Dür 2007b). The creation of NAFTA was perceived to be a key cause of the decline in the EU's share of Mexican imports from 11.4 percent in 1994 to 8.5 percent in 2000 (calculated from data in Inter-American Development Bank 2004, 69).[32] NAFTA's discriminatory effect was reinforced by the Mexican decision to increase its tariffs against non-NAFTA countries in 1995 and 1999 (the unweighted average tariff rose from 12.4 percent in 1994 to 16.1 percent in 1999; see Preuße 2000, 28), augmenting the tariff advantage for U.S. and Canadian companies in the Mexican market. As expected by the protection-for-exporters argument, in this situation European exporters voiced concerns about losses of market access in Mexico. Illustratively, the German peak business associations stressed the competitive disadvantages they faced in the Mexican market vis-à-vis U.S. competitors and therefore demanded the rapid conclusion of a preferential trade agreement with Mexico (*Frankfurter Allgemeine Zeitung*, 6 September 1999, 21; 26 October 1999, 26; and 8 November 1999, 18).

Heeding this pressure, the EU engaged in trade negotiations with Mexico beginning in 1995. Decision makers clearly understood that a trade agreement with this country was necessary to protect the interests of European exporters. A French ambassador, for example, when defending the need for such an agreement, stated:

> It is urgent for us to form a bond between the European Union and Mexico. Why? Because, due to NAFTA, the Americans and Canadians

---

32. In absolute terms, however, EU exports to Mexico grew throughout this period, with the exception of 1993 and 1995.

> have a tariff advantage which, in many cases, is around 18 percent. The French exporters are pulverized by an 18 percent difference. Our interest, due to NAFTA, is to have an agreement with Mexico, and we are going to do it. (Tordjman 2000, 115)

After several years of negotiation, the EU and Mexico signed a trade agreement in March 2000 that established free trade in industrial goods by 2007. The schedule of tariff reductions was specifically chosen to help European exporters reestablish equal conditions with the NAFTA countries as soon as possible.[33] In addition, EU companies achieved NAFTA parity with respect to public procurement and trade in services. Accordingly, the EU's commissioner for trade Pascal Lamy praised the agreement for "neutralising the distorting impact of NAFTA."[34] The *Economist* (29 January 2000) concluded: "The European Union…was eager for a deal with Mexico because its exports to that country have slumped since Mexico signed the North American Free Trade Agreement with America and Canada in 1992."

The EU and the United States also competed over market access in the southern part of the Western Hemisphere (*Economist,* 29 January 2000). In April 2002, and several months before the United States could complete a similar agreement, the EU was successful in concluding an association agreement with Chile. The European decision to negotiate with Chile clearly was a reaction to the potential for discrimination resulting from the parallel U.S.-Chile negotiations, with studies estimating trade diversion costs for the EU from such an agreement to amount to as much as $749 million (Hilaire and Yang 2003, 14; see also Harrison, Rutherford, and Tarr 2001). The EU-Chile agreement became particularly urgent as the EU had suffered substantial losses in the absolute level of exports to Chile from 1997 onward, mainly owing to Chile's closer relations with Mercosur. Once the agreement was concluded, the Spanish Ministry for Commerce declared that it helped the EU "to get one step ahead [of the United States], which will help avoid the problems [we had] in Mexico when that country signed the NAFTA agreement with the U.S. and Canada" (Subdirección General de Coordinación y Evaluación Comercial 2002, 19, my translation).

The agreement with Chile was actually thought to be part of a larger agreement that would also include the member countries of Mercosur. Again, the EU's

---

33. "Entry into Force of EU-Mexico Free Trade Agreement Signals Start of New Era in Europe's Relations with Mexico," *Rapid,* 3 July 2000.

34. "Mexico and the EU: Married Partners, Lovers, or Just Good Friends?" Speech held at the Institute of European Integration Studies, Instituto Technológico Autónomo de Mexico (ITAM), Mexico City, 29 April 2002. Available at http://trade.ec.europa.eu/doclib/docs/2004/september/tradoc_118831.pdf (accessed 1 April 2009).

objective in negotiating with Mercosur was to ensure continued access to this market in the face of U.S. plans for an FTAA (Thorstensen and Peña 1999, 270; Wiesebron 2002, 183). In this vein, the *New York Times* (9 January 2003, C1) quoted a European representative in Washington as saying: "It is obvious we are in stiff competition right now. Our agreement with Mexico came after Nafta, and we don't want to lose out again, especially not with Mercosur." In addition, as Mercosur itself had trade diverting consequences (Yeats 1998), an agreement with Mercosur had the advantage of protecting EU exporters in that market independent of U.S. trade policies. In July 2001, the EU proposed liberalizing 100 percent of trade in industrial products and 90 percent of trade in agricultural products over a ten-year period. By 2004 it appeared as if the two sides were very close to a final deal. Once the U.S. initiative for a FTAA came to a stop, however, a free trade agreement with Mercosur lost much of its appeal for the EU, and the negotiations have since stalled. This state of affairs is in line with Hypothesis 2, as exporter lobbying in the EU has been too weak to offset a strong mobilization by import-competing (agricultural) groups.

Some authors argue that geopolitical considerations are a major motivation for the EU when engaging in theses preferential trade negotiations (Sapir 1998, 726–27; Messerlin 2001, 226; Maur 2005, 1578). The argument is that since the EU does not have many means of conducting a common foreign policy, it resorts to trade agreements to achieve political objectives. Contrary to this argument, however, commercial aspirations seem to have been central in the decision of the EU to conclude trade agreements with Mexico, Chile, and some other countries (Brown 2003, 172). Protecting exporters' and investors' access to these emerging markets was a commercial objective pushed by European domestic interests. While geopolitical motives—such as stabilizing governments in neighboring countries and reducing immigration—were highly significant in the agreements concluded with geographically adjacent countries, even in these agreements commercial objectives were present. One indication of this is the strong emphasis that the EU put on the export of its standards to the partner countries. As the *Economist* (29 January 2000) concluded: "But economics is a bigger spur [than geopolitics]. Thanks to its bilateral deals, the EU is an export and investment hub with preferential access to markets in a great many spokes. That helps European exporters corner foreign markets."

The Turn to the Multilateral Arena

Despite these successes in concluding preferential trade agreements, in the early 2000s the EU turned its focus to the multilateral realm, at the same time devoting less attention to the preferential track. This turn to the multilateral arena was largely a result of a perception that the EU had more to loose than to gain from a further spread of preferential trade agreements (*Financial Times*, 6 August 1996, 5). By December 2002, some 250 regional trade agreements had been notified to the WTO, with a majority of them concluded after January 1995. It was clear that the EU with its dispersed trading interests could not keep pace in negotiating with all countries where European exporters might be hurt as a result of a preferential agreement among foreign countries. In addition, negotiating preferential deals had become increasingly difficult for the EU as foreign countries asked for concessions with respect to agricultural trade. The U.S.-Australian agreement, for example, had the potential to hurt European exporters (Hilaire and Yang 2003, 14), but a bilateral agreement with Australia, a highly efficient exporter of agricultural goods, was politically not feasible for the EU.

In view of this, pushing for multilateral negotiations following the nondiscrimination principle appeared to be the most reasonable strategy. Already in the mid-1990s, there had been first indications of a change in the European trade strategy, when in response to the spread of free trade agreements, the EU called on the WTO to tighten its rules for such agreements (*Financial Times*, 25 July 1996, 5). Initially, however, the need to reach trade agreements with Mexico and Chile, in particular, still inhibited a more thorough shift in EU trade policy. It was only after these agreements had been concluded that European exporting interests clearly favored a greater concentration on multilateral negotiations in the WTO.[35] Commissioner for Trade Lamy, in turn, felt compelled to warn about a shift away from the WTO resulting from the spread of bilateral trade deals (*Wall Street Journal*, 20 March 2003, 16).

Notwithstanding strong European support for multilateral trade negotiations, a first attempt at starting a new trade round failed during the WTO ministerial conference in Seattle in 1999. In an effort at overcoming this setback for the trade policies of the EU, the European Commission continued to advocate for a new global trade round, and on 16 June 2001, the European Council in Gothenburg confirmed the EU's commitment to a new round. In November 2001, finally, the WTO members launched the Doha Development Agenda, which soon became the EU's trade policy priority. Since then, however, the negotiations have hardly progressed. In July 2006, the negotiations were even suspended for half a year. It was in response to this suspension of negotiations that the EU revived its strategy of concluding preferential trade agreements. In 2007 it started to negotiate trade agreements with ASEAN, India, and South Korea. While the choice of India may

---

35. Interviews with business associations, Brussels, 10–13 January 2006; "CEOs Speak Out on WTO Doha Round: A Word From Business Association Leaders," available at http://www.esf.be (accessed 1 April 2009).

have been largely driven by the fact that this country has no competitive agricultural exports, the other two entities were obvious candidates from the perspective of the protection-for-exporters argument because of previous U.S. agreements with two ASEAN members (Malaysia and Singapore) and South Korea. BusinessEurope, for example, explicitly called for an agreement with South Korea that would establish "a level playing field for EU companies in all sectors in Korea, equal to that enjoyed by its main competitors."[36]

In this chapter I have provided additional evidence supporting the protection-for-exporters argument. I have drawn attention to the external effects of U.S. and European trade policies in the 1990s, focusing on the quest for preferential access to emerging markets. In the late 1990s and early 2000s, the EU, reacting to prior U.S. initiatives, concluded a series of preferential trade agreements. In turn, these agreements had discriminatory consequences that mobilized U.S. exporters, which finally put enough pressure on Congress to allow for the passage of trade legislation in 2002. The United States and the EU thus engaged in competition for market access, especially in Latin America. Although quite successful in defending its stance in Latin America, in the early 2000s the EU changed its strategy, concentrating all of its resources on the multilateral trade negotiations in the framework of the WTO. I have suggested that this change in strategy was largely driven by exporters' and decision-makers' recognition that the EU would not be able to protect European export interests by way of preferential deals alone. With the Doha Development Agenda deadlocked, however, the EU had to revive its preferential strategy in late 2006. The EU's strategy now is to conclude free trade agreements with South Asian and East Asian countries to ensure that European exporters are not "left behind" when Japan and the United States conclude agreements with these countries (*Frankfurter Allgemeine Zeitung*, 20 November 2004, 11–12).

---

36. "BusinessEurope Position on the EU-Korea Free-Trade Agreement," 2007, available at http://www.bilaterals.org/IMG/pdf/EU-Korea_position_BusinessEurope_180707.pdf (accessed 1 April 2009).

CONCLUSION

Despite its objective importance, the process of transatlantic trade liberalization has received only scant scholarly attention. In particular, two major gaps exist in the literature on this subject. On the one hand, most existing research explains either American or European trade policies, while neglecting that for reciprocal trade liberalization to take place, both sides have to agree to trade liberalization. Studies of the trade policies of either side provide interesting insights into trade policymaking but cannot explain negotiated trade policy outcomes. On the other hand, the majority of studies concentrate on specific, temporally very limited developments such as transatlantic bargaining in the Uruguay round or the Doha Development Agenda. Longer-term developments have been neglected, and some epochs have hardly been studied at all. My objective with this book has been to fill some of these gaps and provide an explanation for transatlantic trade liberalization from the 1930s until the early 2000s.

For this purpose, I have set out an argument, labeled protection-for-exporters argument, which is based on the premise that for a variety of reasons exporters mostly fail to mobilize in pursuit of opportunities. Rather, they become politically active in response to losses of foreign market access, often caused by preferential trade agreements among foreign countries that discriminate against exporters in excluded countries. The resulting increase in exporter lobbying influences the trade policy choices of political actors in these countries. Decision makers, in an attempt to protect the interests of exporters, choose among various options of how to respond to discrimination, with the choice of strategy determined by the vulnerability of a country to changes in foreign trade flows.

Highly vulnerable countries are likely to opt for a negotiated agreement with the member countries of a preferential agreement. Less vulnerable countries may pick more aggressive strategies, such as retaliation, in response to discrimination abroad. The protection-for-exporters argument also allows for predictions about the trade policy choices of member countries in the aftermath of the creation of a preferential trade agreement: they should see their bargaining power in international trade negotiations increased, allowing them to achieve a favorable balance of concessions. This advantageous balance makes member-country exporters back an agreement, creating incentives for member governments to accept a trade agreement with excluded countries that satisfies exporter interests without too much harming import-competing interests.

The Findings

The goal of the six case studies, which cover a period of seventy years, has been to see how well this argument can explain the process of transatlantic trade liberalization. The empirical evidence has largely supported the hypotheses set out in the theoretical part. For one, the evidence has confirmed the argument that the mobilization of exporter interests comes about mainly as a defensive reaction to the preferential trade policies of foreign countries (Hypothesis 1). In the five cases in which European countries pursued preferential trade policies, namely when setting up imperial preferences; establishing, enlarging, and deepening the EEC; and extending trade preferences to emerging markets, this led to a mobilization of exporters in the United States. This mobilization sharply contrasts with the case of the 1950s, when U.S. exporters, in the absence of a long-term challenge to their market access in Europe, failed to mobilize. These observations provide robust support for the hypothesis that exporters' motivation to become politically active is higher in response to losses of foreign market access than in pursuit of opportunities.

The presence or absence of exporter lobbying has strongly influenced the actions of the U.S. Congress and administration (Hypothesis 2). In the five cases in which American exporters mobilized, U.S. trade policies changed to accommodate demands for the protection of exporter interests. In the 1950s, by contrast, when American exporters failed to mobilize, U.S. trade policies strongly favored import-competing interests. The fact that in most instances it was the United States that had to react to European discriminatory policies explains why the United States was the driver behind most of the GATT trade rounds; only recently, with European exporters facing discrimination, has the EU become a principal advocate for the Doha Development Agenda. Interest-group pressures thus go a long way in explaining transatlantic trade policies over the last century. This is not to say that the preferences of decision makers did not play a role: in some instances, changes in trade policies were delayed because decision makers were committed to supporting a specific coalition even after that coalition's relative strength had declined. In other instances, decision-makers' preferences reinforced a policy change caused by a shift in the balance of domestic interests. When adopting a long-term view and abstracting from day-to-day politics, however, a strong correlation between the balance of demands and the policies implemented becomes evident.

The narrative has also confirmed Hypothesis 3, which links an excluded country's choice of strategy to its vulnerability. From the 1930s until the 1960s, successive U.S. administrations adhered to a nondiscriminatory strategy in response to discrimination in Europe. My argument has been that this choice was a result of the relatively high degree of vulnerability of the United States at that time. As a country with strong exporting interests in Europe and a trade surplus with European countries, the United States was not in a position to threaten with retaliation when facing discriminatory trade policies in that region. The content of domestic deliberations has also supported the argument that links the choice of strategy to the degree of vulnerability. In the late 1950s and early 1960s, for example, when discussing various options of how to react to the creation of the EEC, U.S. decision makers clearly alluded to the issue of vulnerability. After considering accession to the EEC, retaliation, and the creation of a rival agreement, they finally opted for multilateral trade negotiations, as this appeared to best protect U.S. exporters' interests given U.S. trade patterns at that time.

In the 1970s, the United States altered its strategy to become more aggressive. Congress included Section 301 in the Trade Act of 1974 that asked the president to retaliate against countries "unduly" restricting international trade. This aggressive approach continued into the 1980s when Congress responded to calls for "fair" rather than free trade, meaning a strategy combining better access to foreign markets with limits on imports into the domestic market (Nollen and Quinn 1994, 495–97). This shift in strategy is in line with the protection-for-exporters argument, as the degree of vulnerability of the United States decreased at that time. For the first time in the postwar years, the United States incurred a bilateral trade deficit with Western Europe in the early 1970s and then again in the 1980s, making retaliation a feasible strategy. Most recently, changes in trade flows, which have increased the importance for U.S. exporters of some countries—especially Canada and Mexico—and reduced the importance of western European countries, has allowed the U.S. administration to use discriminatory trade policies when pursuing the aim of preserving foreign market access. In the 1990s and early 2000s, consequently, the U.S. administration first concluded

NAFTA and then engaged in a series of preferential trade negotiations with countries in different regions of the world.

The empirical evidence has also supported Hypothesis 4, which stipulates that the mobilization of exporters makes excluded countries more willing to offer concessions to member countries with the objective of achieving a reduction of discrimination. In the 1930s and 1940s, the United Kingdom managed to gain substantial concessions from the United States, although it was in a structurally weak position, owing to, first, the threat created by Germany and, later, wartime destruction. In the 1960s and 1970s, the EC disposed of major bargaining power in the trade realm, which explains why it engaged in foot-dragging in the Kennedy and Tokyo rounds. Empirical support for Hypothesis 4 is less clear-cut from the 1980s onward, when changes in trade flows that improved the structural position of the United States partly offset the impact of discrimination on bargaining power.

Finally, the narrative has offered support for the hypothesis that this increase in bargaining power provides member countries with an incentive to accept trade liberalization (Hypothesis 5). In 1947 the United Kingdom agreed to quite far-reaching tariff cuts and the establishment of international rules concerning trade policy at a time when its economy was weak. It did so not least because British exporters anticipated major U.S. concessions in exchange for a dent in the system of imperial preference. In the 1960s, the EEC accepted trade liberalization, although it engaged in the parallel liberalization of intra-European trade. Again, an important precondition for this was that European export interests realized that the United States would be willing to make considerable concessions to achieve a reduction in discrimination in the Kennedy round.

Overall, therefore, the protection-for-exporters argument has fared very well when exposed to empirical scrutiny. As could be expected from a parsimonious argument, however, some developments have proved difficult to explain without recourse to ad hoc reasoning. This is most evident in the treatment of the 1980s, as the start of the Uruguay round of trade negotiations is only partly compatible with the protection-for-exporters argument. A larger number of exporter interests than expected supported the launch of these negotiations in the United States at a time when they hardly faced any new discrimination in foreign markets. In addition, in this case state actors acted more autonomously from the balance of domestic economic interests than had been postulated in the theoretical part. Nevertheless, with many other aspects of transatlantic trade relations in the 1980s consistent with the protection-for-exporters argument, these anomalies detract little from the plausibility of the argument.

A partial explanation for the anomalies that arise in the case of the 1980s derives from the observation that the international trading system became more complex in that decade. Up to the late 1970s, the United States and European countries paid relatively little attention to the trade policies of third countries. For the analysis of the four cases covering the period from the 1930s until the 1970s, the abstraction from developments outside of the transatlantic region thus not only has the advantages of parsimony and analytical rigor, but also is empirically accurate. With the weakening of transatlantic dominance of the international trading system, however, the specific geographic focus is more difficult to sustain from the 1980s onward. In the 2000s, for example, U.S. trade policies, although still in line with the expectations derived from the protection-for-exporters argument, are no longer just a response to European trade policies (and vice versa for the EU). This is not surprising considering that in 2007 U.S. merchandise exports to Canada exceeded the combined exports to the twenty-seven EU member countries (in fact, only 21 percent of U.S. exports went to the EU). What is more, U.S. exports to China and Japan in that year were larger than those to the United Kingdom, Germany, and France combined.

The anomalies that hamper the protection-for-exporters argument are clearly less significant than the difficulties that the narrative unveiled for potential alternative explanations. In particular, the empirical analysis has cast doubt on interpretations of the process of transatlantic trade liberalization that stress either the importance of institutional changes or the role of geopolitical concerns. With respect to institutional changes, a prominent explanation in the literature on U.S. trade policy is that the RTAA enabled liberalization by empowering exporters (Bailey, Goldstein, and Weingast 1997; Gilligan 1997a). Little evidence, however, suggests that the RTAA was a "magic bullet" (for this term, see Hiscox 1999) that brought about trade liberalization. Instead, the RTAA may usefully be seen as a solution to a problem faced by decision makers, namely how to protect American exporters' access to foreign markets in the face of widespread discrimination. Neither does the collusive-delegation argument, as the most prominent institutional argument for the case of the EU (Meunier 2005, 8–9; Woolcock 2005, 247), fare particularly well in accounting for European trade-policy choices. European governments did not pursue trade liberalization because they gained autonomy from protectionist societal interests; rather, their actions closely reflected the demands voiced by societal interests.

It is undeniable that geopolitical interests play a role in shaping trade-policy choices (Cooper 1973; Nelson 1989; Eckes 1995; Skålnes 1998). This also applies to transatlantic trade relations over the last eighty years. In 1938, for example, the United Kingdom partly used its trade agreement with the United States to signal strength vis-à-vis Germany. In the 1970s, similarly, security interests were important in shaping the U.S. administration's reaction to American economic difficulties. Nevertheless, the historical narrative has showed that the importance of geopolitics is easily exaggerated. In the 1950s, when in the United States security concerns should have been most prominent during the hottest phase of the cold war, domestic economic interests largely determined trade policy choices, as is witnessed in the protectionist orientation of U.S. trade policies at that time. In fact, domestic interests often use geopolitical arguments in a strategic manner, as was the case with the import-competing oil industry from the U.S. South asking for a national security clause that would limit the importation of petroleum in the 1950s. A more recent example is provided by export interests arguing that free trade agreements are an important instrument in the "war on terror" after 9/11. In other instances, trade and security were linked, but in the other direction than the one postulated in the literature. In the 1960s, for example, some U.S. decision makers proposed reducing the number of U.S. military forces in Europe if U.S. trading interests were not given enough consideration in the process of European integration (*Economist*, 4 May 1963, 429).

In short, the protection-for-exporters argument has stood up well in light of the empirical findings. Given that the argument had to exclude many context-dependent variables to explain a wide range of different cases, its success is particularly significant. What is more, the cases included here could be considered crucial cases for a test of the argument more generally. The United States, due to its size and economic weight, is unlikely to change its trade policies because of external factors. Having provided ample evidence that it did indeed react to discrimination in Europe, it seems plausible that the causal mechanism set out to explain transatlantic trade relations over a seventy-year period has explanatory power for other cases as well.

Extending the Empirical Scope

Whereas my aim in this book has been to explain transatlantic trade relations from 1930 until 2010, the protection-for-exporters argument should also be able to cast light on trade-policy episodes in other time epochs and involving other countries. In the nineteenth century, the Zollverein (1818–70), a customs union among a large number of German states, was the result of a dynamic that is similar to the one discussed here, in that an initial agreement created a pull effect that made other states join (Mattli 1999, 115–21). The establishment of the Zollverein, in turn, created concerns among excluded countries, even motivating the British government to commission an investigation into the consequences of the Zollverein for British trading interests (O'Brien 1976, 552). As hypothesized here, the Zollverein also endowed its members with additional bargaining power, hereby ending "the centuries-old political impotence of Germany" (Pollard 1974, 115). It would be interesting to study in more detail the political processes underlying the creation of the Zollverein, and its external effects, to examine the causal mechanism set out here.

The argument may also be of help in explaining European countries' competition for colonies in the late nineteenth century. From 1879 on, when some governments embarked on fostering exclusive trade ties with their colonies, many other colonial powers felt the need to follow suit, and the area comprising formal colonies increased sizably. The present argument explains this development as protection for exporters in the face of a closing of markets in Europe. Indeed, in 1885, Jules Ferry, a defender of French colonial ambitions, legitimized the French expansion in parts of Africa with the following words: "[Colonial expansion] was a question of finding outlets for our industries, exports, and capital. That was an absolute necessity, since Europe was closing itself to Europe; to Europe, too, North America was being closed by covering itself with almost prohibitive tariffs.... That was why France had to expand in West Africa, on the Congo, in Madagascar" (quoted in Dietrich 1939, 305). Even within the British Empire, there was strong pressure to establish preferential trade relations to protect the interests of British exporters, which however did not materialize before the twentieth century.

The protection-for-exporters argument is also likely to have explanatory power for developments in the twenty-first century. The "new regionalism," that is, the rapid proliferation of preferential trade agreements since the early 1990s, can largely be understood as the outcome of many countries struggling to avoid a loss of market access resulting from other countries concluding preferential trade agreements. This not only applies to the trade agreements concluded by the EU and the United States as argued in chapter 7, but also to those signed by other countries.[1] For example, the creation of NAFTA and Mexico's trade agreement with the EU created a strong incentive for Japan to sign its own agreement (Manger 2009). The peak business association in Japan, Keidanren, strongly advocated a free trade agreement with Mexico, arguing that Japanese companies found themselves in an "uncompetitive position relative to European and U.S. companies."[2] It is estimated that Mexico's free trade agreements cost Japan as much as 400 billion yen in exports in 1999 (that is, approximately 3.5 billion

---

1. Baccini and Dür (2009) provide quantitative support for the protection-for-exporters argument based on a spatial econometric analysis of the diffusion of trade agreements among 168 countries between 1990 and 2007.

2. "Request for Bilateral Negotiations on a Japan-Mexico Economic Partnership Agreement," 2003, available at http://www.keidanren.or.jp/english/policy/2003/060.html (accessed 1 April 2009).

U.S. dollars at the 1999 exchange rate). In early 2004, supporters of a free trade agreement with Mexico established a "national council" to promote this policy vis-à-vis the Japanese government. The pressure by business interests on the Japanese bureaucracy and government finally became so strong that not even intense counterlobbying by agricultural interests could impede the conclusion of an "economic partnership agreement" in 2004. This agreement reflects a substantial policy shift for Japan, which up until that time only had a preferential agreement with Singapore, concluded one year earlier.

Many of these twenty-first-century agreements do not include parties of approximately equal size, thus calling for an attempt at relaxing the scope condition introduced in chapter 1. A cursory analysis of a few agreements suggests that this should not be problematic. China and Chile, for example, signed a preferential trade agreement in 2004, which seems perfectly compatible with the protection-for-exporters argument. Chile has been one of the most active countries in terms of signing preferential trade agreements. As discussed in chapter 7, it signed agreements with both the EU (2002) and the United States (2003). It also concluded agreements with direct competitors of China such as Mexico (1999) and South Korea (2003) and became an associate member of Mercosur (1996). China, in turn, was in the process of concluding preferential agreements, among others with the ASEAN countries, at that time. Both sides thus faced an incentive to respond to discrimination in the market of the other. In the ensuing negotiations, China does not seem to have been able to exploit its larger structural power to achieve a result that is particularly close to its preferences. This observation backs the assumption made in chapter 1 that power is not fungible, and leads to an optimistic evaluation of the possibility of extending the protection-for-exporters argument to negotiations involving parties with different capabilities.

Another issue that may have to be addressed when applying the protection-for-exporters argument to twenty-first-century trade politics is the role of importers. In the theoretical part, I introduced the assumption that only two types of interests are relevant for trade politics: exporters and import competitors. Recently, however, the retail industry has become increasingly vocal in developed countries. The so-called Bra Wars between the EU and China in 2005, during which European retail interests successfully opposed the imposition of new restrictions against imports of garments from China, provides an illustration of this (Heron 2007). Since importers have a strong interest in avoiding a trade war, their lobbying activity changes the expectation about the determinants of a government's choice of strategy in response to foreign discrimination. In particular, the point that a bilateral trade deficit strengthens a government's position in international trade talks no longer holds if import interests engage in a major lobbying effort. In short, the detailed analysis of additional cases beyond the transatlantic relationship over the eighty-year period covered here could help both further specify the protection-for-exporters argument and delineate its empirical scope.

Broader Contributions

The argument and empirical evidence presented in this book have implications for a range of debates in the fields of trade-policy analysis, international political economy, and international relations. For one, the argument shows how the domestic balance of interests can change relatively quickly as a result of varying incentives for political action by different groups. Most existing trade-policy studies within the societal-demands approach have a hard time explaining rapid shifts in trade-policy outcomes, as they draw attention to long-drawn-out changes in the production process, the regional concentration of industries, and the multinationalization of firms as the determinants of policy changes over time. In this book I resolve this issue by focusing on levels of mobilization, rather than just economic factors that strengthen or weaken exporting and import-competing interests.

The argument also provides a causal mechanism that shows how policy choices in different countries can interact with each other. Very little research has been undertaken on such interaction effects in the field of trade policy. As John Odell (1990, 163) pointed out, "many works [in the field of trade policymaking] have abstracted from overseas influences, concentrating on the domestic sources of policy." Similarly, Robert Pahre (1998, 468) criticized theories of trade policymaking for assuming "that each state chooses its tariff in a political vacuum, unaffected by the choices of others." Scott C. James and David A. Lake (1989), as an exception, argued that in the mid-nineteenth century the British decision to liberalize agricultural imports shifted U.S. trade policies toward free trade, as well. Only very recently, largely quantitative research on the spread of preferential trade agreements has started to tackle this question (Egger and Larch 2008). In this present book I have presented an innovative argument and a detailed qualitative study of interdependence in trade-policy formation.

Protection of domestic interests in the face of foreign discrimination is not necessarily limited to the trade field. In fact, cooperation among a few countries that has negative externalities for excluded countries should have a contagion effect in other policy fields as well. The expansion of participation in the initiative for a European Higher Education Area illustrates this effect. Initially, only four European countries signed an agreement that had the aim of increasing the attractiveness of the university systems of the participating countries. As this initiative posed a threat to excluded countries, the latter rushed to join, making sure that membership in the "Bologna process" increased to forty-six countries by 2007. The process has been seen as a challenge to countries even as geographically distant as Australia, leading to debates about how that country could avoid becoming a "Bologna outsider."[3] It seems very plausible that the protection-for-exporters argument, which sees domestic interests mobilizing in response to threats, is able to shed light on this development.

The protection-for-exporters argument also contributes to a recent suite of studies that stress the importance of power as an explanatory factor in the analysis of international relations (Gruber 2000; Barnett and Duvall 2005). In particular, this book has developed an operationalization of bargaining power for the trade realm that differs from existing attempts at conceptualizing power in that issue area. It uses the concept of the best alternative to negotiated agreement that is well established in studies of negotiations and makes it applicable to trade negotiations. In this view, the relative balance of domestic interests determines bargaining power. In providing this specific operationalization, I also take a position in the debate on the fungibility of power (Baldwin 2002). Since the balance of domestic interests is specific to a policy field, I suggest that power should not be considered fungible. The lack of fungibility explains why the United States, despite its military superiority, was relatively weak in the trade field for the first decades after World War II.

Moreover, this book is another link in a chain of studies in the field of international political economy that are looking at the past as a laboratory to develop and test parsimonious theories. I have tried to show that studying past developments can help shed new light on supposedly well-established knowledge. It is largely accepted, for example, that the U.S. acted as a benign hegemon in the years following World War II. A closer analysis of that period, however, reveals many inconsistencies in that account. By taking into account developments that occur over a long time span, studies can also assess important changes in the trade policies of specific countries over time. The United States, for instance, shifted from a stance in defense of the nondiscrimination principle to a policy in which it pursues preferential trade policies. The EU, by contrast, was accused of having an "addiction to discrimination" (Wolf 1994, 17), but now has moved toward a position of preferring multilateral trade liberalization. Studies that fail to take into account a longer time horizon will be incapable of explaining these important shifts.

---

3. Australian Department of Education, Science, and Training, "The Bologna Process and Australia: Next Steps," 2006, available at http://www.dest.gov.au/ (accessed 1 April 2009).

Furthermore, the argument provides a distinct evaluation of the consequences of trade discrimination for the multilateral trading system, an issue that is of high current relevance given the spread of bilateral agreements across the globe. Economists have hotly debated the question whether preferential trading arrangements are "building blocks" or "stumbling blocks" for multilateral trade liberalization (Panagariya 2000, 317–25). While some authors come to an optimistic assessment (Lawrence 1991), others argue that preferential agreements inhibit further multilateral trade liberalization (Bhagwati 1992). Although much has been written on this topic, this book is one of only a few that try to outline the *specific circumstances* under which preferential trade agreements set off a process of multilateral trade liberalization.[4] Preferential liberalization should do so if the excluded country is relatively vulnerable and has geographically diffuse export interests.

More generally, the argument leads to the conclusion that in most circumstances the creation of a preferential trade agreement leads to further liberalization, albeit often of a preferential kind. As long as the member and excluded countries coincide in their perception of the distribution of bargaining power between the two sides, no trade war should ensue, as the excluded countries either make concessions that are enticing enough for the member countries to change their trade policies or issue a threat that is credible enough to achieve the same goal. Only when an excluded country overplays its hand and uses retaliation in a situation in which it is vulnerable, will a trade war, and hence a stumbling block scenario, ensue. (Alternatively, a member country may overestimate its power and fail to back down when facing a threat, again leading to a trade war.) This discussion suggests that both building-block and stumbling-block scenarios can result in the wake of the creation of a preferential trade agreement, although the former is more likely.

The protection-for-exporters argument also has some policy implications. First, for some years the United States has been following a strategy of competitive liberalization that builds on the idea that it can use regional trade agreements to "jump-start" multilateral trade negotiations (Evenett and Meier 2008). In this book I suggest that there are limits to this strategy. In particular, the argument leads to the expectation that exporter support for proactive agreements that could lead to discrimination against excluded countries should be weak. It should be difficult for the United States, or for any other country, to sign an

---

4. Kono (2007) provides another attempt at doing so; however, his causal mechanism, which focuses on the disappearance or continued presence of import-competing firms in the aftermath of regional integration, can only explain long-term developments, as a trade policy change hardly ever leads to the vanishing of a large numbers of firms over a short period of time.

agreement with a large trading entity unless this move is already a response to discrimination. Second, many governments openly state that they want to pursue preferential trade agreements to increase their bargaining power in future trade negotiations. Although such an effect is probable, the analysis shows that, due to the progressively lower levels of trade barriers, it will become less important in the future, since low levels of trade barriers also minimize the potential for trade diversion. Moreover, if a country indeed manages to increase its bargaining power, the outcome is not necessarily normatively desirable: the EU's bargaining power, for example, allowed it to maintain high barriers in the agricultural sector, which are very costly, not only for the European economy, but also for developing countries that could benefit from exporting agricultural commodities.

References

Aaronson, Susan A. 1996. *Trade and the American Dream: A Social History of Postwar Trade Policy.* Lexington: University of Kentucky Press.

Ahearn, Raymond J. 1992. "U.S. Access to the EC-92 Market: Opportunities, Concerns and Policy Challenges." In *Europe and the United States: Competition and Cooperation in the 1990s,* edited by Committee on Foreign Affairs, U.S. House of Representatives, 177–92. Washington, D.C.: Government Printing Office.

Aitken, Norman D. 1973. "The Effect of the EEC and EFTA on European Trade: A Temporal Cross-Section Analysis." *American Economic Review* 63(5): 881–92.

Alkema, Ynze. 1999. "European-American Trade Policies, 1961–1963." In *John F. Kennedy and Europe,* edited by Douglas Brinkley and Richard T. Griffiths, 212–34. Baton Rouge: Louisiana State University Press.

Allen, William R. 1953. "The International Trade Philosophy of Cordell Hull, 1907–1933." *American Economic Review* 43(1): 101–16.

Alt, James E., and Michael Gilligan. 1994. "Survey Article: The Political Economy of Trading States: Factor Specificity, Collective Action Problems and Domestic Political Institutions." *Journal of Political Philosophy* 2(2): 165–92.

Aminoff, Nicholas A. 1991. "The United States-Israel Free Trade Area Agreement of 1985: In Theory and Practice." *Journal of World Trade* 25(1): 5–42.

Anderson, Kim, and Robert E. Baldwin. 1987. "The Political Market for Protection in Industrial Countries." In *Protection, Cooperation, Integration and Development: Essays in Honour of Hiroshi Kitamura,* edited by Ali El-Agraa, 20–37. London: Macmillan.

Anderson, Kym, and Hege Norheim. 1993. "From Imperial to Regional Preferences: Its Effect on Europe's Intra- and Extra-Regional Trade." *Weltwirtschaftliches Archiv* 129:78–102.

Asbeek Brusse, Wendy. 1997. *Tariffs, Trade, and European Integration, 1947–1957: From Study Group to Common Market.* New York: St. Martin's Press.

Baccini, Leonardo, and Andreas Dür. 2009. "The New Regionalism and Policy Interdependence." Unpublished manuscript, available at http://andduer.googlepages.com/BacciniDuer_ISA2009.pdf (accessed 1 April 2009).

Bagwell, Kyle, and Robert Staiger. 1999. "An Economic Theory of GATT." *American Economic Review* 89(1): 215–48.

———. 2001. "Reciprocity, Non-Discrimination and Preferential Agreements in the Multilateral Trading System." *European Journal of Political Economy* 17(2): 281–325.

Bailey, Michael A., Judith Goldstein, and Barry R. Weingast. 1997. "The Institutional Roots of American Trade Policy: Politics, Coalitions, and International Trade." *World Politics* 49(3): 309–38.

Bailey, S. H. 1932. "The Political Aspect of Discrimination in International Economic Relations." *Economica* 12(35): 89–115.

Balassa, Bela. 1967a. "Trade Creation and Trade Diversion in the European Common Market." *Economic Journal* 77(1): 1–21.

———. 1967b. *Trade Liberalization among Industrial Countries: Objectives and Alternatives.* New York: McGraw-Hill.

———. 1989. "Europe 1992 and Its Possible Implications for Nonmember Countries." In *Free Trade Areas and U.S. Trade Policy,* edited by Jeffrey J. Schott, 293–312. Washington, D.C.: Institute for International Economics.

Baldwin, David A. 2002. "Power and International Relations." In *Handbook of International Relations,* edited by Walter Carlsnaes, Thomas Risse, and Beth A. Simmons, 177–91. London: SAGE.

Baldwin, Richard E. 1993. "A Domino Theory of Regionalism." NBER Working Paper 4465.

———. 1997. "The Causes of Regionalism." *World Economy* 20(7): 865–88.

———. 2006. "Multilateralising Regionalism: Spaghetti Bowls as Building Blocs on the Path to Global Free Trade." *World Economy* 29(11): 1451–518.

Baldwin, Richard E., and Frédéric Robert-Nicoud. 2007. "Entry and Asymmetric Lobbying: Why Governments Pick Losers." *LSE Political Science and Political Economy Group WP3–07.*

Baldwin, Robert E. 1985. *The Political Economy of U.S. Import Policy.* Cambridge: MIT Press.

Baldwin, Robert E., and Anthony J. Venables. 1995. "Regional Economic Integration." In *Handbook of International Economics,* vol. 3, edited by Gene M. Grossman and Kenneth Rogoff, 1597–644. Amsterdam: Elsevier.

Ball, George W. 1982. *The Past Has Another Pattern: Memoirs.* New York: Norton.

Barfield, Claude E. 1996. "Regionalism and U.S. Trade Policy." In *The Economics of Preferential Trade Agreements,* edited by Jagdish N. Bhagwati and Arvind Panagariya, 136–59. Washington, D.C.: AEI Press.

Barnett, Michael, and Raymond Duvall, eds. 2005. *Power in Global Governance.* Cambridge: Cambridge University Press.

Barrie, Robert W. 1987. *Congress and the Executive: The Making of United States Foreign Trade Policy, 1789–1968.* New York: Garland.

Bauer, Raymond A., Ithiel De Sola Pool, and Lewis Anthony Dexter. 1972. *American Business and Public Policy: The Politics of Foreign Trade.* New York: Atherton Press.

Bayard, Thomas O., and Kimberly A. Elliott. 1994. *Reciprocity and Retaliation in U.S. Trade Policy.* Washington, D.C.: Institute for International Economics.

Bayoumi, Tamim, and Barry Eichengreen. 1997. "Is Regionalism Simply a Diversion? Evidence from the Evolution of the EC and EFTA." In *Regionalism versus Multilateral Trade Arrangements,* edited by Takatoshi Ito and Anne O. Krueger, 141–67. Chicago: University of Chicago Press.

Beckett, Grace. 1941. *The Reciprocal Trade Agreements Program.* New York: Columbia University Press.

Benham, Frederic. 1941. *Great Britain Under Protection.* New York: Macmillan.

Benoit, Emile. 1961. *Europe at Sixes and Sevens: The Common Market, the Free Trade Association, and the United States.* New York: Columbia University Press.

Bergsten, C. Fred. 1971. "Crisis in U.S. Trade Policy." *Foreign Affairs* 49(July): 619–35.

———. 1999. "America and Europe: Clash of the Titans." *Foreign Affairs* 78(2): 20–34.

Bhagwati, Jagdish N. 1988. *Protectionism.* Cambridge: MIT Press.

———. 1992. "Regionalism Versus Multilateralism." *World Economy* 15(5): 535–55.

Bilal, Sanousi. 1998. "Why Regionalism May Increase the Demand for Trade Protection." *Journal of Economic Integration* 13(1): 30–61.

Bivens, Karen Kraus. 1968. *After the Kennedy Round: Outlook for World-Wide Trade Liberalization.* New York: National Industrial Conference Board.

Bordo, Michael D., Barry Eichengreen, and Douglas A. Irwin. 1999. "Is Globalisation Today Really Different from Globalisation a Hundred Years Ago?" In *Brookings Trade Forum 1999,* edited by Susan M. Collins and Robert Z. Lawrence, 1–50. Washington, D.C.: Brookings Institution Press.

Brenner, Steven R. 1977. Economic interests and the trade agreements program, 1937–1940: A study of institutions and political influence. PhD diss., Stanford University.

Brown, Andrew G. 2003. *Reluctant Partners: A History of Multilateral Trade Cooperation, 1850–2000.* Ann Arbor: University of Michigan Press.

Brown, William Adams Jr. 1950. *The United States and the Restoration of World Trade: An Analysis and Appraisal of the ITO Charter and the General Agreement on Tariffs and Trade.* Washington, D.C.: Brookings Institution.

Buigues, Pierre-André, and Carlos Martinez-Mongay. 1999. "Marché unique et pays tiers: Y a-t-il eu détournement ou création du commerce?" *Economie internationale* 80(4): 75–102.

Bundesverband der Deutschen Industrie. 1963. *Jahresbericht 1963 des Bundesverbandes der Deutschen Industrie.* Berlin: BDI.

———. 1989. *Completion of the Single European Market: Consequences for the European Community's External Economic Relations—German Industry's View.* Cologne, DE: BDI.

Butler, Michael A. 1998. *Cautious Visionary: Cordell Hull and Trade Reform, 1933–1937.* Kent, Ohio: Kent State University Press.

Calingaert, Michael. 1988. *The 1992 Challenge from Europe: Development of the European Community's Internal Market.* Washington, D.C.: National Planning Association.

———. 1996. *European Integration Revisited: Progress, Prospects, and U.S. Interests.* Boulder, Colo.: Westview Press.

Camps, Miriam. 1957. "Trade Policy and American Leadership." Princeton University, Center of International Studies, Memorandum 12.

Capie, Forrest. 1983. *Depression and Protectionism: Britain between the Wars.* London: Allen and Unwin.

Carter, Susan B., Scott S. Gartner, Michael R. Haines, Alan L. Olmstead, Richard Sutch, and Gavin Wright, ed. 2005. *Historical Statistics of the United States: Millennial Edition.* Cambridge: Cambridge University Press.

Cassing, James, Timothy McKeown, and Jack Ochs. 1986. "The Political Economy of the Tariff Cycle." *American Political Science Review* 80(3): 843–62.

CEPES-CED. 1964. *Die freie Weltwirtschaft in der Bewährung: Drei Studien zur Kennedy-Runde.* Frankfurt a.M.: CEPES.

Chang, Won, and L. Alan Winters. 2001. "Preferential Trading Arrangements and Excluded Countries: Ex-Post Estimates of the Effects on Prices." *World Economy* 24(6): 797–807.

Chase, Kerry A. 2005. *Trading Blocs: States, Firms, and Regions in the World Economy.* Ann Arbor: University of Michigan Press.

Chorev, Nitsan. 2007. *Remaking U.S. Trade Policy: From Protectionism to Globalization.* Ithaca: Cornell University Press.

Coffey, Peter. 1976. *The External Economic Relations of the EEC.* London: Macmillan.

Cohen, Stephen D., ed. 1994. *The Making of United States International Economic Policy: Principles, Problems, and Proposals for Reform.* 4th ed. Westport, Conn.: Praeger.

Commission of the European Communities. 1971. *Consequences of the Present Situation for the Common Agricultural Policy.* Brussels: CEC.

———. 1973. "Development of an Overall Approach to Trade in View of the Coming Multilateral Negotiations in GATT (Memorandum from the Commission to the Council forwarded on 9 April and amended on 22 May 1973)." *Bulletin of the European Communities* (Supplement 2/73).

———. 1985. *Completing the Internal Market: White Paper from the Commission to the European Council (Milan, 28–29 June 1985).* Brussels: CEC.

———. 1988. *Europe 1992: Europe World Partner.* Brussels: EC Office of Press and Public Affairs.

Commission on International Trade and Investment Policy. 1971. *United States International Economic Policy in an Interdependent World: Report to the President Submitted by the Commission on International Trade and Investment Policy.* Washington, D.C.: Government Printing Office.

Conybeare, John A. C. 1984. "Public Goods, Prisoner's Dilemmas and the International Political Economy." *International Studies Quarterly* 28(1): 5–22.

———. 1987. *Trade Wars: The Theory and Practice of International Commercial Rivalry.* New York: Columbia University Press.

———. 1993. "1992, The Community, and the World: Free Trade or Fortress Europe?" In *The 1992 Project and the Future of Integration in Europe,* edited by Dale L. Smith and James Lee Ray, 143–63. Armonk, N.Y.: M. E. Sharpe.

Cooney, Stephen. 1991. "The Impact of Europe 1992 on the United States." *Proceedings of the Academy of Political Science* 38(1): 100–112.

Cooper, Richard N. 1973. "Trade Policy Is Foreign Policy." In *A Reordered World: Emerging International Economic Problems,* edited by Richard N. Cooper, 46–61. Washington, D.C.: Potomac Associates.

Corbet, Hugh. 1979. "Importance of Being Earnest about Further GATT Negotiations." *World Economy* 2(2): 319–41.

Corden, W. Max. 1972. "Economies of Scale and Customs Union Theory." *Journal of Political Economy* 80(3): 465–75.

———. 1997. *Trade Policy and Economic Welfare.* 2nd ed. Oxford: Oxford University Press.

Cowles, Maria Green. 1996. "The EU Committee of AmCham: The Powerful Voice of American Firms in Brussels." *Journal of European Public Policy* 3(3): 339–58.

Culbert, Jay. 1987. "War-time Anglo-American Talks and the Making of GATT." *World Economy* 10(4): 381–408.

Curtis, Thomas B., and John R. Vastine. 1971. *The Kennedy Round and the Future of American Trade.* New York: Praeger.

Curzon, Gerard. 1965. *Multilateral Trade Diplomacy: An Examination of the Impact of the General Agreement on Tariffs and Trade on National Commercial Policies and Techniques.* London: Michael Joseph.

Curzon, Gerard, and Victoria Curzon. 1976. "The Management of Trade Relations in the GATT." In *Politics and Trade.* Vol. 1 of *International Economic Relations of the Western World 1959–1971,* edited by Andrew Shonfield, 141–283. London: Oxford University Press.

Dallek, Robert. 1979. *Franklin D. Roosevelt and American Foreign Policy: 1932–1945.* New York: Oxford University Press.

De Bièvre, Dirk, and Andreas Dür. 2005. "Constituency Interests and Delegation in European and American Trade Policy." *Comparative Political Studies* 38(10): 1271–96.

Dell, Sidney. 1963. *Trade Blocs and Common Markets.* London: Constable.

Destler, I. M. 1978. "United States Trade Policymaking during the Tokyo Round." In *The Politics of Trade: US and Japanese Policymaking for the GATT Negotiations,* edited by Michael Blaker, 15–73. New York: East Asian Institute, Columbia University.

———. 1992. *American Trade Politics.* 2nd ed. Washington, D.C.: Institute for International Economics.

———. 2005. *American Trade Politics.* 4th ed. Washington, D.C.: Institute for International Economics.

Destler, I. M., and John S. Odell. 1987. *Anti-Protection: Changing Forces in United States Trade Politics.* Washington, D.C.: Institute for International Economics.

Diebold, William Jr. 1962. "Trade Policies since World War II." *Current History* 42:356–61.

———. 1999. "A Watershed with Some Dry Sides: The Trade Expansion Act of 1962." In *John F. Kennedy and Europe,* edited by Douglas Brinkley and Richard T. Griffiths, 235–60. Baton Rouge: Louisiana State University Press.

Dietrich, Ethel B. 1939. *World Trade.* New York: Henry Holt and Co.

Dolan, Michael B. 1983. "European Restructuring and Import Policies for a Textile Industry in Crisis." *International Organization* 37(4): 583–615.

Douglas, Paul H. 1966. *America in the Market Place: Trade, Tariffs and the Balance of Payments.* New York: Holt, Rinehart and Winston.

Drahos, Peter 2003. "When the Weak Bargain with the Strong: Negotiations in the World Trade Organization." *International Negotiation* 8(1): 79–109.

Drummond, Ian M., and Norman Hillmer. 1989. *Negotiating Freer Trade: The United Kingdom, the United States, Canada, and the Trade Agreements of 1938.* Waterloo, Ont.: Wilfried Laurier University Press.

Dür, Andreas. 2007a. "Discriminating among Rival Explanations: Some Tools for Small-n Researchers." In *Research Design in Political Science: How to Practice What They Preach?* edited by Thomas Gschwend and Frank Schimmelfennig, 183–200. Houndmills, UK: Palgrave.

———. 2007b. "EU Trade Policy as Protection for Exporters: The Agreements with Mexico and Chile." *Journal of Common Market Studies* 45(4): 833–55.

———. 2008. "Interest Groups in the European Union: How Powerful Are They?" *West European Politics* 31(6): 1212–30.

Eckes, Alfred E. 1995. *Opening America's Market: U.S. Foreign Trade Policy since 1776.* Chapel Hill: University of North Carolina Press.

———. 1999. "U.S. Trade History." In *U.S. Trade Policy: History, Theory, and the WTO,* edited by William A. Lovett, Alfred E. Eckes, and Richard L. Brinkman, 51–105. Armonk, N.Y.: M. E. Sharpe.

Eckes, Alfred E., ed. 2000. *Revisiting U.S. Trade Policy: Decisions in Perspective.* Athens: Ohio University Press.

Eckes, Alfred E., and Thomas W. Zeiler. 2003. *Globalization and the American Century.* Cambridge: Cambridge University Press.

Eckstein, Harry. 1975. "Case Study and Theory in Political Science." In *Strategies of Inquiry.* Vol. 7 of *Handbook of Political Science,* edited by Fred I. Greenstein and Nelson W. Polsby, 79–137. Reading, Mass.: Addison-Wesley.

Economic Research Department. 1959. "A List of Companies with New Operations in Western Europe During 1958–1959 (Since the Start of the European Common Market)."

Economist Intelligence Unit. 1957. *Britain and Europe: A Study of the Effects on British Manufacturing Industry of a Free Trade Area and the Common Market.* London: EIU.

Egger, Peter, and Mario Larch. 2008. "Interdependent Preferential Trade Agreement Memberships: An Empirical Analysis." *Journal of International Economics* 76(2): 384–99.

Eisenhower, Dwight D. 1965. *Waging Peace: 1956–1961.* Garden City, N.Y.: Doubleday.

Ellingsen, Tore, and Karl Wärneryd. 1999. "Foreign Direct Investment and the Political Economy of Protection." *International Economic Review* 40(2): 357–79.

Europäisches Parlament. 1963a. "Die Vereinigung der Industrien der Europäischen Gemeinschaften zum Trade Expansion Act." *Europäische Dokumentation: Ein Überblick* (4).

———. 1963b. "EWG-Handelskammern über die Beziehungen der EWG zu Drittländern." *Europäische Dokumentation: Ein Überblick* (8/9).

European Commission. 1995. *Communication from the Commission: Free Trade Areas: An Appraisal, SEC(95) 322 final.* Brussels: EC.

———. 1997. *Trade Creation and Trade Diversion: The Single Market Review, Subseries IV (Impact on Trade and Investment),* vol. 3. Luxembourg: EC.

European Council. 1988. "Declaration of the European Council on the International Role of the European Community." Rhodes, EL: European Council.

European Free Trade Association. 1972. *The Trade Effects of EFTA and the EEC 1959–1967.* Geneva: EFTA.

Eurostat. 2003. *External and Intra-European Union Trade—Statistical Yearbook, Data 1958–2002.* Luxembourg: Office for Official Publications of the European Communities.

———. Various. "Monthly External Trade Bulletin."

Evans, John W. 1971. *The Kennedy Round in American Trade Policy: The Twilight of GATT?* Cambridge: Harvard University Press.

Evenett, Simon J., and Michael Meier. 2008. "An Interim Assessment of the U.S. Trade Policy of 'Competitive Liberalization.'" *World Economy* 31(1): 31–66.

Fanis, Maria. 2004. "Collective Action Theory Meets Prospect Theory: An Application to Coalition Building in Chile, 1973–75." *Political Psychology* 25(3): 363–88.

Farrands, Chris. 1979. "Textile Diplomacy: The Making and Implementation of European Textile Policy 1974–78." *Journal of Common Market Studies* 18(1): 22–39.

Feinberg, Richard E. 2003. "The Political Economy of United States' Free Trade Agreements." *World Economy* 26(7): 1019–40.

Feis, Herbert. 1966. *1933: Characters in Crisis.* Boston: Little, Brown and Co.

Ferguson, Thomas. 1984. "From Normalcy to New Deal: Industrial Structure, Party Competition, and American Public Policy in the Great Depression." *International Organization* 38(1): 41–94.

Fisher, Roger, and William L. Ury. 1981. *Getting to Yes: Negotiating Agreement without Giving In.* London: Hutchinson Business.

Fishlow, Albert, and Stephan Haggard. 1992. *The United States and the Regionalisation of the World Economy.* Paris: OECD.

Fordham, Benjamin O., and Timothy J. McKeown. 2003. "Selection and Influence: Interest Groups and Congressional Voting on Trade Policy." *International Organization* 57(3): 519–49.

Frankel, Jeffrey. 1997. *Regional Trading Blocs in the World Economic System.* Washington, D.C.: Institute for International Economics.

Freeman, Harry L. 1998. "The Role of Constituents in U.S. Policy Development towards Trade in Financial Services." In *Constituent Interests and U.S. Trade Policies,* edited by Alan V. Deardorff and Robert M. Stern, 183–91. Ann Arbor: University of Michigan Press.

Frey, Bruno S., and Heinz Buhofer. 1986. "Integration and Protectionism: A Comparative Institutional Analysis." In *Protectionism and Structural Adjustment,* edited by Heinz Hauser, 167–88. Grüsch: Verlag Rüegger.

Frieden, Jeffry A. 1988. "Sectoral Conflict and Foreign Economic Policy, 1914–1940." *International Organization* 42(1): 59–90.

Frieden, Jeffry, and Ronald Rogowski. 1996. "The Impact of the International Economy on National Policies: An Analytical Overview." In *Internationalization and Domestic Politics,* edited by Robert O. Keohane and Helen Milner, 25–47. Cambridge: Cambridge University Press.

Fusfeld, Daniel R. 1956. *The Economic Thought of Franklin D. Roosevelt and the Origins of the New Deal.* New York: Columbia University Press.

Gaddis, John Lewis. 1972. *The United States and the Origins of the Cold War, 1941–1947.* New York: Columbia University Press.

Gantzer, Hans. 1956. "Die vierte Zollkonferenz des GATT in Genf." *Europa-Archiv* 11(August): 9069–71.

Gardner, Lloyd C. 1964. *Economic Aspects of New Deal Diplomacy.* Madison: University of Wisconsin Press.

Gardner, Richard N. 1980. *Sterling-Dollar Diplomacy in Current Perspective: The Origins and the Prospects of Our International Economic Order.* New York: Columbia University Press.

Garrett, Garet. 1947. "More About the World Trade Charter." *American Affairs* 9(2): 75–83.

Geiger, Theodore. 1970. *Transatlantic Relations in the Prospect of an Enlarged European Community.* London: British–North American Committee.

George, Alexander, and Tim McKeown. 1985. "Case Studies and Theories of Organizational Decision Making." In *Advances in Information Processing in Organizations,* vol. 2, edited by Robert Coulam and Richard Smith, 21–58. Greenwich, Conn.: JAI Press.

George, Alexander L., and Andrew Bennett. 2005. *Case Studies and Theory Development in the Social Sciences.* Cambridge: MIT Press.

Geroski, P. A. 1995. "What Do We Know about Entry?" *International Journal of Industrial Organization* 13(4): 421–40.

Gianaris, Nicholas V. 1991. *The European Community and the United States: Economic Relations.* New York: Praeger.

Gilligan, Michael J. 1997a. *Empowering Exporters: Reciprocity, Delegation, and Collective Action in American Trade Policy.* Ann Arbor: University of Michigan Press.

——. 1997b. "Lobbying as a Private Good with Intra-Industry Trade." *International Studies Quarterly* 41(3): 455–74.

Gilpin, Robert. 1987. *The Political Economy of International Relations.* Princeton, N.J.: Princeton University Press.

——. 2001. *Global Political Economy.* Princeton, N.J.: Princeton University Press.

Glejser, Herbert, and Sueli Moro. 1996. "Estimates of Trade Effects of Portugal's and Spain's Entry to the European Union." *De Economist* 144(2): 285–304.

Glickman, David L. 1947. "The British Imperial Preference System." *Quarterly Journal of Economics* 61(3):4 39–70.

Goldstein, Judith. 1993. *Ideas, Interests, and American Trade Policy.* Ithaca: Cornell University Press.

——. 1998. "International Institutions and Domestic Politics: GATT, WTO, and the Liberalization of International Trade." In *The WTO as an International Organization,* edited by Anne O. Krueger, 133–52. Chicago: University of Chicago Press.

Goldstein, Judith, and Lisa L. Martin. 2000. "Legalization, Trade Liberalization, and Domestic Politics: A Cautionary Note." *International Organization* 54(3): 603–32.

Golembe, Carter H., and David S. Holland. 1990. "Banking and Securities." In *Europe 1992: An American Perspective,* edited by Gary Clyde Hufbauer, 65–118. Washington, D.C.: Brookings Institution.

Golt, Sidney. 1978. *The GATT Negotiations, 1973–79: The Closing Stage.* London: British–North American Committee.

Goodman, John B., Debora Spar, and David B. Yoffie. 1996. "Foreign Direct Investment and the Demand for Protection in the United States." *International Organization* 50(4): 565–91.

Gourevitch, Peter. 1986. *Politics in Hard Times: Comparative Responses to International Economic Crises.* Ithaca: Cornell University Press.

Gowa, Joanne. 1994. *Allies, Adversaries, International Trade.* Princeton, N.J.: Princeton University Press.

Grady, Henry. 1936. "The New Trade Policy of the United States." *Foreign Affairs* 14(2): 283–96.

Graham, Edward M. 1991. "Strategic Responses of U.S. Multinational Firms to the Europe-1992 Initiative." In *Europe and America, 1992: US-EC Economic Relations and the Single European Market,* edited by George N. Yannopoulos, 177–204. Manchester, UK: Manchester University Press.

Grieco, Joseph M. 1990. *Cooperation Among Nations: Europe, America, and Non-Tariff Barriers to Trade.* Ithaca: Cornell University Press.

Grossman, Gene M., and Elhanan Helpman. 1995. "Trade Wars and Trade Talks." *Journal of Political Economy* 103(4): 675–708.

Gruber, Lloyd. 2000. *Ruling the World: Power Politics and the Rise of Supranational Institutions.* Princeton, N.J.: Princeton University Press.

Haftel, Yoram Z. 2004. "From the Outside Looking In: The Effect of Trading Blocs on Trade Disputes in the GATT/WTO." *International Studies Quarterly* 48(1): 121–42.

Haggard, Stephan. 1988. "The Institutional Foundations of Hegemony: Explaining the Reciprocal Trade Agreements Act of 1934." *International Organization* 42(1): 91–119.

Hall, Richard L., and Alan V. Deardorff. 2006. "Lobbying as Legislative Subsidy." *American Political Science Review* 100(1): 69–84.

Hanson, Brian T. 1998. "What Happened to Fortress Europe? External Trade Policy Liberalization in the European Union." *International Organization* 52(1): 55–85.

Hardin, Russell. 1982. *Collective Action.* Baltimore: Johns Hopkins University Press.

Harrison, Glenn W., Thomas F. Rutherford, and David G. Tarr. 2001. "Chile's Regional Arrangements and the Free Trade Agreement of the Americas: The Importance of Market Access." World Bank, Policy Research Working Paper 2634.

Harrison, Richard A. 1984. "The Runciman Visit to Washington in January 1937: Presidential Diplomacy and the Non-Commercial Implications of Anglo-American Trade Negotiations." *Canadian Journal of History* 19(2): 217–39.

Hathaway, Oona A. 1998. "Positive Feedback: The Impact of Trade Liberalization on Industry Demands for Protection." *International Organization* 52(3): 575–612.

Helleiner, G. K. 1977. "Transnational Enterprises and the New Political Economy of U.S. Trade Policy." *Oxford Economic Papers* 29(1): 102–16.

Henderson, David. 1989. "1992: The External Dimension." Group of Thirty Occasional Papers.

Heron, Tony. 2007. "European Trade Diplomacy and the Politics of Global Development: Reflections on the EU-China 'Bra Wars' Dispute." *Government and Opposition* 42(2): 190–214.

Hieronymi, Otto. 1973. *Economic Discrimination against the United States in Western Europe (1945–58): Dollar Shortage and the Rise of Regionalism.* Geneva: Librairie Droz.

Hilaire, Alvin, and Yongzheng Yang. 2003. "The United States and the New Regionalism/ Bilateralism." IMF Working Paper.

Hillman, Arye L., and Heinrich W. Ursprung. 1993. "Multinational Firms, Political Competition, and International Trade Policy." *International Economic Review* 34(2): 347–63.

Hine, R. C. 1985. *The Political Economy of European Trade: An Introduction to the Trade Policies of the EEC.* Sussex, UK: Wheatsheaf Books.

Hirschman, Albert O. 1945. *National Power and the Structure of Foreign Trade.* Berkeley: University of California Press.

Hiscox, Michael J. 1999. "The Magic Bullet? The RTAA, Institutional Reform, and Trade Liberalization." *International Organization* 53(4): 669–98.

———. 2002. *International Trade and Political Conflict: Commerce, Coalitions, and Mobility.* Princeton, N.J.: Princeton University Press.

Hocking, Brian, and Michael Smith. 1997. *Beyond Foreign Economic Policy: The United States, the Single European Market and the Changing World Economy.* London: Pinter.

Hody, Cynthia A. 1996. *The Politics of Trade: American Political Development and Foreign Economic Policy.* Hanover, N.H.: Dartmouth College.

Hudec, Robert E. 1971. "GATT or GABB? The Future Design of the General Agreement on Tariffs and Trade." *The Yale Law Journal* 80(7): 1299–386.

Hufbauer, Gary Clyde. 1990. "An Overview." In *Europe 1992: An American Perspective,* edited by Gary Clyde Hufbauer, 1–64. Washington, D.C.: Brookings Institution.

Hull, Cordell. 1938. "The Outlook for the Trade-Agreements Program." Address by Cordell Hull, Secretary of State, before the Twenty-Fifth National Foreign Trade Convention, 1 November, in New York.

———. 1948. *The Memoirs of Cordell Hull.* New York: Macmillan.

Humphrey, Don D. 1961. "The Effects of a Customs Union in Western Europe." *Southern Economic Journal* 27(4): 283–92.

Ikenberry, G. John. 1992. "A World Economy Restored: Expert Consensus and the Anglo-American Postwar Settlement." *International Organization* 46(1): 289–321.

Ilgen, Thomas Lee. 1976. The politics of economics: United States–West European monetary and trade relations, 1958–1971. PhD diss., University of California, Santa Barbara.

Inter-American Development Bank. 2004. *Integration and Trade in the Americas. III EU-LAC Summit: Special Issue on Latin American and Caribbean Economic Relations with the European Union.* Washington, D.C.: IADB.

Irwin, Douglas A., and Randall S. Kroszner. 1999. "Interests, Institutions, and Ideology in Securing Policy Change: The Republican Conversion to Trade Liberalization after Smoot-Hawley." *Journal of Law and Economics* 42(2): 643–73.

James, Scott C., and David A. Lake. 1989. "The Second Face of Hegemony: Britain's Repeal of the Corn Laws and the American Walker Tariff of 1846." *International Organization* 43(1): 1–29.

Johnson, G. Griffith. 1963. "Western Europe and the American Balance of Payments." *Annals of the American Academy* 348(1): 110–20.

Johnston, Eric. 1962. "Joining the Common Market." In *U.S. Foreign Trade Policy,* edited by Ronald Steel, 153–59. New York: H. W. Wilson.

Jones, Joseph M. Jr. 1934. Tariff retaliation: Repercussions of the Hawley-Smoot bill. PhD diss., University of Pennsylvania.

Junker, Detlef. 1975. *Der unteilbare Weltmarkt: Das ökonomische Interesse in der Außenpolitik der USA, 1933–1941.* Stuttgart, DE: Klett.

Kahneman, Daniel, and Amos Tversky. 1979. "Prospect Theory: An Analysis of Decision under Risk." *Econometrica* 47(2): 263–91.

Kakabadse, Mario. 1980. The negotiating role of the Commission of the European Community in the GATT Tokyo Round 1973–79. PhD diss., London School of Economics.

Kaplan, Edward S. 1996. *American Trade Policy, 1923–1995.* Westport, Conn.: Greenwood Press.

Karol, David. 2000. "Divided Government and U.S. Trade Policy: Much Ado about Nothing?" *International Organization* 54(4): 825–44.

Kaufman, Burton J. 1982. *Trade and Aid: Eisenhower's Foreign Economic Policy, 1953–1961.* Baltimore: Johns Hopkins University Press.

Keech, William R., and Kyoungsan Pak. 1995. "Partisanship, Institutions, and Change in American Trade Politics." *Journal of Politics* 57(4): 1130–42.

Keohane, Robert O. 1980. "The Theory of Hegemonic Stability and Changes in International Economic Regimes, 1967–1977." In *Change in the International System,* edited by Ole Holsti, Randolph Siverson, and Alexander L. George, 131–62. Boulder, Colo.: Westview Press.

———. 1984. *After Hegemony: Cooperation and Discord in the World Political Economy.* Princeton, N.J.: Princeton University Press.

———. 1989. *International Institutions and State Power: Essays in International Relations Theory.* Boulder, Colo.: Westview Press.

Keohane, Robert O., and Joseph S. Nye, eds. 1989. *Power and Interdependence: World Politics in Transition.* 2nd ed. Boston: Little, Brown and Co.

Kerremans, Bart. 1999. "The U.S. Debate on Trade Negotiating Authority between 1994 and 1999." *Journal of World Trade* 33(5): 49–85.

Kindleberger, Charles P. 1973. *The World in Depression, 1929–1939.* London: Penguin Press.

———. 1975. "The Rise of Free Trade in Western Europe." *Journal of Economic History* 35(1): 20–55.

———. 1989. "Commercial Policy between the Wars." In *The Industrial Economies: The Development of Economic and Social Policies.* Vol. 8 of *The Cambridge Economic History of Europe,* edited by Peter Mathias and Sidney Pollard, 161–96. Cambridge: Cambridge University Press.

King, Gary, Robert Keohane, and Sidney Verba. 1994. *Designing Social Inquiry: Scientific Inference in Qualitative Reserach.* Princeton, N.J.: Princeton University Press.

Kock, Karin. 1969. *International Trade and the GATT 1947–1967.* Stockholm: Almquist and Wiksell.

Kollman, Ken. 1998. *Outside Lobbying: Public Opinion and Interest Group Strategies.* Princeton, N.J.: Princeton University Press.

Kono, Daniel Y. 2007. "When Do Trade Blocs Block Trade?" *International Studies Quarterly* 51(1): 165–81.

Kottman, Richard N. 1968. *Reciprocity and the North Atlantic Triangle, 1932–1938.* Ithaca: Cornell University Press.

Krasner, Stephen D. 1976. "State Power and the Structure of International Trade." *World Politics* 28(3): 317–47.

———. 1979. "The Tokyo Round: Particularistic Interests and Prospects for Stability in the Global Trading System." *International Studies Quarterly* 23(4): 491–531.

Krause, Lawrence B. 1959. "United States Imports and the Tariff." *American Economic Review* 49(2): 542–51.

———. 1962. "United States Imports, 1947–1958." *Econometrica* 30(2): 221–38.

———. 1968. *European Economic Integration and the United States.* Washington, D.C.: Brookings Institution.

Krauss, Melvyn B. 1979. *The New Protectionism: The Welfare State and International Trade.* Oxford: Basil Blackwell.

Kravis, Irving B. 1962. "The U.S. Trade Position and the Common Market." In *Factors Affecting the United States Balance of Payments,* edited by U.S. Congress, Joint Economic Committee, Subcommittee on International Exchange and Payments, 87–104. Washington, D.C.: Government Printing Office.

Kreider, Carl. 1943. *The Anglo-American Trade Agreement: A Study of British and American Commercial Policies, 1934–1939.* Princeton, N.J.: Princeton University Press.

Kreinin, Mordechai E. 1959. "European Integration and American Trade." *American Economic Review* 49(4): 615–27.

———. 1973. "The Static Effects of EEC Enlargement on Trade Flows." *Southern Economic Journal* 39(4): 559–68.

———. 1976. "U.S. Trade Interests and the EEC Mediterranean Policy." In *The EEC and the Mediterranean Countries,* edited by Avi Shlaim and G. N. Yannopoulos, 33–51. Cambridge: Cambridge University Press.

———. 1991. "EC-1992 and World Trade and the Trading System." In *Europe and America, 1992: U.S.-EC Economic Relations and the Single European Market*, edited by George N. Yannopoulos, 47–74. Manchester, UK: Manchester University Press.

Krueger, Anne O. 1997. "Trade Policy and Economic Development: How We Learn." *American Economic Review* 87(1): 1–22.

———. 1999. "Are Preferential Trading Arrangements Trade-Liberalizing or Protectionist?" *Journal of Economic Perspectives* 13(4): 105–24.

Krugman, Paul. 1991. "Is Bilateralism Bad?" In *International Trade and Trade Policy*, edited by Elhanan Helpman and Assaf Razin, 9–23. Cambridge: MIT Press.

Lake, David A. 1988. *Power, Protection, and Free Trade: International Sources of U.S. Commercial Strategy, 1887–1939.* Ithaca: Cornell University Press.

———. 1993. "Leadership, Hegemony, and the International Economy: Naked Emperor or Tattered Monarch with Potential?" *International Studies Quarterly* 37(4): 459–89.

Lavergne, Réal P. 1983. *The Political Economy of U.S. Tariffs: An Empirical Analysis.* Toronto: Academic Press.

Lawrence, Robert Z. 1991. "Emerging Regional Arrangements: Building Blocks or Stumbling Blocks?" In *The AMEX Bank Review Prize Essays.* Vol. 5 of *Finance and the International Economy*, edited by Richard O'Brien, 23–35. Oxford: Oxford University Press.

Lazer, David. 1999. "The Free Trade Epidemic of the 1860s and Other Outbreaks of Economic Discrimination." *World Politics* 51(4): 447–83.

Leith, J. Clark, and John Whalley. 2004. "Competitive Liberalization and a U.S.-SACU FTA." In *Free Trade Agreements: U.S. Strategies and Priorities*, edited by Jeffrey J. Schott, 331–55. Washington, D.C.: Institute for International Economics.

Lindeen, James Walter. 1970. "Interest-Group Attitudes toward Reciprocal Trade Legislation." *Public Opinion Quarterly* 34(1): 108–12.

Lipson, Charles. 1982. "The Transformation of Trade: The Sources and Effects of Regime Change." *International Organization* 36(2): 417–55.

Lohmann, Susanne. 1998. "An Information Rationale for the Power of Special Interests." *American Political Science Review* 92(4): 809–27.

Lohmann, Susanne, and Sharyn O'Halloran. 1994. "Divided Government and U.S. Trade Policy: Theory and Evidence." *International Organization* 48(4): 595–632.

Louis, Jean-Victor. 1984. "The European Economic Community and the Implementation of the GATT Tokyo Round Results." In *Implementing the Tokyo Round: National Constitutions and International Economic Rules*, edited by John H. Jackson, Jean-Victor Louis, and Mitsuo Matsushita. Ann Arbor: University of Michigan.

Lundestad, Geir. 2003. *The United States and Europe since 1945: From "Empire" by Invitation to Transatlantic Drift.* Oxford: Oxford University Press.

Lusztig, Michael. 2004. *The Limits of Protectionism: Building Coalitions for Free Trade.* Pittsburgh, Penn.: Pittsburgh University Press.

Luyten, Paul. 1989. "Multilateralism Versus Preferential Bilateralism: A European View." In *Free Trade Areas and U.S. Trade Policy*, edited by Jeffrey J. Schott, 271–79. Washington, D.C.: Institute for International Economics.

Lynch, Frances M. B. 1997. *France and the International Economy: From Vichy to the Treaty of Rome.* London: Routledge.

MacDougall, Donald, and Rosemary Hutt. 1954. "Imperial Preference: A Quantitative Analysis." *Economic Journal* 64(254): 233–57.

Magee, Stephen P. 1978. "Three Simple Tests of the Stolper-Samuelson Theorem." In *Issues in International Economics*, edited by Peter Oppenheimer, 138–53. London: Oriel Press.

Malmgren, Harald B. 1973. "Coming Trade Wars? Neo-Mercantilism and Foreign Policy." In *A Reordered World: Emerging International Economic Problems*, edited by Richard N. Cooper, 22–45. Washington, D.C.: Potomac Associates.

Manger, Mark. 2009. *Investing in Protection: The Politics of Preferential Trade Agreements between North and South.* Cambridge: Cambridge University Press.

Mansfield, Edward D., and Helen V. Milner. 1999. "The New Wave of Regionalism." *International Organization* 53(3): 589–627.

Marsh, John S. 1971. *British Entry to the European Community—Implications for British and North American Agriculture.* London: British–North American Committee.

Mason, Mark. 1994. "Elements of Consensus: Europe's Response to the Japanese Automotive Challenge." *Journal of Common Market Studies* 32(4): 433–53.

Mattli, Walter. 1999. *The Logic of Regional Integration: Europe and Beyond.* Cambridge: Cambridge University Press.

Maur, Jean-Christophe. 2005. "Exporting Europe's Trade Policy." *World Economy* 28(11): 1565–90.

McLaren, John. 2002. "A Theory of Insidious Regionalism." *Quarterly Journal of Economics* 117(2): 571–608.

Medick-Krakau, Monika. 1995. *Amerikanische Außenhandelspolitik im Wandel: Handelsgesetzgebung und GATT-Politik 1945–1988.* Berlin: Akademie Verlag.

Messerlin, Patrick A. 2001. *Measuring the Costs of Protection in Europe: European Commercial Policy in the 2000s.* Washington, D.C.: Institute for International Economics.

Meunier, Sophie. 2005. *Trading Voices: The European Union in International Commercial Negotiations.* Princeton, N.J.: Princeton University Press.

Meyer, F. V. 1978. *International Trade Policy.* London: Croom Helm.

Milner, Helen V. 1988. *Resisting Protectionism: Global Industries and the Politics of International Trade.* Princeton, N.J.: Princeton University Press.

——. 2002. "International Trade." In *Handbook of International Relations,* edited by Walter Carlsnaes, Thomas Risse, and Beth A. Simmons, 448–61. London: SAGE.

Milward, Alan S. 1984. *The Reconstruction of Western Europe, 1945–51.* London: Methuen.

——. 1992. *The European Rescue of the Nation-State.* London: Routledge.

Mitchell, B. R. 1992. *International Historical Statistics: Europe, 1750–1988.* New York: Stockton.

——. 1998. *European Historical Statistics, 1750–1993.* London: Macmillan.

Moley, Raymond. 1939. *After Seven Years.* New York: Harper and Brothers.

Moravcsik, Andrew. 1998. *The Choice for Europe: Social Purpose and State Power from Messina to Maastricht.* Ithaca: Cornell University Press.

Morrow, James. 1992. "Signaling Difficulties with Linkage in Crisis Bargaining." *International Studies Quarterly* 36(2): 153–72.

——. 1994. *Game Theory for Political Scientists.* Princeton, N.J.: Princeton University Press.

Nagarajan, Nigel. 1998. "Regionalism and the WTO: New Rules for the Game?" European Commission, Economic Papers 128.

Nedergaard, Peter. 1993. "The End of Special Interests? The Political Economy of EC Trade Policy Changes in the 1990s." In *The European Community in World Politics,* edited by Ole Nørgaard, Thomas Pedersen, and Nicolaj Petersen, 52–73. London: Pinter.

Nelson, Douglas. 1988. "Endogenous Tariff Theory: A Critical Survey." *American Journal of Political Science* 32(3): 796–837.

——. 1989. "The Domestic Political Preconditions of U.S. Trade Policy: Liberal Structure and Protectionist Dynamics." *Journal of Public Policy* 9(1): 83–108.

Neunreither, Karlheinz. 1968. "Wirtschaftsverbände im Prozeß der europäischen Integration." In *Politische Dimensionen der europaischen Gemeinschaftsbildung,* edited by Carl J. Friedrich, 358–445. Cologne, DE.: Westdeutscher Verlag.

Nicolaïdis, Kalypso, and Sophie Meunier. 2002. "Revisiting Trade Competence in the European Union: Amsterdam, Nice, and Beyond." In *Institutional Challenges in the European Union,* edited by Madleine Hosli, Adrian M. A. van Deemen, and Mika Widgrén, 173–201. London: Routledge.

Nivola, Pietro S. 1986. "The New Protectionism: U.S. Trade Policy in Historical Perspective." *Political Science Quarterly* 101(4): 577–600.

Nollen, Stanley D., and Dennis P. Quinn. 1994. "Free Trade, Fair Trade, Strategic Trade, and Protectionism in the U.S. Congress, 1987–88." *International Organization* 48(3): 491–525.

Nownes, Anthony J. 2001. *Pressure and Power: Organized Interests in American Politics.* Boston: Houghton Mifflin.

O'Brien, Denis. 1976. "Customs Unions: Trade Creation and Trade Diversion in Historical Perspective." *History of Political Economy* 8(4): 540–63.

Odell, John S. 1990. "Understanding International Trade Policies: An Emerging Synthesis." *World Politics* 43(1): 139–67.

———. 1993. "International Threats and Internal Policies: Brazil, the European Community, and the United States, 1985–1987." In *Double-Edged Diplomacy: International Bargaining and Domestic Politics,* edited by Peter B. Evans, Harold K. Jacobson, and Robert D. Putnam, 233–64. Berkeley: University of California Press.

Odell, John, and Barry Eichengreen. 1998. "The United States, the ITO, and the WTO: Exit Options, Agent Slack, and Presidential Leadership." In *WTO as an International Organization,* edited by Anne O. Krueger, 181–209. Chicago: University of Chicago Press.

O'Halloran, Desmond H. P. 1970. "The Kennedy Round": An analysis of bilateral tariff bargaining within the multilateralism of GATT. PhD diss., University College of Dublin.

O'Halloran, Sharyn. 1994. *Politics, Process, and American Trade Policy.* Ann Arbor: University of Michigan Press.

Olson, Mancur. 1965. *The Logic of Collective Action.* Cambridge: Harvard University Press.

Organization for Economic Cooperation and Development. Various. *Revenue Statistics.* Paris: OECD.

Organization for European Economic Cooperation. 1958. *A Decade of Co-Operation: Achievements and Perspectives.* Paris: OEEC.

Oye, Kenneth A. 1992. *Economic Discrimination and Political Exchange: World Political Economy in the 1930s and 1980s.* Princeton, N.J.: Princeton University Press.

Page, S. A. B. 1981. "The Revival of Protectionism and Its Consequences for Europe." *Journal of Common Market Studies* 20(1): 17–40.

Pahre, Robert. 1998. "Reactions and Reciprocity: Tariffs and Trade Liberalization from 1815 to 1914." *Journal of Conflict Resolution* 42(4): 467–92.

———. 1999. *Leading Questions: How Hegemony Affects the International Political Economy.* Ann Arbor: University of Michigan Press.

———. 2008. *Politics and Trade Cooperation in the Nineteenth Century: The "Agreeable Customs" of 1815–1914.* Cambridge: Cambridge University Press.

Panagariya, Arvind. 2000. "Preferential Trade Liberalization: The Traditional Theory and New Developments." *Journal of Economic Literature* 38(2): 287–331.

Pastor, Robert. 1980. *Congress and the Politics of U.S. Foreign Economic Policy, 1929–1976.* Berkeley: University of California Press.

Pastor, Robert A. 1983. "The Cry and Sigh Syndrome: Congress and Trade Policy." In *Making Economic Policy in Congress,* edited by Allen Schick, 158–95. Washington, D.C.: American Enterprise Institute.

Patterson, Gardner. 1966. *Discrimination in International Trade: The Policy Issues, 1945–1965.* Princeton, N.J.: Princeton University Press.

Peek, George N., and Samuel Crowther. 1936. *Why Quit Our Own?* New York: D. Van Nostrand.

Pelkmans, Jacques, and Paul Brenton. 1999. "Bilateral Trade Agreements with the EU: Driving Forces and Effects." In *Multilateralism and Regionalism in the Post–Uruguay Round Era: What Role for the EU?* edited by Olga Memedovic, Arie Kuyvenhoven, and Willem T. Molle, 87–120. Boston: Kluwer Academic Publishers.

Penrose, E. F. 1953. *Economic Planning for the Peace.* Princeton, N.J.: Princeton University Press.

Peterson, Peter G. 1972. *The United States in the Changing World Economy,* vol. I, *A Foreign Economic Perspective.* London: British–North American Research Association.

Piquet, Howard S. 1958. "First Effects of the Common Market: The Impact of Changing Tariffs on U.S. Exports." In *The European Common Market: New Frontier for American Business,* edited by American Management Association, 124–59. New York: American Management Association.

Pollard, Robert A. 1985. *Economic Security and the Origins of the Cold War, 1945–1950.* New York: Columbia University Press.

Pollard, Sidney. 1974. *European Economic Integration, 1815–1970.* London: Thames and Hudson.

Pomfret, Richard. 2001. *The Economics of Regional Trading Arrangements.* Oxford: Oxford University Press.

Postan, M. M. 1967. *An Economic History of Western Europe, 1945–1964.* London: Methuen.

Potters, Jan, and Randolph Sloof. 1996. "Interest Groups: A Survey of Empirical Models that Try to Assess Their Influence." *European Journal of Political Economy* 12(3): 403–42.

Preeg, Ernest H. 1970. *Traders and Diplomats: An Analysis of the Kennedy Round of Negotiations under the General Agreement on Tariffs and Trade.* Washington, D.C.: Brookings Institution.

Preuße, Heinz Gert. 2000. "Sechs Jahre nordamerikanisches Freihandelsabkommen (NAFTA)—eine Bestandsaufnahme." Tübinger Diskussionsbeitrag 183.

Pugel, Thomas A., and Ingo Walter. 1985. "U.S. Corporate Interests and the Political Economy of U.S. Trade Policy." *Review of Economics and Statistics* 67(3): 465–73.

Resnick, Stephen A., and Edwin M. Truman. 1975. "An Empirical Examination of Bilateral Trade in Western Europe." In *European Economic Integration,* edited by Bela Balassa, 41–78. Amsterdam: North-Holland.

Ribicoff, Abraham. 1971. *Trade Policies in the 1970s: Report by Senator Abraham Ribicoff to the Committee on Finance United States Senate.* Washington, D.C.: Government Printing Office.

Rode, Reinhard. 1980. *Amerikanische Handelspolitik gegenüber Westeuropa: Von der Handelsreform zur Tokio-Runde.* Frankfurt: Campus.

Rodrik, Dani. 1995. "Political Economy of Trade Policy." In *Handbook of International Economics,* vol. 3, edited by Gene M. Grossman and Kenneth Rogoff, 1457–94. Amsterdam: Elsevier.

Romer, Paul. 1990. "Endogenous Technological Change." *Journal of Political Economy* 98(5): 71–102.

Romero, Frederico. 1996. "U.S. Attitudes towards Integration and Interdependence: The 1950s." In *The United States and the Integration of Europe: Legacies of the Postwar Era,* edited by Francis H. Heller and John R. Gillingham, 103–21. New York: St. Martin's Press.

Rose, Andrew K. 2004. "Do WTO Members Have More Liberal Trade Policy?" *Journal of International Economics* 63(2): 209–35.

Rosen, Howard. 2004. "Free Trade Agreements as Foreign Policy Tools: The U.S.-Israel and U.S.-Jordan FTAs." In *Free Trade Agreements: U.S. Strategies and Priorities,* edited by Jeffrey J. Schott, 51–78. Washington, D.C.: Institute for International Economics.

Rowland, Benjamin M. 1987. *Commercial Conflict and Foreign Policy: A Study in Anglo-American Relations, 1932–1938.* New York: Garland.

Ruggie, John Gerard. 1982. "International Regimes, Transactions, and Change: Embedded Liberalism in the Postwar Economic Order." *International Organization* 36(2): 379–415.

Sandholtz, Wayne, and John Zysman. 1989. "1992: Recasting the European Bargain." *World Politics* 42(4): 95–128.

Sapir, André. 1998. "The Political Economy of EC Regionalism." *European Economic Review* 42(3–5): 717–32.

Sarris, Alexander H. 1983. "European Community Enlargement and World Trade in Fruits and Vegetables." *American Journal of Agricultural Economics* 65(2): 235–46.

Saxonhouse, Gary R. 1996. "Regionalism and U.S. Trade Policy in Asia." In *The Economics of Preferential Trade Agreements,* edited by Jagdish N. Bhagwati and Arvind Panagariya, 108–35. Washington, D.C.: AEI Press.

Sayre, Francis B. 1939. *The Way Forward: The American Trade Agreements Program.* New York: Macmillan.

——. 1940. *The Protection of American Export Trade.* Chicago: University of Chicago Press.

Schattschneider, E. E. 1935. *Politics, Pressures, and the Tariff: A Study of Free Private Enterprise in Pressure Politics, as Shown in the 1929–1930 Revision of the Tariff.* New York: Prentice Hall.

Schiff, Maurice. 2002. "Chile's Trade and Regional Integration Policy: An Assessment." *World Economy* 25(7): 973–90.

Schlesinger, Arthur M. Jr. 1959. *The Coming of the New Deal.* Boston: Houghton Mifflin.

Schmidt, Stephen C. 1972. "United Kingdom Entry into the European Economic Community: Issues and Implications." *Illinois Agricultural Economics* 12(2): 1–11.

Schnietz, Karen E. 2000. "The Institutional Foundation of U.S. Trade Policy: Revisiting Explanations for the 1934 Reciprocal Trade Agreements Act." *Journal of Policy History* 12(4): 417–44.

——. 2003. "The Reaction of Private Interests to the 1934 Reciprocal Trade Agreements Act." *International Organization* 57(1): 213–33.

Schnietz, Karen E., and Timothy Nieman. 1999. "Politics Matter: The 1997 Derailment of Fast-Track Trade Authority." *Business and Politics* 1(2): 233–51.

Schott, Jeffrey J. 1998. "Whither U.S.-EU Trade Relations?" In *Transatlantic Economic Relations in the Post-Cold War Era,* edited by Barry Eichengreen, 36–68. New York: Council on Foreign Relations.

Schuknecht, Ludger. 1992. *Trade Protection in the European Community.* Chur, CH: Harwood Academic Publishers.

Schwab, Susan C. 1994. *Trade-Offs: Negotiating the Omnibus Trade and Competitiveness Act.* Boston: Harvard Business School Press.

Schwok, René. 1991. *US-EC Relations in the Post-Cold War Era: Conflict or Partnership?* Boulder, Colo.: Westview.

Scott, Hal S. 1971. "The United States Response to Common Market Trade Preferences and the Legality of the Import Surcharge." *The University of Chicago Law Review* 39(1): 177–243.

Sherman, Richard. 2002. "Endogenous Protection and Trade Negotiations." *International Politics* 39(4): 491–509.

Shoch, James. 2001. *Trading Blows: Party Competition and U.S. Trade Policy in a Globalizing Era.* Chapel Hill: University of North Carolina Press.

Shonfield, Andrew. 1976. "International Economic Relations of the Western World: An Overall View." In *Politics and Trade.* Vol. 1 of *International Economic Relations of the Western World, 1959–1971,* edited by Andrew Shonfield, 1–140. London: Oxford University Press.

Siegler, Heinrich. 1964. *Dokumentation der Europäischen Integration,* vol. 2, *1961–1963.* Bonn: Siegler and Co.

Simmons, Beth and Zachary Elkins. 2004. "The Globalization of Liberalization: Policy Diffusion in the International Political Economy." *American Political Science Review* 98(1): 171–89.

Skålnes, Lars. 1998. "Grand Strategy and Foreign Economic Policy: British Grand Strategy in the 1930s." *World Politics* 50(4): 582–616.

Smith, Adam. 1937. *An Inquiry into the Nature and Causes of the Wealth of Nations.* New York: Random House.

Soloaga, Isidro, and L. Alan Winters. 2001. "Regionalism in the Nineties: What Effect on Trade?" *North American Journal of Economics and Finance* 12(1): 1–29.

Srinivasan, T. N., and Jagdish Bhagwati. 2001. "Outward-Orientation and Development: Are Revisionists Right?" In *Trade, Development and Political Economy. Essays in Honor of Anne O. Krueger,* edited by Deepak Lal and Richard H. Snape, 3–26. Houndmills, UK: Palgrave.

Stigler, Joseph. 1971. "The Theory of Economic Regulation." *Bell Journal of Economic and Management Science* 2:3–21.

Stiles, Kendall W. 1995. "The Ambivalent Hegemon: Explaining the 'Lost Decade' in Multilateral Trade Talks, 1948–1958." *Journal of International Political Economy* 2(1): 1–26.

Strange, Susan. 1979. "The Management of Surplus Capacity: Or, How Does Theory Stand Up to Protectionism 1970s Style?" *International Organization* 33(3): 303–34.

———. 1985. "Protectionism and World Politics." *International Organization* 39(2): 233–60.

Subdirección General de Coordinación y Evaluación Comercial. 2002. "Acuerdo de Asociación entre la UE y Chile." *Boletín Económico ICE* 2748:7–20.

Taber, George M. 1969. *John F. Kennedy and a Uniting Europe: The Politics of Partnership.* Bruges, BE: College of Europe.

Talbot, Ross B. 1978. *The Chicken War: An International Trade Conflict between the United States and the European Economic Community, 1961–1964.* Ames: Iowa State University Press.

Tasca, Henry Joseph. 1938. *The Reciprocal Trade Policy of the United States: A Study in Trade Philosophy.* Philadelphia: University of Pennsylvania Press.

Taylor, Paul. 1983. *The Limits of European Integration.* London: Croom Helm.

Thorstensen, Vera, and Felix Peña. 1999. "The View from Latin America." In *Multilateralism and Regionalism in the Post-Uruguay Round Era: What Role for the EU?* edited by Olga Memedovic, Arie Kuyvenhoven, and Willem T. Molle, 235–74. Boston: Kluwer Academic Publishers.

Tordjman, Jean-Daniel. 2000. "The Future of World Politics of Commerce." In *Security, Trade, and Environmental Policy: A U.S./European Union Transatlantic Agenda,* edited by Charles Bonser, 111–18. Boston: Kluwer Academic Publishers.

Toye, Richard. 2003. "The Attlee Government, the Imperial Preference System and the Creation of the GATT." *English Historical Review* 118(478): 912–39.

Truman, Edwin M. 1969. "The European Economic Community: Trade Creation and Trade Diversion." *Yale Economic Essays* 9:201–57.

Tsoukalis, Loukas, and Antonio da Silva Ferreira. 1980. "Management of Industrial Surplus Capacity in the European Community." *International Organization* 34(3): 355–76.

Twiggs, Joan E. 1987. *The Tokyo Round of Multilateral Trade Negotiations: A Case Study in Building Domestic Support for Diplomacy.* Lanham, Md.: University Press of America.

UNCTAD (United Nations Conference on Trade and Development). 1968. *The Kennedy Round Estimated Effects on Tariff Barriers: Report by the Secretary-General of UNCTAD.* New York: United Nations.

U.S. Council of the International Chamber of Commerce. 1961. "Principles of an International Trade Policy for the United States."

U.S. Department of State. 1946. "Suggested Charter for an International Trade Organization of the United Nations."

U.S. General Accounting Office. 2004. *International Trade: Intensifying Free Trade Negotiating Agenda Calls for Better Allocation of Staff and Resources, GAO-04–233.* Washington, D.C.: GAO.

U.S. International Trade Commission. 1989. *The Effects of Greater Economic Integration within the European Community on the United States.* Washington, D.C.: USITC.

———. 2006. *Value of U.S. Imports for Consumption, Duties Collected, and Ratio of Duties to Values, 1891–2005.* Washington, D.C.: USITC.

U.S. Tariff Commission. 1919. *Reciprocity and Commercial Treaties.* Washington, D.C.: Government Printing Office.

———. 1969. *Operation of the Trade Agreements Program, 19th Report, January–December 1967.* Washington, D.C.: USTC.

Uri, Pierre. 1969. "Final Report of the Colloquium on Atlantic Relations after the Kennedy Round." In *Economic Relations after the Kennedy Round,* edited by Frans A. M. Alting von Geusau, 213–16. Leyden, NL: A. W. Sijthoff.

Venables, Anthony J. 1991. "International Trade and the Internal Market." In *The Economics of the Single European Act,* edited by George McKenzie and Anthony J. Venables, 51–69. Houndmills, UK: Macmillan.

Verdier, Daniel. 1994. *Democracy and International Trade: Britain, France, and the United States, 1860–1990.* Princeton, N.J.: Princeton University Press.

———. 1998. "Democratic Convergence and Free Trade?" *International Studies Quarterly* 42(1): 1–24.

Verdoorn, P. J., and A. N. R. Schwartz. 1972. "Two Alternative Estimates of the Effects of EEC and EFTA on the Pattern of Trade." *European Economic Review* 3(3): 291–335.

Vernon, Raymond. 1958. "Trade Policy in Crisis." *Essays in International Finance* 29.

Viner, Jacob. 1950. *The Customs Union Issue.* New York: Carnegie Endowment for International Peace.

Vollrath, Thomas L. 1998. "RTA's and Agricultural Trade: A Retrospective Assessment." In *Regional Trade Agreements and U.S. Agriculture,* edited by Mary E. Burfisher and Elizabeth A. Jones, 27–34. Washington, D.C.: Economic Research Service, U.S. Department of Agriculture.

Warley, T. K. 1976. "Western Trade in Agricultural Products." In *Politics and Trade.* Vol. 1 of *International Economic Relations of the Western World 1959–1971,* edited by Andrew Shonfield, 285–402. London: Oxford University Press.

Watson, Richard A. 1956. "The Tariff Revolution: A Study of Shifting Party Attitudes." *Journal of Politics* 18(4): 678–701.

Wei, Shang-Jin, and Jeffrey A. Frankel. 1998. "Open Regionalism in a World of Continental Trade Blocs." IMF Staff Papers 45.

Weintraub, Sidney. 1986. "A Note on Trade Discrimination." *Rivista Internazionale di Scienze Economiche e Commerciali* 33(4): 353–70.

Wiesebron, Marianne L. 2002. "Transformation in Latin America: Integration, Cooperation and Reforms." In *Competing for Integration: Japan, Europe, Latin America, and Their Strategic Partners,* edited by Kurt Werner Radtke and Marianne Wiesebron, 166–92. Armonk, N.Y.: M. E. Sharpe.

Wilcox, Clair. 1949. *A Charter for World Trade.* New York: Macmillan.

Wilkins, Mira. 1996. "U.S. Multinationals and the Unification of Europe, 1945–1960." In *The United States and the Integration of Europe: Legacies of the Postwar Era,* edited by Francis H. Heller and John R. Gillingham, 341–63. New York: St. Martin's Press.

Winand, Pascaline. 1993. *Eisenhower, Kennedy, and the United States of Europe.* Houndmills, UK: Macmillan.

———. 1999. "United States–European Relationships, 1961–1963." In *Widening, Deepening and Acceleration: The European Economic Community, 1957–1963,* edited by Anne Deighton and Alan S. Milward, 17–30. Baden-Baden, DE: Nomos.

Winham, Gilbert R. 1986. *International Trade and the Tokyo Round Negotiation.* Princeton, N.J.: Princeton University Press.

Winters, L. Alan. 1984. "British Imports of Manufactures and the Common Market." *Oxford Economic Papers* 36(1): 103–18.

———. 1999. "Regionalism vs. Multilateralism." In *Market Integration, Regionalism and the Global Economy,* edited by Richard Baldwin, Daniel Cohen, Andre Sapir, and Anthony Venables, 7–49. Cambridge: Cambridge University Press.

Wolf, Martin. 1994. *The Resistible Appeal of Fortress Europe.* London: Centre for Policy Studies.

Woll, Cornelia. 2008. *Firm Interests: How Governments Shape Business Lobbying on Global Trade.* Ithaca: Cornell University Press.

Woolcock, Stephen. 1991. *Market Access Issues in EC-US Relations: Trading Partners or Trading Blows?* London: Pinter.

———. 2005. "European Union Trade Policy: Domestic Institutions and Systemic Factors." In *The Politics of International Trade in the Twenty-First Century: Actors, Issues and Regional Dynamics,* edited by Dominic Kelly and Wyn Grant, 234–51. Houndsmill, UK: Palgrave Macmillan.

World Trade Organization. 1995. *Regionalism and the World Trading System.* Geneva: WTO.

———. 2003. *World Trade Report 2003.* Geneva: WTO.

Yannopoulos, George N. 1988. *Customs Unions and Trade Conflicts: The Enlargement of the European Community.* London: Routledge.

Yeats, Alexander J. 1998. "Does Mercosur's Trade Performance Raise Concerns about the Effect of Regional Trading Arrangements?" *World Bank Economic Review* 12(1): 1–28.

Yoffie, David B., and Sigrid Bergenstein. 1985. "Creating Political Advantage: The Rise of the Corporate Political Entrepreneur." *California Management Review* 28(1): 124–39.

Zeiler, Thomas W. 1992. *American Trade and Power in the 1960s.* New York: Columbia University Press.

———. 1999. *Free Trade, Free World: The Advent of GATT.* Chapel Hill: University of North Carolina Press.

Zeng, Ka. 2002. "Trade Structure and the Effectiveness of America's 'Aggressively Unilateral' Trade Policy." *International Studies Quarterly* 46(1): 93–115.

Index

Agricultural Adjustment Act (1933), 65
Agricultural Adjustment Act (1938), 95
agricultural goods
    trade in, 64, 73, 95, 134, 141–42, 163, 165,
        222
    trade barriers for, 97, 142n, 172,
    See also agricultural interests, citrus fruit,
        Common Agricultural Policy
agricultural interests
    European, 124, 177, 204
    U.S., 54–61, 63, 72, 75, 77, 107–10, 136–38,
        156, 161, 166, 195–96
    See also American Farm Bureau Federa-
        tion, National Farmers Union, National
        Grange
American Farm Bureau Federation, 59, 77,
    109, 138, 171t, 195
American selling price
    Kennedy round and, 122, 125, 127
    Tokyo round and, 151, 156–67
antidumping, 7, 122, 125, 145, 147, 178
    Kennedy round code on, 127–28
    Tokyo round code on, 158n
Asia-Pacific Economic Cooperation, 161, 180,
    202t, 205
Association of South East Asian Nations, 190,
    209–10, 218
Atlantic Charter, 77

Ball, George, 114–17
banking sector, 106, 164, 168, 181
BATNA. *See* best alternative to negotiated
    agreement
Belgium, 86, 92, 100, 103
    See also Benelux
Benelux, 35, 98, 104
    See also Belgium, Netherlands
best alternative to negotiated agreement, 40, 220
    See also power
Bogor Declaration, 197, 205
    See also Asia-Pacific Economic Cooperation
Bretton Woods, 144
    See also monetary policy
broadcasting directive, 164, 168, 174
    See also single market programme

Bundesverband deutscher Industrie.
    See Federation of German Industry
Bush, George W., 185, 198–201
Business Roundtable, 166–67, 191, 193
Buy America Act. *See* public procurement

Canada
    Asia-Pacific Economic Cooperation forum
        and, 205
    free trade agreement with Chile, 194, 201–2
    imperial preference and, 52–54
    trade agreements with the United States, 69,
        73–77, 80n, 172, 176, 180, 207
    transatlantic free trade area and, 116–17
    See also Commonwealth
Cancún ministerial meeting, 201, 204
CAP. *See* Common Agricultural Policy
capital flight, 114, 144
cars
    American producers of, 6, 56, 59–60, 87,
        106–8, 167, 169
    European producers of, 73, 121, 123,
        152, 178–79
    Japanese producers of, 169
Casey-Soames understanding, 155
Central American Free Trade Agreement,
    195, 202–3
Chamber of Commerce
    British, 71–73, 78, 152
    EC, 121n, 151
    French, 122–23
    International, 107–8, 121, 152,
    United States, 47, 59, 77, 106–7, 115,
        136–37, 167, 169, 192–93
Chamberlain, Neville, 70, 72, 75
chemical industry
    American, 57n, 60–61, 89, 108, 111–12, 196t
    European, 122, 138, 140
Chile, 35
    China and, 218,
    EU agreement with, 14, 32, 188–89,
        200, 207–8
    U.S. agreement with, 190, 192–94, 201–2
citrus fruit
    EC tariffs on, 155

citrus fruit *(continued)*
 Mediterranean agreements and, 109, 135,
  138, 141, 143, 147n
 Ottawa agreements and, 54, 60
 See also agricultural goods, Common Agricultural Policy
Clinton, William J., 185, 197–98
cold war, 9, 51, 102, 149, 216
 end of, 185
 reciprocal trade agreements program and, 91
 U.S. support for European allies during, 119
 See also geopolitics
collective action problems, 3, 18, 67, 197
Collier bill, 62
collusive delegation argument, 7–8, 102, 124,
  215
Committee for a National Trade Policy, 88, 104,
  106, 115, 171t
Common Agricultural Policy
 and discrimination, 104–5, 142, 165, 172
 EC defense of, 152–54, 157
 expansion to the United Kingdom, 134
 introduction of, 104, 125
 U.S. exporters' complaints about, 109,
  137–38
 See also agricultural goods, agricultural
  interests
Commonwealth, 64, 88, 114
 British accession to the EC and, 134
 Geneva negotiations and, 79
 Ottawa agreements and, 52–54
 United Kingdom trade links with, 103
 See also Canada
competitive liberalization, 201, 205
Confederation of British Industry, 70–74, 152
Conseil national du patronat français, 121–23
Council of Ministers, 8, 126, 143, 160, 181
countervailing duties, 7, 122, 156–57

de Gaulle, Charles, 126
Democratic party, 173
 position on trade policy, 5–6, 94–95, 197–98
 support for Collier bill, 62
 support for textile industry, 118
 support for the RTAA, 67–68
 Trade Act of 2002 and, 200
 Trade Reform Act and, 146
 unified government by, 50, 120
 See also Republican party
Deutscher Industrie und Handelstag, 152
Dillon round, 101, 113, 120
divided and unified government, 68, 102, 120,
  185
 See also party politics

Doha Development Agenda, 185, 201, 204,
  209–12

economic growth, 10, 16, 20n, 28, 36, 40, 51,
  105, 119, 163
 See also endogenous growth theory
economies of scale, 5–6, 27–29, 40, 51, 61, 160,
  183
EFTA. *See* European Free Trade Association
Eisenhower, Dwight D., 88, 93, 112
Emergency Committee for American Trade,
  136, 166, 191, 193
Empire Industries Association, 72–73
endogenous growth theory, 28
enlargement of the EU
 1973, 45, 133–57
 Eastern, 195–96
 Southern, 159, 165–66, 172, 183,
EU free trade agreements
 Chile and, 14, 188–90, 192, 200–202, 207–9
 EFTA countries and, 106, 132–37, 142–44, 154
 Mediterranean countries and, 132–33,
  135–36, 141, 143, 148, 155, 188–89
 Mexico and, 14, 189, 206–9, 217
 South Africa and, 188–89, 194, 203
Europe 1992. *See* single market programme
European Coal and Steel Community, 88,
  98–99, 133
European Commission, 7–8, 102, 121,
 Kennedy round and, 126
 new regionalism and, 186, 205–6, 209
 single market programme and, 165, 167,
  173, 177n, 180
 Tokyo round and, 154
European Economic Area, 165
European Free Trade Association
 adoption of EC standards by, 182
 creation of, 35, 133
 free trade agreements with the EEC, 106,
  135, 137, 142–44, 154
 and a transatlantic free trade area, 116
 See also European Economic Area
European Higher Education Area, 219–20
European Payments Union, 85, 92

fair trade, 159, 170, 175–76, 213
fast-track authority, 147, 173, 185, 191, 193–99
Federation of British Industry (FBI). *See* Con-
  federation of British Industry
Federation of German Industry, 121, 151, 179
film industry, 164
 American, 60, 168
 Motion Picture Association, 107, 117, 168, 194
 See also services trade

foreign direct investments, 6, 20n, 30, 109, 167, 183

Fortress Europe, 13, 160, 165, 167–181, 183–84

France, 43, 143
agreement with the United States, 69
agreements with colonies, 52, 217
British accession to the EEC and, 133–34
EU-U.S. preferential trade agreement and, 205–6
Franco-Italian customs union, 97–98
in the Kennedy round, 123–26
monetary policy of, 105
single market programme and, 181–82
in the Tokyo round, 153–54

Free Trade Area of the Americas, 193–95, 197, 203, 208

GATT. *See* General Agreement on Tariffs and Trade

General Agreement on Tariffs and Trade, 8, 36, 92, 94n, 96–97, 132, 148, 153–55, 180–81
creation of, 12, 76–82
MFN clause and, 25
trade conflicts and, 92, 110, 143–44, 155, 174
U.S. stance vis-à-vis, 93, 147
See also World Trade Organization

generalized system of preferences, 148

geopolitics, 9–10, 26, 74–76, 83, 102, 112–13, 160, 215–16
1950s U.S. trade policy and, 92–96
1970s U.S. trade policy and, 149–50
Kennedy round and, 119–20, 126
new regionalism and, 186, 198, 200–201, 208

Germany, 43–44, 70, 88, 98–99, 215, 217
Kennedy round, 103, 123–26
Tokyo round, 151, 153

Glass-Steagall Act, 164, 168

government procurement, 157, 160, 162, 165, 168, 173, 179, 182–83, 203, 207
Buy America Act, 68, 122, 151, 156, 179n

gravity model, 47

Great Britain. *See* United Kingdom

Great Depression, 1, 7, 51, 55, 61–62, 89

Gulf Cooperation Council, 190, 203

hegemonic stability thesis, 9–10, 12, 38n, 76, 83
decline of U.S. hegemony and, 131–32, 158, 175
international trade organization and, 93
Japanese accession to GATT and, 94n
See also geopolitics

Hoover, Herbert, 50, 62

Hull, Cordell, 62–64, 74
at the London Monetary and Economic Conference, 65–66
negotiations with the United Kingdom and, 72, 74, 77
and the Reciprocal Trade Agreements Act, 56, 62, 66

import-competing interests, 3, 5, 7, 11, 18–20, 23, 26, 32, 34
American, 60–61, 63, 69, 88–90, 110–12, 136, 138–39, 169–70, 195–96, 216
European, 123–24, 152–53, 177

institutionalism, 7–9, 14, 50–51, 56, 96, 102, 112, 118–19, 132, 183–84

interdependence, economic, 6, 132

International Banking Act, 164

International Trade Organization, 79, 93
See also General Agreement on Tariffs and Trade, World Trade Organization

intra-industry trade, 5–6, 27

Israel
free trade agreement with the EU, 118n, 135, 138, 154–55, 188
free trade agreement with the United States, 176

Italy
Franco-Italian customs union, 97–98
single market programme and, 181–82
trade agreement with the United Kingdom, 70

Japan
accession to the GATT, 94n
APEC and, 205
and free trade agreements, 210, 217–18
rising competition from, 102, 132, 138–39, 169
Smithsonian agreement and, 145
trade restrictions against, 131, 177–78, 184

Keidanren, 217
See also Japan

Kennedy, John F., 106, 110, 114–19, 129

Kennedy round, 12–13, 35
aftermath of, 132–33, 134, 140
EEC position in, 124–26
European societal interests and, 121–24
results of, 126–29
start of, 126

labor unions, 115, 118, 170, 191, 195, 197, 199

legislative subsidy, 18

lesson thesis, 10, 51, 67

Lomé agreements, 155
London Monetary and Economic Conference, 56, 65–66

Marshall Plan, 96
McFadden Act, 164
Mediterranean countries
    EC agreements with, 132–33, 135–36, 141, 143, 148, 155, 188–89
Mercado Común del Sur, 35, 191, 194
    negotiations with the EU, 189, 194, 203, 207–8
Mercosur. *See* Mercado Común del Sur
Mexico, 199, 201, 213
    agreement with Japan, 217–18
    agreement with the EU, 14, 189, 206–9, 217
    North American Free Trade Agreement and, 35,
MFN. *See* most-favored-nation clause
Mills bill, 140, 151
monetary policy, 31n, 58, 80n, 85, 105–6, 145, 150–53
    London Monetary and Economic Conference and, 65–66
most-favored-nation clause, 35
    British position on, 70–72
    in the GATT, 25, 79
    U.S. trade agreements and, 63–67, 142
multinational companies, 5–6, 111–12, 137
    single market programme and, 168–69
    trade liberalization in the 1970s and, 132, 140, 148
Mutual Aid Agreement, 77

NAFTA. *See* North American Free Trade Agreement
National Association of Manufacturers, 60, 201
    single market programme and, 167
    Trade Act of 2002 and, 193
    Trade Expansion Act and, 115, 117
    Uruguay round and, 166
National Farmers Union, 77
    Common Agricultural Policy and, 109–10, 138
    Reciprocal Trade Agreements Act and, 58
National Grange, 61
    EC enlargement and, 166
    Trade Expansion Act and, 109
Netherlands, 98
New Deal, 63, 65
new economic policy, 144, 151
    See also Nixon, Richard
new protectionism, 132, 170
Nixon, Richard, 136, 138, 140, 144–46, 149

Nixon round. *See* Tokyo Round
nontariff barriers, 162
    negotiations on, 125, 127–28
    restrictions on use of, 1, 157
    U.S. trade legislation and, 146–47
    voluntary export restrictions, 131, 162, 170, 177–79
    See also American selling price, fast-track authority, public procurement, standards, Tokyo round codes
North American Free Trade Agreement, 31–32, 35, 195n, 205
    Chile and, 35, 190
    discriminatory effect of, 197, 205–6
    EU agreement with Mexico and, 206–7
North Atlantic free trade agreement, 205

OEEC. *See* Organization for European Economic Cooperation
Omnibus Trade and Competitiveness Act, 173
Organization for European Economic Cooperation, 85, 98, 100
Organization for Trade Cooperation, 93, 97
    See also General Agreement on Tariffs and Trade, International Trade Organization
Ottawa agreements, 35, 52, 63

party politics, 185–86, 198, 200
    Reciprocal Trade Agreements Act and, 67–68
    Trade Expansion Act and, 120
    U.S. trade policy in the 1950s and, 94–95
Peek, George N., 62–66
peril-point provision, 90–91, 116
Pflimlin, Pierre, 97
power, 14, 220
    definition of, 40
    fungibility of, 17, 218, 220
    measurement of, 48
    preferential trade agreements and, 41–44, 222
    reciprocity and, 44
    sources of, 20
President's Commission on Foreign Economic Policy, 91, 97
prospect theory, 33
protectionism
    explanation for, 17–25
Prussia, 34–35
    See also Zollverein
public procurement
    Buy America Act (1933), 68, 122, 151, 156, 173n
    EU-Mexico agreement and, 207
    single market program and, 165, 182–83
    Tokyo round and, 157

Randall, Clarence, 91
  See also President's Commission on Foreign Economic Policy
Randall Commission. *See* President's Commission on Foreign Economic Policy
Reagan, Ronald, 171–73, 176
Reciprocal Trade Agreements Act (1934)
  contents of, 66–67
  explanations for, 7–10, 67–69
  exporter support for, 55–58
  passage of, 65–66
Reciprocal Trade Agreements Act (1958), 12, 101
  hearings for, 106–7
  passage of, 113
reciprocity
  demand for, 121, 124, 154, 156
  in negotiations, 44
  principle in U.S. trade legislation, 62, 68
  provisions in the single market programme, 163–64, 181, 183
regionalism, 14, 221–22
Republican party
  1997 trade bill and, 197–98
  position on trade of, 5–6, 94–95
  RTAA and, 59, 67
  Trade Act of 2002 and, 200
  Trade Expansion Act and, 120
  See also Democratic party, party politics
Roosevelt, Franklin D., 57–59
  meeting with British Prime Minister, 65
  New Deal and, 63
  presidential campaign of 1932, 62
  support for the RTAA, 64–66
RTAA. *See* Reciprocal Trade Agreements Act (1934)
rules of origin, 28–29
  single market programme and, 160, 163–64, 167, 168, 174, 178

Sayre, Francis, 62, 66, 69
secondary trade expansion, 27
Second Banking Directive, 164, 181
Section 301, 147, 171, 173, 213
  See also Trade Act of 1974
sectoral attrition, 40, 124
services trade, 163, 168
  audiovisual, 174, 206
  financial, 164, 166, 181
set of feasible agreements, 20, 40–43
single market programme
  discrimination against U.S. exports, 161–65
  European industry and, 178–79
  negotiations in the wake of, 181–83

passage of, 162
  U.S. exporters' reaction to, 166–69
  U.S. reaction to, 172–75
Smithsonian agreement, 145
Smoot-Hawley Tariff Act, 3, 6
  Great Depression and, 10, 50
  hearings for, 55
  repeal of, 61
  See also lesson thesis
South Africa
  agreement with the EU, 189, 194
  negotiations with the United States, 192, 203
South Korea
  APEC and, 205
  Chile and, 218
  negotiations with the EU, 190, 209–10
Soviet Union, 9, 83, 93, 129
  diplomatic recognition of, 58
  easing of tensions with, 102
  Jewish emigration from, 146
  trade offensive by, 119
  See also cold war
Spain
  accession to the EC, 165–66, 172
  agreement with the EC, 135, 143, 154,
standards
  harmonization of, 156, 162–68, 182
  international agreement on, 182
  labor and environmental, 198
  protectionist impact of, 29
steel
  European producers of, 123, 151, 177
  restrictions on imports of, 131, 140, 170, 200
  U.S. producers of, 88, 138, 169, 195
Stikker Plan of Action, 98
Strackbein, O. R., 89
Summit of the Americas, 197, 203
  See also Free Trade Area of the Americas
Swiss formula, 157

textiles
  European producers of, 73, 123, 178
  trade restrictions on, 131, 140, 162
  U.S. producers of, 61, 77, 95n, 118, 138, 169–70, 195
Tokyo round
  results, 157–58
  See also Tokyo round codes
Tokyo round codes, 157, 158n, 173
Trade Act of 1974
  contents of, 146–48, 156
  explanations of, 147, 149–50
  hearings for, 138, 140
  passage of, 146

Trade Act of 2002, 186–87
    passage of, 199–201
trade creation, 26–28
trade diversion
    EC accession of Portugal and Spain and, 165
    EEC accession of the United Kingdom and,
        133–134
    EEC and, 103–6
    EU free trade agreements and, 135, 187–90
    Ottawa agreements and, 52–55
    single market programme and, 162–65
Trade Expansion Act (1962), 12
    contents of, 115–16, 147n, 173n
    explanations for, 118–20
    opposition to, 110–12
    passage of, 113–15
    support for, 106–10
trade promotion authority. *See* fast-track
    authority
trade war, 36, 37, 221
    Chicken War, 110, 116, 121, 143
    French and Russian, 43–44
Treaty of Rome, 7, 99, 103, 124
Truman, Harry S., 92

unified government. *See* divided and unified
    government
United Kingdom
    accession to the EEC, 45, 133–34
    Benelux trade agreement and, 35
    European Free Trade Association and, 35
    negotiations with the US, 48, 63–65, 69–81
    Ottawa agreements and, 26, 52–55
Uruguay round, 14, 160–61, 167, 214
    agreements reached in, 182–83
    EC participation in, 177–78
U.S. Commission on International Trade and
    Investment Policy, 141–42
U.S. free trade agreements
    Australia and, 195, 203, 209
    Central America and, 195, 202–3
    Chile and, 190, 192–94, 201–2
    See also North American Free Trade
    Agreement
Utilities Directive, 182–83

Vietnam War, 150

World Economic Conference. *See* London
    Monetary and Economic Conference
World Trade Organization, 93, 187,
    ministerial meeting of, 200n, 203–4, 209
    See also Doha Development Agenda, Gen-
    eral Agreement on Tariffs and Trade
WTO. *See* World Trade Organization

Yaoundé association agreement, 135
    See also Lomé agreements

Zollverein, 43, 216–17